A GRAMMAR WRITER'S COOKBOOK

CSLI Lecture Notes
Number 95

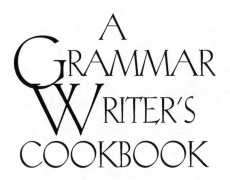

A GRAMMAR WRITER'S COOKBOOK

Miriam Butt, Tracy Holloway King,
María-Eugenia Niño, & Frédérique Segond

CSLI
PUBLICATIONS
Center for the Study of
Language and Information
Stanford, California

Library of Congress Cataloging-in-Publication Data

A grammar writer's cookbook / Miriam Butt ... [et al.].
    p.   cm. — (CSLI lecture notes ; no. 95)
Includes bibliographical references (p.) and index.
                ISBN 1-57586-171-2
            ISBN 1-57586-170-4 (pbk.)
    1. Grammar, Comparative and general—Data processing.
    2. Computational linguistics. I. Butt, Miriam, 1966–   . II. Series.
                P98.G73   1999
            415′.0285—dc21   99-13457
                    CIP

∞ The acid-free paper used in this book meets the minimum
requirements of the American National Standard for Information
Sciences—Permanence of Paper for Printed Library Materials, ANSI
                    Z39.48-1984.

CSLI was founded early in 1983 by researchers from Stanford University,
SRI International, and Xerox PARC to further research and development
of integrated theories of language, information, and computation. CSLI
headquarters and CSLI Publications are located on the campus of
Stanford University.

CSLI Publications reports new developments in the study of language,
information, and computation. In addition to lecture notes, our
publications include monographs, working papers, revised dissertations,
and conference proceedings. Our aim is to make new results, ideas, and
approaches available as quickly as possible. Please visit our web site at
            http://csli-www.stanford.edu/publications/
for comments on this and other titles, as well as for changes and
corrections by the author and publisher.

Contents

Part II Grammar Engineering 153

Acknowledgements

We would like to thank Mary Dalrymple for first suggesting that we write this book. The following people have given us invaluable comments and suggestions: Caroline Brun, Max Copperman, Mary Dalrymple, Stefanie Dipper, Ron Kaplan, Veronika Knüppel, Jonas Kuhn, John Maxwell, Christian Rohrer, Hadar Shemtov, and Annie Zaenen. Special thanks go to John Maxwell for all his help with XLE and to Anette Frank, who patiently answered many and varied questions about the French Grammar. We are further indebted to Christine Kaschny, who helped with the proofreading and indexing.

We would like to acknowledge the Xerox Palo Alto Research Center, the Xerox Research Centre Europe in Grenoble, and the Institut für Maschinelle Sprachverarbeitung at Universität Stuttgart for funding both for the ParGram project and for the writing of this book. For their technical and general support, many thanks to Emma Pease and Jeanette Figueroa. Finally, it was as usual a pleasure to work with the CSLI staff and we would like to thank Dikran Karagueuzian, Tony Gee and Maureen Burke. In particular, we would like to thank Dikran for the many interesting and entertaining moments and conversations.

Abbreviations

Acc	accusative	NTAG	noun tag
Adj	adjective	P	person
Akk	accusative	Part	participle
Art	article	PART	particle
AVM	attribute value matrix	Pass	passive
Comp	comparative degree	PerfP	perfect participle
ConjQue	conjunction *que*	Pl	plural
Dat	dative	POSTNEG	postposed
Dem	demonstrative		negative marker
Det	determiner	Pres	present tense
DPL	double plural	Pro	pronoun
F	feminine gender	Prog	progressive
FMN	feminine, masculine	Pron	pronoun
	or neuter gender	PrPrt	present participle
Fut	future tense	REFL	reflexive
Gen	genitive	Rel	relative
GEND	gender	S	strong inflection
Imp	imperative	Sg	singular
Inf	infinitive	SP	singular/plural
Int	interrogative	St	strong inflection
InvGen	invariant gender	Subj	subjunctive
InvPL	invariant plural	VNBR	verb number
M	masculine gender	W	weak inflection
N	neuter gender	Wh	*wh*-word
NBR	number	1	first person
NEG	negative marker	2	second person
Nom	nominative	3	third person
NomObl	nominative/oblique and	3P	third person
Non3Sg	not third singular		

1

Introduction

This book is meant to be a cookbook in several senses. One aim of the book is to present analyses of core constructions in a crosslinguistically valid manner which also takes into account the particular demands of grammar development. In particular, the analyses we document are motivated by our experiences in the development of parallel grammars for English, French and German. We thus provide the potential grammar writer with a handbook in which sample analyses and their linguistic motivations can be looked up and used in the development of further grammars. To that end, we have tried to couch our solutions in terms that are sufficiently independent from the particular framework of LFG used in our grammar development effort. The presentation of the linguistic analyses and their implementation constitutes the substance of Part I. In Part II we report on the grammar engineering issues such as modularity, performance, and testing. As these issues are central to any grammar development effort, we have again tried to present the discussion of our experiences and results so that they may be of use in further grammar development efforts.

1.1   Parallel Grammars

The grammar development we report on in this book involves three languages: English, French and German. The overall aim of our project is to produce collaboratively written large Lexical-Functional Grammar (LFG) computational grammars for English, French, and German. Of central concern is the issue of how to balance grammar maintainability while at the same time still achieving large coverage. The project is therefore characterized by an attention to parallelism and crosslinguistic validity. The grammars are parallel in the sense that they are guided by a common set of linguistic principles and a commonly agreed upon set of grammatical analyses and features. This approach was taken in order

1

to maximize compatibility between the different grammars with regard to the phenomena being treated, and to ensure a maximal degree of generality.

Within a given linguistic theory (e.g., LFG), there are often several possible analyses for syntactic constructions such as prepositional phrases or relative clauses. In many cases, despite agreement on the general direction of the solution, no consensus has been reached by linguists. In any given language, three or four differing solutions might be possible for a particular construction, with one perhaps being the most attractive. Parallel grammar development involves looking at a syntactic construction in several different languages and, within the chosen linguistic theory, finding the one analysis among the various possibilities that is the most elegant and attractive for all of the languages under consideration, while simultaneously allowing for linguistically motivated divergences. Thus, parallel grammars are grammars with similar coverage in different languages which explore how similarly one can treat various phenomena crosslinguistically. This issue of the parallelism is a central concern in opening the door to a possible (unproblematic) extension of the analyses to other grammars and languages. An unproblematic extension is especially desirable in light of machine translation applications.

Another aspect of parallelism is embodied by the phenomena treated in this project. In our case, the grammar development effort was initially oriented by a user manual for tractors, available in French, German, and English. A plus of having used this corpus is that the texts are aligned so that the translation equivalents in the three languages are given sentence by sentence. An additional advantage is the immediate applicability of the resulting grammar towards machine translation in industrial contexts. One problem with using the tractor manual corpus is that certain core constructions, such as questions, do not occur in the text, while certain other constructions, such as imperatives, are statistically over-represented. In order to be able to parse standard sentences of each of the languages within our project, we included an implementation of core grammar constructions that do not necessarily appear in the base corpus. However, the technical text provided a good basis for the initial phase of parallel grammar development.

As LFG presents a modular conception of linguistic information, we have chosen to write grammars which concentrate on doing syntactic analyses only, but in such a way that the representations arrived at could serve as direct and useful input for further semantic interpretation (Halvorsen 1987, Dalrymple et al. 1993, Dalrymple 1999) or machine translation (Kaplan et al. 1989, Emele and Dorna 1998). Since the functional structures which primarily serve to represent predicate argument, head-modifier and control relations in LFG have shown to be translatable into QLFs (Quasi Logical Formulas) quite straightforwardly (van Genabith and Crouch 1996), we see the contribution of the work presented in this book as complementing the efforts represented by the Core Language Engine (CLE) (Alshawi 1992).

The grammar development reported on here took place within the ParGram (Parallel Grammars) project, which is a joint effort involving researchers from Xerox Palo Alto Research Center in California, the Xerox Research Centre Europe in Grenoble, France, and the Institut für Maschinelle Sprachverarbeitung at the University of Stuttgart, Germany.

In the remainder of this chapter, we provide a short overview of LFG, the syntactic theory underlying ParGram, and finally provide an introductory look at the architecture of the grammars.

1.2 Overview of LFG

LFG assumes two syntactic levels of representation: c(onstituent)-structure encodes phrasal dominance and precedence relations and is represented as a phrase structure tree; f(unctional)-structure encodes syntactic predicate argument structure and is represented as an attribute-value matrix (see section 1.3 for a more detailed discussion of the role these levels of representation play in the ParGram project). The c-structure is the product of a context free grammar; the f-structure reflects the collection of constraints imposed on the context free skeleton. The f-structure thus contains attributes, such as PRED, SUBJ, and OBJ, whose values can be other f-structures, as in (1b). Note that the ordering of the attributes in the f-structure is irrelevant since it is an unordered set. The (simplified) c-structure and f-structure for sentence (1a) are given in (1b) and (1c) respectively.

The value of the attribute PRED is considered to be a *semantic* value in that items like 'COFFEE' or 'DRINK' are taken to be a pointer to a more elaborated entry in which the precise lexical semantics of the item are encoded (Kaplan and Bresnan 1982). In the case of argument taking predicates it has been the convention to write the subcategorization frame as part of the entry.[1]

---

[1]With the advent of linking theory in LFG (Bresnan and Kanerva 1989, Bresnan and Moshi 1990), the explicit listing of grammatical functions in the subcategorization frame of a predicate became inapplicable, as the explicit mapping from argument structure (lexical semantics) to grammatical functions takes place in terms of linking principles. The f-structure in (1) does not reflect this, but would make it appear that *drink* subcategorizes directly for a SUBJ and an OBJ rather than, for example, an agent and a patient. As the f-structures are much easier to read with the subcate-

(1) a. Peter drinks coffee.

b. c-structure:

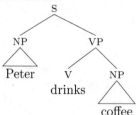

c. f-structure:

$$\begin{bmatrix} \text{PRED} & \text{'DRINK}\langle\text{SUBJ,OBJ}\rangle\text{'} \\ \text{SUBJ} & \begin{bmatrix} \text{PRED} & \text{'PETER'} \end{bmatrix} \\ \text{OBJ} & \begin{bmatrix} \text{PRED} & \text{'COFFEE'} \end{bmatrix} \end{bmatrix}$$

The relationship between c-structure trees and the corresponding f-structures is given by a *functional projection* function ϕ from c-structure nodes to f-structure attribute-value matrices. For example, the following annotated phrase-structure rules were used in the analysis of sentence (1a).

(2) S $\longrightarrow$ NP VP
$(\uparrow\text{SUBJ})=\downarrow$ $\uparrow=\downarrow$

VP $\longrightarrow$ V NP
$\uparrow=\downarrow$ $(\uparrow\text{OBJ})=\downarrow$

In each rule or lexical entry constraint, the $\uparrow$ metavariable refers to the ϕ-image of the mother c-structure node, and the $\downarrow$ metavariable refers to the ϕ-image of the nonterminal labeled by the constraint (Kaplan and Bresnan 1982:183). The annotations on the rules indicate that the f-structure for the S has a SUBJ attribute ($\uparrow$ in the annotation on the NP node) whose value is the f-structure for the NP daughter ($\downarrow$ in the annotation on the NP node), and that the S node corresponds to an f-structure which is the same as the f-structure for the VP daughter. The functional projection of a c-structure node is the solution of constraints associated with the phrase-structure rules and lexical entries (see below)

---

gorization frame spelled out in terms of grammatical functions, and since we have not implemented a version of linking theory, we have retained the earlier convention. Note that in the original version of LFG, semantic forms encoded the relation between grammatical functions and thematic roles.

used to derive the node.

When the phrase-structure rule for s is used in the analysis of a particular sentence, the metavariables ↑ and ↓ are instantiated to particular f-structures placed in correspondence with nodes of the c-structure. We refer to actual f-structures by giving them indices such as 1, 2, 3, and 4. The instantiated phrase structure rule is given in (3), with the ϕ correspondence between c-structure nodes and f-structures indicated by arrows leading from phrase-structure nodes to attribute-value matrices.

(3)   S ⟶   NP   VP
                (1 SUBJ)=2   1 = 4

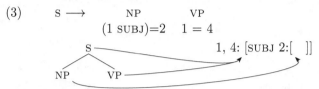

Lexical entries also use the metavariable ↑ to encode information about the f-structures of the preterminal nodes that immediately dominate them. A partial lexical entry for the word 'Peter' is:

(4) Peter NP   (↑PRED) = 'PETER'
                 (↑NUM)=SG
                 (↑PERS)=3
                 (↑GEND)=MASC

The constraint (↑PRED)='PETER' states that the preterminal node immediately dominating the terminal symbol 'Peter' has an f-structure whose value for the attribute PRED is 'PETER'. The entry also contains information as to person, number, and gender, which is relevant, for example, for determining agreement with the verb *drinks* whose lexical entry is shown in (5). If there is a conflict, the result is an illformed f-structure.

(5) drinks V   (↑PRED)='DRINK<SUBJ,OBJ>'
                 (↑TENSE)=PRESENT
                 (↑SUBJ PERS)=3
                 (↑SUBJ NUM)=SG

For a particular instance of use of the word *Peter*, the following c-structure and f-structure configuration results:

(6)   (2 PRED) = 'PETER'
         NP   2: [PRED 'PETER']
        ╱──╲
        Peter

There are three wellformedness conditions on the f-structure: functional uniqueness, completeness, and coherence (see Kaplan and Bresnan

1982 for the original definitions).

(7) **Functional Uniqueness:** In a given f-structure, a particular attribute may have at most one value.

Functional uniqueness guarantees that an attribute does not have more than one value. This, for example, rules out an f-structure in which the TENSE attribute is specified as both PAST and PRESENT. This does not mean that a particular attribute may not receive its value from more than one source. As long as the values can unify, this is no problem.[2] For example, if the PERS attribute of the subject is specified as first person both by the lexical entry of the subject noun and by the verb, the f-structure still satisfies functional uniqueness.

(8) **Completeness:** An f-structure is *locally complete* if and only if it contains all the governable grammatical functions that its predicate governs. An f-structure is *complete* if and only if it and all its subsidiary f-structures are locally complete.

Completeness states that all of the grammatical functions for which the predicate subcategorizes must be assigned values. This rules out clauses such as *John likes* in which the OBJ attribute of the predicate is not assigned a value.

(9) **Coherence:** An f-structure is *locally coherent* if and only if all the governable grammatical functions it contains are governed by a local predicate. An f-structure is *coherent* if and only if it and all its subsidiary f-structures are locally coherent.

Coherence requires every semantic form in the f-structure to be the PRED value of a grammatical function in that f-structure. That is, all items with a PRED must be assigned to a grammatical function. This results in clauses like *Kim appears the dog* being illformed because *the dog* is not associated with any argument of the verb nor can it be interpreted as an adjunct and hence it receives no grammatical function.

1.3 Levels of Representation

One of the primary purposes of the modularity assumed in LFG is the idea that one ought to be able to represent differing generalizations about languages at the level of representation most appropriate for that generalization. Syntactic, phonological, or semantic analyses of a given sentence within linguistic theory have most successfully been tackled under

---

[2]There are two exceptions to this. The first is semantic forms, i.e., the value of PREDs, which by definition cannot unify. The second are instantiated forms, which are defined by the user as attributes whose values cannot unify.

an approach which used differing tools and concepts for each of these areas (e.g., formal logic for semantics, notions of segments, syllables, and prosody for phonology). The modular organization of LFG allows the statement of generalizations relevant for a particular aspect of language at an independent level of representation. However, since the differing levels of representation are related to one another through the projection architecture, they are also *mutually constraining*, thus allowing for the modeling of the interactions between phonology, semantics, syntax and morphology that are observed in natural language. Most of the work in LFG has been done primarily from a syntactic point of view, so that the syntactic levels of representation are the best understood to date.

The grammars developed in ParGram make use of c-structure and f-structure (but see section 3.5.4 on morphosyntactic-structure) since our primary purpose is to provide a syntactic analysis for given sentences. This primary emphasis on syntax does not, however, preclude the possibility of subsequent semantic analysis at a level of s(emantic)-structure (see Halvorsen 1983 or Dalrymple et al. 1993 for some proposals on the representation of semantics in LFG) or machine translation based on f-structures (Kaplan, Netter, Wedekind and Zaenen 1989).

As discussed in section 1.2, there are two primary levels of syntactic representation in LFG. Facts about linear precedence and constituency are encoded in the c-structure. Information about predicate-argument, head modifier or control relationships, along with morphosyntactic properties such as tense, aspect, case, number and gender, are represented at f-structure. Besides this division of labor, another guiding idea for distinguishing the two levels of representation is that one would like to be able to factor out language universal properties from language particular properties. An examination of a wide variety of languages has shown that surface properties, such as word order and constituency, can vary quite drastically from language to language. However, a remarkable number of phenomena across languages express the same generalizations with respect to notions such as subject, object, complementation, control, anaphor binding, and head modifier relationships in general. These more language universal properties are expressed at f-structure, while the more language particular properties are encoded at c-structure.

One aspect of parallel grammar development that we set ourselves to explore within ParGram is how far one can develop parallel (ultimately language universal) analyses in English, French and German for various phenomena such as auxiliaries, control, coordination, relative clauses, comparatives and predicatives. In developing each of these analyses, we pursued the strategy that the analysis in terms of f-structure for each of the three languages should only differ where very good linguistic reasons could be provided. The analysis in terms of c-structure, however, was allowed to differ from language to language as this level of representation encodes the language particular facts such as word order or constituency.

The linguistic desirability of providing language universal analyses which produce parallel representations for German, French and English at the level of f-structure also proves to be an attractive feature in terms of machine translation. If machine translation can operate on a fairly deep, i.e., language universal, level of representation, it can operate more efficiently. Furthermore, a systematic and parallel representation at f-structure also ensures the viability of subsequent semantic interpretation. Rather than being faced with the task of developing a specially designed semantic construction and interpretation system for each language, the semanticist can formulate language universal principles of semantic interpretation on the basis of parallel f-structure representations. So, although f-structures are syntactic representations, they represent an interface to the semantics, and as such can be used as direct input for the purposes of translation.[3]

Within ParGram we therefore instituted strict guidelines for the kinds of information in terms of features and values that could be used in the development the f-structure analyses (see the Appendix for examples). In addition, despite the relative language dependent variability of German, French, and English c-structures, we aimed to set standards that would keep the structures readable. That is, the phrase structures were not allowed to vary so idiosyncratically across languages as to become mysterious, uninterpretable objects to anyone not thoroughly familiar with the language particular implementation. To that end, while we do not adhere to a strict X′ system, we use generally accepted categories like NP, VP and CP.[4] Where we needed to say something special about these categories, as in VPperf or CPrel, we maintain a standard that any such "extra" subscripts are represented with lower case letters. Illustrative examples from German and English are shown below.

---

[3]This is currently being experimented with at the University of Stuttgart with respect to Underspecified DRSs (Discourse Representation Structures) based on Discourse Representation Theory (Kamp and Reyle 1993) and at PARC with respect to linear logic (Dalrymple et al. 1993).

[4]The phrase structures generated by the analyses loosely adhere to common X′ principles, so that NPs dominate nouns or pronouns, VPs dominate verbs, APs dominate adjectives, etc. (see Bresnan 1982b for X′ Theory within LFG and Sells 1985 for a summary and comparison across theories). However, we avoided using explicit X′ terminology such as N′ or V′ in order to avoid any potential confusions as to what the phrase structure trees are expressing: they are not always binary branching, as is assumed in many current approaches to syntax (see Kayne 1984 as one of the original proponents of this idea), and the expansion of an NP, VP, or AP node may result in more than just the two levels of X′ and X.

(10) a. Wir haben eine Grammatik entwickelt.
          we have a   grammar   developed
          'We have developed a grammar.' (German)

      b. c-structure:

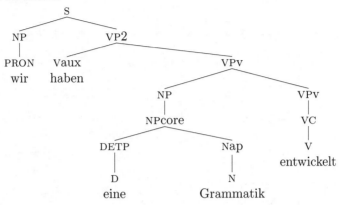

      c. f-structure:

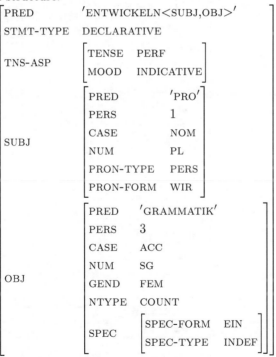

(11) a. We have developed a grammar.

  b. c-structure:

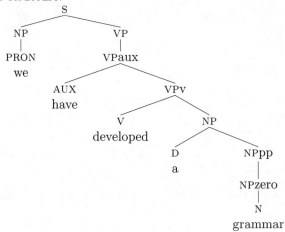

  c. f-structure:

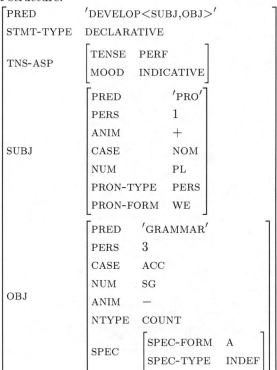

A comparison of the f-structures in (10c) and (11c) shows that at this level the analyses of the English and German sentences look very similar. There is a minor difference in that the English grammar makes use of an ANIM feature. In English, a syntactic differentiation between animate and inanimate is necessary for the distinction between the uses of *who* and *which* in relative clauses.

(12) The woman, who/*which is good, is laughing.
      The book, which/*who is good, is on the shelf.

As there is no such syntactic distinction in German, it has not been adopted in our grammar, although it could have been implemented vacuously in order to ensure complete parallelism. This, however, was not done as it could not be linguistically motivated. The general guideline towards establishing treatments of phenomena in the languages thus primarily consists of finding a linguistically motivated analysis. Gratuitous parallelism was avoided. Thus, the two f-structures in (10c) and (11c) only differ where necessary.

The two c-structures in (10b) and (11b), on the other hand, are fairly different in appearance. For example, the English grammar provides an analysis of the NP that has a depth of at least four levels, thus allowing for at least four differing possible attachment levels (see (11b)). This structurally rigid analysis of NPs is possible for English, but not for German, since English mandates very fixed word order, but German allows comparatively flexible word order patterning. The NP analysis in German, therefore, does not rely on structurally complex phrase structure schemata for an analysis and instead makes use of other tools (see section 4.2.2).

On the other hand, the German pattern of verb-second in main clauses and verb-final in subordinate clauses in combination with the rather free word order effects among the arguments gives rise to a structurally complex treatment of the VP in German. An example is shown in (13). Here the main clause contains the finite auxiliary *haben* 'have', which is in clause-second position, while the subordinate clause places the finite verb in clause-final position. Notice that the nonfinite main verb of the main clause *entwickelt* 'developed' is also in clause-final position: the generalization is that only the finite verbal element can appear in clause-second position.

(13) Wir haben eine Grammatik entwickelt, weil   wir gerne am
    We have a   grammar   developed because we like   at.the
    Rechner   sitzen.
    computer sit
    'We have developed a grammar because we like to sit at the com-
    puter.' (German)

The grammar represents this pattern by making a distinction as to whether a VP is verb-second (VP2) or verb final (VPv), and whether the finite verb-second clause was headed by an auxiliary or by a main verb. This difference in turn determines the possible realizations of the verb complex (VC) in clause-final position: if the finite auxiliary already appeared in clause-second position, then it should not be able to appear in the clause-final position, and the phrase structure rules are formulated accordingly. The English grammar, on the other hand, has taken the rigid positioning of the auxiliaries and modals with respect to the main verb, as in (14), into account and thus distinguishes VPs on the basis of whether or not they contain an auxiliary or a modal (see section 3.5)

(14)   a. The tractor will have been being started.

     b.*The tractor will have being been started.

To reiterate, the level of c-structure serves to encode language particular properties such as linear order, position, and constituent structure, and thus may differ widely from language to language. In contrast, the level of f-structure encodes analyses in terms of predicate-argument structure and head-modifier relationships, which are taken to hold at a "deeper", i.e., a language universal level.

1.4   Implementation and Environment

The grammar development environment used at the beginning of the ParGram project was the Xerox LFG Grammar Writer's Workbench (Kaplan and Maxwell 1996). This environment is written in Medley Lisp, a variant of Interlisp, and provides a cut-and-paste morphology which the grammar writer specifies by hand. It was designed mainly as a teaching tool for LFG theory and to be used by linguists to test particular linguistic constructions. Although it is a complete implementation of the LFG formalism, the Grammar Writer's Workbench turned out to be difficult to use with real-size on-line dictionaries, as well as producing unacceptable run-times for more complex sentences.[5]

---

[5]The Grammar Writer's Workbench remains a useful system in that it provides a complete implementation of the range of formal devices available in an LFG formalism. As such, it is highly recommended for teaching purposes, and smaller (perhaps

As such, grammar development efforts within ParGram now use the Xerox Linguistic Environment (XLE) as a platform for grammar development. XLE is an efficient C language reimplementation of the LFG Grammar Writer's Workbench which preserves the original spirit while operating within Unix and Tcl/Tk. Given ParGram's goal of producing parallel grammars that cover more than just a fragment of each particular language, XLE on the whole is a more appropriate platform. For example, within XLE it is possible to load real-size on-line lexicons, and parse complex forty word sentences in a reasonable amount of time. Another advantage of XLE is that it can be used for both parsing and generation.

The general architecture of the implementation is shown in (15).

(15)

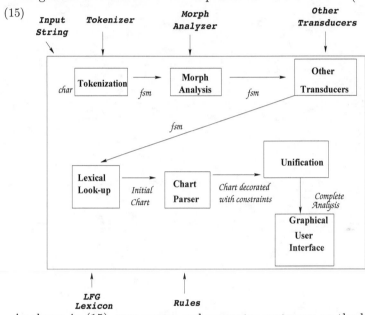

As shown in (15), XLE parses and generates sentences on the basis of grammar rules, one or more LFG lexicons (see section 11.4), a tokenizer (see 11.3.1), and a finite state morphological analyzer (see 11.3.2), as well as other finite state modules such as a guesser and a normalizer.

A more complete discussion of the various parts of the XLE architecture in (15) as pertaining to grammar development within ParGram can be found in Part II. In addition, an XLE "user manual" documenting its various features is currently being compiled. Part II also addresses

experimental) grammars. It is available at
http://www.parc.xerox.com/istl/groups/nltt/medley/.

some of the grammar engineering issues that were of particular relevance in the ParGram grammar development efforts, such as grammar modularity, maintainability, and transparency, blocking of ambiguity and overgeneration, and the vexing question of how to measure grammar performance in an objective and hardware independent way. But first we turn to the general analyses developed for the three languages within ParGram in Part I and hope that Parts I and II together will provide an informative and useful basis for further grammar development efforts.

Part I

The Grammars: General Analyses

2

The Clause

A clause is taken to encompass a constituent which contains a verb and all of its arguments, in addition to any adjuncts such as prepositional phrases or adverbs. In some cases, one or more of the arguments of the verb (usually the subject) may not be overt, e.g., in imperatives, or may have been pulled out of the clause and "fronted" for topicalization or other purposes. However, this is not generally seen as detracting from the nature of a clause. In most languages, a number of basic root or matrix clauses can be distinguished in terms of verb placement, verb morphology, intonation, or the presence and position of interrogative words. In our grammars we represent the distinctive syntax of various types of root clauses by distinguishing between declaratives, interrogatives and imperatives. The grammars also distinguish between various types of subordinate clauses such as conditionals, concessives, and subcategorized versus adjunct subordinate clauses.

2.1 Root Clauses

Root clauses appear independently. Subordinate clauses, such as *that* or *when* clauses (section 2.2 and 2.3) cannot occur without a matrix clause. Root clauses encompass several semantically and syntactically distinct types. We present differing c-structure analyses for these types and mark their distinctive semantic import in terms of a STMT-TYPE feature[1] at f-structure. This feature may then be fed into a separate semantic evaluation module.

2.1.1 Declaratives

The c-structure of declaratives is often considered the most basic clause structure of the language (as opposed to interrogatives (section 2.1.2),

---

[1] This feature does not reflect the type of speech act. Instead, it represents a very basic syntactic distinction among types of clauses according to their syntax.

imperatives (section 2.1.3), or embedded clauses (section 2.2)). All declaratives are assigned STMT-TYPE DECLARATIVE; this is treated as a default, while special constructions like interrogatives and imperatives will provide their own STMT-TYPE. One important characteristic of root declaratives is that they are tensed. We ensure this by annotating the c-structure rules with a condition that demands the existence of a TENSE feature, which is provided by a finite verb.[2]

Some languages allow practically any order of constituents in declarative clauses; these orders are usually associated with varying discourse functions and there may be specific constructional interpretations of certain orders (É. Kiss 1995, Vallduví 1992). However, many languages have relatively strict c-structure requirements on root declaratives. For example, English and French require the subject to precede the VP in simple declaratives, as in (1), and have further requirements on the internal structure of the VP, e.g., the verb is followed by the object which is followed by other arguments and adjuncts. In contrast, German allows relatively free order among the verb's arguments and adjuncts, but requires the finite verb to be in second position (i.e., to follow the first constituent), as in (2).

(1) a. The driver starts the tractor with the key.
    b. Le conducteur fait   demarrer le tracteur avec la   clef.
       the driver   makes start   the tractor with the key
       'The driver starts the tractor with the key.' (French)

(2) a. [Der   Fahrer] **startet** den   Traktor mit dem
       the.Nom driver starts   the.Acc tractor with the.Dat
       Schlüssel.
       key
       'The driver starts the tractor with the key.' (German)
    b. [Den Traktor] **startet** der Fahrer mit dem Schlüssel.
    c. [Mit dem Schlüssel] **startet** der Fahrer den Traktor.
    d. [Mit dem Schlüssel] **startet** den Traktor der Fahrer.

In the three grammars, declaratives are taken to be the default type of root clause and are analyzed as a simple S. In French and English, the S expands into a structure which requires a subject preceding a VP

---

[2]In addition, root declaratives are generally punctuated with a period in German, French, and English. When dealing with punctuated input, we parse the punctuation as part of the input (punctuation differs widely crosslinguistically, but not in our sample set — see Nunberg 1990 for a discussion of the linguistics of punctuation). However, when dealing with text derived from natural speech recordings, in which punctuation is not part of the original input, punctuation is not parsed.

in declaratives, and the VP expands into a verb with an optional object following it. Further arguments such as secondary objects and obliques may follow, and adjuncts are interspersed among the arguments (not shown here).

(3) S ⟶   NP   VP
                   (↑SUBJ)=↓   ↑=↓

     VP ⟶   V   (NP)   (NP)   (PP)
                    ↑=↓   (↑OBJ)=↓   (↑OBJ2)=↓   (↑OBL)=↓

The rules presented here are an abstraction over the actual implementation, which involves the treatment of such phenomena as *that* clauses in subject position, the role of topics, and the addition of further constraining annotations to prevent the grammar from overgenerating. The essential backbone of the logic and structure of the analysis, however, is as described here. In all three languages, the f-structure analyses are parallel and are essentially the same as the one given for English in (4c).

(4) a. The driver starts the tractor.

     b.

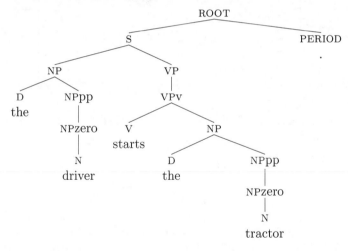

c.
$$
\begin{bmatrix}
\text{PRED} & \text{'START<SUBJ,OBJ>'} \\
\text{STMT-TYPE} & \text{DECLARATIVE} \\
\text{TNS-ASP} & \begin{bmatrix} \text{TENSE} & \text{PRES} \\ \text{MOOD} & \text{INDICATIVE} \end{bmatrix} \\
\text{SUBJ} & \begin{bmatrix} \text{PRED} & \text{'DRIVER'} \\ \text{PERS} & 3 \\ \text{ANIM} & + \\ \text{CASE} & \text{NOM} \\ \text{NUM} & \text{SG} \\ \text{NTYPE} & \text{COUNT} \\ \text{SPEC} & \begin{bmatrix} \text{SPEC-FORM} & \text{THE} \\ \text{SPEC-TYPE} & \text{DEF} \end{bmatrix} \end{bmatrix} \\
\text{OBJ} & \begin{bmatrix} \text{PRED} & \text{'TRACTOR'} \\ \text{PERS} & 3 \\ \text{CASE} & \text{ACC} \\ \text{NUM} & \text{SG} \\ \text{ANIM} & - \\ \text{NTYPE} & \text{COUNT} \\ \text{SPEC} & \begin{bmatrix} \text{SPEC-FORM} & \text{THE} \\ \text{SPEC-TYPE} & \text{DEF} \end{bmatrix} \end{bmatrix}
\end{bmatrix}
$$

In German, the relatively free word order demonstrated by (2) is handled via functional uncertainty (see Kaplan and Zaenen 1989, and Kaplan and Maxwell 1996 for a discussion of the phenomena and the introduction of functional uncertainty). Functional uncertainty allows a characterization of long-distance dependencies without traces, gaps, or chains. That is, the free word order effects of German, in which arguments and adjuncts can appear in any order within a given clause (the particular order in any given sentence is determined by factors such as definiteness, phonological weight, and discourse "packaging" considerations) and can be extracted out of the clause, can be modeled without having to assume an invariant deep structure from which all other orders are derived. Instead, arguments and adjuncts can be base generated in all of the positions they might be found in and connected to the clause they belong to via a functional uncertainty path.

In the German grammar, for example, root clauses are taken to be an S which expands into a single constituent preverbal position and a VP in which the finite V must precede all other arguments and adjuncts. On the face of it, this does not appear to be so different from what is done for the English and French grammars. The crucial difference, however, lies not in the expansion of S, but in the functional annotations associated with these expansions, as shown in (5) (leaving aside PPs for ease of exposition).

(5) S $\longrightarrow$ NP   VP
                  ($\uparrow$XCOMP* GF)=$\downarrow$ $\uparrow$=$\downarrow$

   VP $\longrightarrow$ V   NP*
                  $\uparrow$=$\downarrow$ ($\uparrow$XCOMP* GF)=$\downarrow$

The functional annotations make use of regular expressions to allow for an infinite disjunction of possibilities. The Kleene star '$*$' on the XCOMP indicates that the NP in question may be embedded under any number of verbal complements, while the GF is shorthand notation for a disjunction of governed (subcategorized for) grammatical functions such as subject, object, and oblique.[3] Thus, (6a) will be instantiated as in (7a) and (6b) as in (7b). For purposes of illustration, the c-structure and f-structure of (6b) are shown in (8). Note that the f-structure of the German (6b) and of the English equivalent are essentially identical, despite the difference in word order. It is only the c-structures which differ.

(6) a. Der   Fahrer startet den   Traktor.
        the.Nom driver starts the.Acc tractor
        'The driver starts the tractor. (German)
     b. Den Traktor startet der Fahrer.

---

[3]The implementation realized within XLE is a nonconstructive one. Layers of complementation (XCOMPs here) are only instantiated if there is evidence for them elsewhere. That is, the expansion of the Kleene star is very constrained in practice. For a detailed discussion on why the power introduced by functional uncertainty does not render the formalism of LFG undecidable see Kaplan and Maxwell 1988a.

(7) a. S ⟶   NP   VP
                    (↑SUBJ)=↓   ↑=↓

          VP ⟶   V   NP
                         ↑=↓   (↑OBJ)=↓

      b. S ⟶   NP   VP
                    (↑OBJ)=↓   ↑=↓

          VP ⟶   V   NP
                         ↑=↓   (↑SUBJ)=↓

(8) a. Den Traktor startet den Fahrer.
     b.

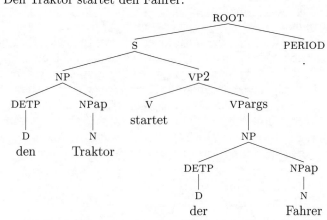

c.
$$\begin{bmatrix} \text{PRED} & \text{'STARTEN}<\text{SUBJ,OBJ}>\text{'} \\ \text{STMT-TYPE} & \text{DECLARATIVE} \\ \text{TNS-ASP} & \begin{bmatrix} \text{TENSE} & \text{PRES} \\ \text{MOOD} & \text{INDICATIVE} \end{bmatrix} \\ \text{SUBJ} & \begin{bmatrix} \text{PRED} & \text{'FAHRER'} \\ \text{PERS} & 3 \\ \text{GEND} & \text{MASC} \\ \text{CASE} & \text{NOM} \\ \text{NUM} & \text{SG} \\ \text{NTYPE} & \text{COUNT} \\ \text{SPEC} & \begin{bmatrix} \text{SPEC-FORM} & \text{DER} \\ \text{SPEC-TYPE} & \text{DEF} \end{bmatrix} \end{bmatrix} \\ \text{OBJ} & \begin{bmatrix} \text{PRED} & \text{'TRAKTOR'} \\ \text{PERS} & 3 \\ \text{GEND} & \text{MASC} \\ \text{CASE} & \text{ACC} \\ \text{NUM} & \text{SG} \\ \text{NTYPE} & \text{COUNT} \\ \text{SPEC} & \begin{bmatrix} \text{SPEC-FORM} & \text{DER} \\ \text{SPEC-TYPE} & \text{DEF} \end{bmatrix} \end{bmatrix} \end{bmatrix}$$

2.1.2 Interrogatives

Interrogatives often have substantially different c-structures from their declarative counterparts. The syntactic encoding of questions also differs widely crosslinguistically. For example, some languages form yes-no questions solely by a change in intonation, whereas others insert a special morpheme indicative of the type of question. Some languages (such as English) place interrogative words (*wh*-words) in a certain position (clause initial in English), while other languages leave the interrogative words *in situ*.

This wide variation in syntactic encoding is reflected by the three ParGram languages. In French, for example, yes-no questions involve the appearance of the special phrase *est-ce que*, as in (9b). In all three languages, yes-no questions may also be formed by subject-auxiliary inversion, as in (9c), (10b) and (11b).

(9) a. Tu as conduit ce tracteur.
   you have driven this tractor
   'You have driven this tractor.' (French)

 b. Est-ce que tu as conduit ce tracteur?
   Is-it that you have driven this tractor
   'Have you driven this tractor?' (French)

 c. As-tu conduit ce tracteur?
   have-you driven this tractor
   'Have you driven this tractor?' (French)

(10) a. They have been flashing repeatedly.

 b. Have they been flashing repeatedly?

(11) a. Die rote Kontrollampe ist aufgeleuchtet.
   the.Nom red control light is lit up
   'The red control light has lit up.' (German)

 b. Ist die rote Kontrollampe aufgeleuchtet?
   is the.Nom red control light lit up
   'Has the red control light lit up?' (German)

For questions formed with so-called *wh*-words (*who, what*, etc.), these differences include the appearance of interrogative phrases. These phrases often appear in restricted c-structure positions. In English and German, for example, one of the interrogative phrases must appear in initial position, as in (12). This may be accompanied by other effects, such as the continued placement of the subject immediately before the finite verb, and the "doubling" of the subject as a clitic in the French (13).

(12) What did he see?

(13) Quel tracteur Jean a-t-il conduit?
   which tractor Jean has-T-he driven
   'Which tractor did Jean drive?' (French)

Due to these substantial differences in c-structure, interrogatives are treated with a separate set of c-structure rules, including one set for yes-no questions and one for *wh*-questions. This allows a simple way of introducing STMT-TYPE INTERROGATIVE, which all interrogatives have, and the special punctuation which usually accompanies root interrogatives. However, a number of problems arise with regard to the appropriate distribution of interrogative phrases, especially in multiple questions, and with ensuring the correct form of the auxiliaries in subject-auxiliary inversion constructions.[4]

---

[4]German also has a "scope-marking" construction which involves the appearance of multiple *was* 'what' markers. We have not handled this construction in the gram-

In keeping with the aim of parallel grammar development and the underlying tenets of LFG, the c-structure analysis of interrogatives differs from language to language as it interacts with other syntactic properties of the language (i.e., auxiliary inversion, English *do*-support, German scrambling, the position of subjects, etc.). However, at the level of f-structure, the analysis aims to encode a more universal representation of the constructions. As such, the c-structures for the German interrogative in (14) and its English counterpart in (15) differ, but the resulting f-structure analyses are essentially identical.[5]

(14) a. Was hat er gesehen?
         what has he seen
         'What did he see?' (German)

   b.

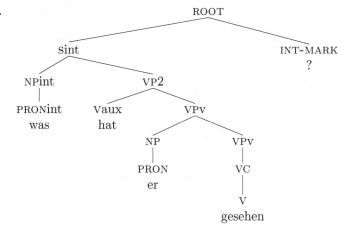

---

mar as yet and as such do not discuss it here.

[5]The value for tense differs in (14c) and (15c). The tense values are based on the language particular morphosyntactic forms. As these differ in (14a) and (15a), this difference is preserved. The fact that the German perfect tense is often interpreted as a simple past tense must be handled in the semantics. The VSEM encodes the properties of unaccusativity vs. unergativity and is instrumental in the treatment of auxiliary selection in French and German.

c.
$$
\begin{bmatrix}
\text{PRED} & \text{'SEHEN<SUBJ,OBJ>'} \\
\text{STMT-TYPE} & \text{INTERROGATIVE} \\
\text{VSEM} & \text{UNERG} \\
\text{TNS-ASP} & \begin{bmatrix} \text{TENSE} & \text{PERF} \\ \text{MOOD} & \text{INDICATIVE} \end{bmatrix} \\
\text{SUBJ} & \begin{bmatrix} \text{PRED} & \text{'PRO'} \\ \text{PERS} & \text{3} \\ \text{GEND} & \text{MASC} \\ \text{CASE} & \text{NOM} \\ \text{NUM} & \text{SG} \\ \text{PRON-TYPE} & \text{PERS} \\ \text{PRON-FORM} & \text{ER} \end{bmatrix} \\
\text{OBJ} & \begin{bmatrix} \text{PRED} & \text{'PRO'} \\ \text{PERS} & \text{3} \\ \text{GEND} & \text{NEUT} \\ \text{CASE} & \text{ACC} \\ \text{NUM} & \text{SG} \\ \text{INT} & + \\ \text{PRON-TYPE} & \text{INT} \\ \text{PRON-FORM} & \text{WAS} \end{bmatrix}
\end{bmatrix}
$$

(15) a. What did he see?

b.

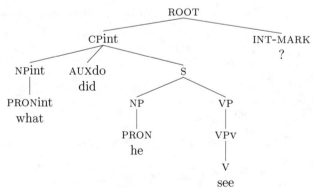

c. $\begin{bmatrix} \text{PRED} & '\text{SEE}<\text{SUBJ,OBJ}>' \\ \text{STMT-TYPE} & \text{INTERROGATIVE} \\ \text{TNS-ASP} & \begin{bmatrix} \text{TENSE} & \text{PAST} \\ \text{MOOD} & \text{INDICATIVE} \end{bmatrix} \\ \text{SUBJ} & \begin{bmatrix} \text{PRED} & '\text{PRO}' \\ \text{PERS} & 3 \\ \text{GEND} & \text{MASC} \\ \text{ANIM} & + \\ \text{CASE} & \text{NOM} \\ \text{NUM} & \text{SG} \\ \text{PRON-TYPE} & \text{PERS} \\ \text{PRON-FORM} & \text{HE} \end{bmatrix} \\ \text{OBJ} & \begin{bmatrix} \text{PRED} & '\text{PRO}' \\ \text{PERS} & 3 \\ \text{INT} & + \\ \text{GEND} & \text{NEUT} \\ \text{CASE} & \text{ACC} \\ \text{NUM} & \text{SG} \\ \text{PRON-TYPE} & \text{INT} \\ \text{PRON-FORM} & \text{WHAT} \end{bmatrix} \end{bmatrix}$

2.1.3 Imperatives

Imperatives have a number of distinctive features which separate them from declaratives and interrogatives. In many languages, they have distinct morphology on the verb and are not tensed, but instead show a different mood. For example, English imperatives use the base form of the verb, while in French and German imperatives can either be bare infinitives or a special imperative form. Some sample imperatives are shown in (16).

(16) a. Push the button.

b. Tourne-le   doucement.
   turn.Imp-it gently
   'Turn it gently.' (French)

c. Den   Hebel vorsichtig drehen.
   the.Acc lever carefully turn
   'Turn the lever carefully.' (German)

    d. Drehe   den   Hebel vorsichtig.
       turn.2.Sg.Imp the.Acc lever carefully
       'Turn the lever carefully.' (German)

A distinctive feature of imperatives crosslinguistically is that they lack an overt subject. The subject is understood to be a second person PRO and must be provided either as part of the imperative rule or by the imperative morphology. Finally, imperatives are often characterized by a distinct c-structure, in part due to the lack of an overt subject. For example, in the basic French and English imperative, the verb is clause initial, in contrast to the order for declaratives (2.1.1). French also has a distinct clitic position and order in imperatives. In German, the verb is clause final if it is in the base form ((16c)), and clause initial if it is finite and is marked by special imperative morphology ((16d)).

Since the imperatives in French, German and English are a different type of construction from declaratives and interrogatives, they are handled by specialized c-structure rules which dictate the different word order, lack of subject, and special imperative morphology. Within these specialized rules, the STMT-TYPE IMPERATIVE is assigned. As should be clear by now, the c-structure representations of imperatives in the various languages differ, but result in essentially identical f-structures. As a representative analysis, the f-structure for the English (16a) is shown below.

(17) a. Push the button.

      b.

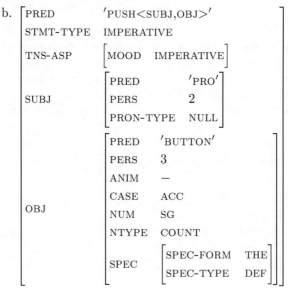

As mentioned above, French and German allow infinitive clauses to function as imperatives, as in (18a). These infinitive imperatives are common in instructional texts, such as the tractor manual used for the ParGram project. Within the grammars, infinitive imperatives are analyzed like the morphological imperatives above, as seen in (18b), though they are handled by different c-structure rules. One difference in the f-structure analysis is the absence of mood marking in the infinitives, which is a reflection of the difference in morphology.

It should be noted that our approach of identifying clauses in terms of a cluster of syntactic properties and then writing clause particular phrase structure rules to account for these properties is very close in spirit to the approach taken within Construction Grammar (Kay and Fillmore 1994), where different types of phenomena are viewed in terms of classes of constructions. Thus, our imperative, interrogative and declarative clause types could be viewed as encoding three different types of constructions.

(18) a. Pousser le tracteur.
push.Inf the tractor
'Push the tractor.' (French)

b.
$$
\begin{bmatrix}
\text{PRED} & \text{'POUSSER<SUBJ,OBJ>'} \\
\text{STMT-TYPE} & \text{IMPERATIVE} \\
\text{SUBJ} & \begin{bmatrix} \text{PRED} & \text{'PRO'} \\ \text{PERS} & 2 \\ \text{PRON-TYPE} & \text{NULL} \end{bmatrix} \\
\text{OBJ} & \begin{bmatrix} \text{PRED} & \text{'TRACTEUR'} \\ \text{SPEC} & \begin{bmatrix} \text{SPEC-TYPE} & \text{DEF} \\ \text{SPEC-FORM} & \text{LE} \end{bmatrix} \\ \text{CASE} & \text{ACC} \\ \text{GEND} & \text{MASC} \\ \text{PERS} & 3 \\ \text{NUM} & \text{SG} \end{bmatrix}
\end{bmatrix}
$$

2.2 Embedded Clauses

Clauses which are subordinate to another (matrix) verb are referred to as embedded clauses. In contrast with adjunct clauses, which are treated separately in 2.3, embedded clauses function as the argument of a verb and must be subcategorized for by that verb. An example is given in (19), where the verb *think* subcategorizes for two arguments: a subject *the driver* and an embedded *that*-clause.

(19) The driver thinks [(that) she has started the tractor].

Following standard LFG analyses as formulated in Bresnan 1982a, we encode the argument status of these embedded clauses by treating them either as a COMP(lement) or XCOMP(lement) argument of the matrix verb. Both these complements are in turn headed by verbs. In (19) above the verb *start* heads the complement clause. The two types of complements differ from one another in terms of how the embedded subject (*she* in (19)) is bound. An XCOMP can be thought of as an "open" function in the sense that the embedded subject must be controlled by an argument in the root (matrix) clause. This is the case in sentences such as *The driver wants to start the tractor*, where the *driver* and the starter of the tractor must be one and the same person. Such occurences of control are referred to as *functional control* and are contrasted with instances of *anaphoric control*, which are argued to occur with the "closed" complement COMP. A COMP either displays an overt subject of its own, as in (19), or it can have an *anaphorically controlled* PRO subject. In other words, the subject of the COMP is not identical with an argument of the matrix clause, but instead must be reconstructed (anaphorically) from the larger context. For details on the notion of control within LFG, and in particular the distinction between functional and anaphoric control, see Bresnan 1982a.

Finally, XCOMPs are generally (but not always) associated with nonfinite complements and COMPs with finite complements. As with root clauses, embedded clauses can be declarative or interrogative (but not imperative). A given verb will require a given type and form of embedded clause; these requirements are stated as part of the verb's lexical entry. For a more detailed exposition on these grammatical functions and the encoding of verbal lexical entries, see Chapter 3. In the remainder of this section we go through various types of embedded clauses and present the analyses implemented in ParGram.

2.2.1 Subcategorized Declaratives

The c-structure of embedded declaratives[6] crosslinguistically usually differs from that of root declaratives. In German, French and English, embedded declaratives must generally be introduced by an overt complementizer, as in (20). In German the position of the finite verb is clause final, as opposed to in a matrix clause, where it appears in second position, as shown in (21).

---

[6]Here the term declarative is used to encompass those embedded clauses which are not interrogative.

(20) a. Elle sait   [que le   tracteur est rouge].
         she knows that the tractor is   red
         'She knows that the tractor is red.' (French)

    b. Le tracteur est rouge.
       the tractor is   red
       'The tractor is red.' (French)

(21) a. Der   Fahrer denkt, [daß er den   Traktor
         the.Nom driver thinks that he the.Acc tractor
         gestartet hat].
         started   has
         'The driver thinks that he started the tractor.' (German)

    b. Er hat den   Traktor gestartet.
       he has the.Acc tractor started
       'He started the tractor.' (German)

Due to such differences, separate c-structure rules instantiate embedded declaratives, e.g., ones which include complementizers and changes in verb position. These rules may, however, in turn call portions of the root clause rules. For example, in English the c-structure rule for embedded clauses consists of a complementizer position followed by the usual root s rule.

Another difference between root and embedded declaratives is tense.[7] Certain verbs have embedded complements that are infinitival and hence untensed, unlike root declaratives which require tense in most languages. Embedded infinitives occur without an overt subject, as in (22a), and with or without a complementizer, as shown in (23).

(22) a. The driver wants [to start the tractor].

    b. The driver thinks [(that) she has started the tractor].

(23) a. Il permet [à Jean de venir].
       he allows to Jean of come
       'He allows Jean to come.' (French)

---

[7]Embedded clauses also involve sequencing of tenses in many languages, including English, French and German. For example, an embedded clause indicating a past event will appear in the pluperfect if the root verb is also past tense.

He said that he had started the tractor.

(=He said, "I started the tractor.")

There are also often constraints on the mood of the embedded clause, e.g., subjunctive or indicative. The rules governing this phenomenon are semantic and are as yet not well understood (Kamp and Reyle 1993, Abush 1994). As such, the ParGram grammars simply parse and record the morphosyntactic tense for potential semantic processing, but do not try to establish semantically based wellformedness constraints.

b. Il veut [venir].
he wants come
'He wants to come.' (French)

A sample analysis of the embedded infinitive in (22a) is shown in (24b). The English *to*, and its German counterpart *zu* are treated as particles which mark an infinitive (see Pullum 1982 on an alternative analysis in which the English *to* is treated as an auxiliary). Note that the embedded subject is identified with the subject of the root clause (*driver*) and that no tense/aspect specification is made in the infinitive embedded clause.

(24) a. The driver wants to start the tractor.

b.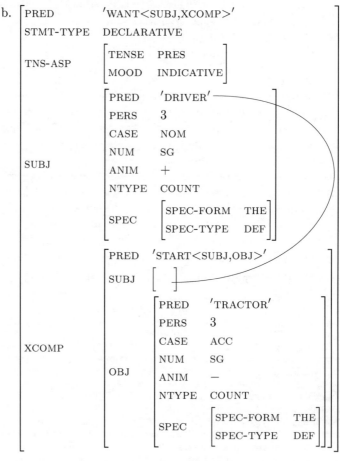

The German and French f-structure analyses are again essentially parallel to (24b). Differences in word order such as the position of the verb in German do not appear as part of the f-structure analysis, but are encoded at c-structure.

The f-structure analysis of embedded finite clauses as in (22b) is similar to that of embedded interrogatives in that the root verb subcategorizes for a COMP. As such, we do not show an explicit example of an embedded finite clause here, but refer the reader to the next section on embedded interrogatives. The two types of embedded clauses differ, of course, in the value of the STMT-TYPE (interrogative vs. declarative) and the fact that the interrogative contains *wh*-elements.

2.2.2 Subcategorized Interrogatives

Embedded interrogatives again differ in terms of c-structures with regard to their matrix counterparts. As illustrated in (26)–(27), subject-auxiliary inversion in English occurs in matrix interrogatives, but not in embedded interrogatives. In German the verb placement differs again, and in French some form of subject (pronoun)-auxiliary inversion also takes place, with the additional insertion of a question morpheme, as illustrated by the *va-t-il* in (27). As such, embedded interrogatives also require the formulation of special c-structure rules.

(25) a. Sie fragte, [ob   der   Traktor lief].
      She asked whether the.Nom tractor ran.
      'She asked whether the tractor was running.' (German)

   b. Sie weiß, [wer den   Traktor gestartet hat].
      She knows who the.Acc Traktor started   has
      'She knows who started the tractor.' (German)

(26) a. They know [which tractor the driver will start].

   b. Which tractor will the driver start?

(27) a. Ils   savent [quel est le   tracteur que   le   conducteur
      they know which is the tractor   which the driver
      fera   demarrer].
      will.make start
      'They know which tractor the driver will start.' (French)

   b. Quel tracteur le   conducteur va-t-il   faire demarrer?
      which tractor the driver   go-T-he make start
      'Which tractor will the driver start?' (French)

Interrogative elements which serve to embed a phrase, such as English *whether* or German *ob* are treated like declarative complementizers such as *that*. As a sample analysis, the f-structure for (25a) is shown below.

(28) a. Sie fragte, [ob   der   Traktor lief].
        She asked whether the.Nom tractor ran.
        'She asked whether the tractor was running.' (German)
    b.

$$
\begin{bmatrix}
\text{PRED} & \text{'FRAGEN<SUBJ,COMP>'} \\
\text{STMT-TYPE} & \text{DECLARATIVE} \\
\text{TNS-ASP} & \begin{bmatrix} \text{TENSE} & \text{PAST} \\ \text{MOOD} & \text{INDICATIVE} \end{bmatrix} \\
\text{SUBJ} & \begin{bmatrix} \text{PRED} & \text{'PRO'} \\ \text{PERS} & 3 \\ \text{CASE} & \text{NOM} \\ \text{NUM} & \text{SG} \\ \text{GEND} & \text{FEM} \\ \text{PRON-TYPE} & \text{PERS} \\ \text{PRON-FORM} & \text{SIE} \end{bmatrix} \\
\text{COMP} & \begin{bmatrix} \text{PRED} & \text{'LAUFEN<SUBJ>'} \\ \text{STMT-TYPE} & \text{INTERROGATIVE} \\ \text{COMP-FORM} & \text{OB} \\ \text{TNS-ASP} & \begin{bmatrix} \text{TENSE} & \text{PAST} \\ \text{MOOD} & \text{INDICATIVE} \end{bmatrix} \\ \text{SUBJ} & \begin{bmatrix} \text{PRED} & \text{'TRAKTOR'} \\ \text{PERS} & 3 \\ \text{GEND} & \text{MASC} \\ \text{CASE} & \text{NOM} \\ \text{NUM} & \text{SG} \\ \text{NTYPE} & \text{COUNT} \\ \text{SPEC} & \begin{bmatrix} \text{SPEC-FORM} & \text{DER} \\ \text{SPEC-TYPE} & \text{DEF} \end{bmatrix} \end{bmatrix} \end{bmatrix}
\end{bmatrix}
$$

The fact that an embedded clause is interrogative is usually signalled by the presence of particular lexical items or with a distinctive c-structure. Some languages use distinctive interrogative pronouns and particles for embedded clauses, e.g., English *whether* and French *ce que* 'what'. As with root interrogatives, embedded interrogatives are assigned STMT-TYPE INTERROGATIVE in the f-structure; this feature can be used to satisfy the subcategorization requirements of verbs which take interrogative complements.

Note that while the matrix clause (headed by the verb *fragte* 'asked') is declarative, the embedded COMP clause is marked as interrogative. As mentioned before, an embedded declarative clause would receive essentially the same f-structure analysis, but the value for the STMT-TYPE and the COMP-FORM would differ. Also note that while the encoding of the features COMP-FORM and STMT-TYPE are used to help in the formulation of wellformedness conditions in minor ways in the grammar, their primary reason for existence is a registration of information that is presumably useful for subsequent semantic analysis.

2.3 Clausal Adjuncts

Clausal adjuncts are subordinate clauses which are not subcategorized for by the verb, as in (29). These can occur with or without a subordinator and can be tensed, infinitival, or participial. Not all languages have all possible combinations, but the types illustrated here are represented in German and French as well.

(29) a. [When the light is red,] push the button.
     b. [To start the engine,] turn the key.
     c. [After closing the door,] lock it carefully.
     d. [Having turned off the lights,] stop the engine.

   In English these clausal adjuncts occur clause initially and clause finally. More than one clausal adjunct can occur in a given clause; they can be sisters, i.e., all modifying the main clause, or nested, i.e., one clausal adjunct modifying the other. Their distribution in German is free in the sense that there is no fixed position that the adjuncts are restricted to. At f-structure the clausal adjuncts are analyzed uniformly as belonging to an ADJUNCT set which modifies the main predicate of the clause.

2.3.1 Infinitival Adjuncts

Infinitival clausal adjuncts can either have a subordinator, as in (30a), or not, as in (30b). The subject of the infinitival is not overt in the string. In the case of clausal adjuncts it is assumed to be an instance of anaphoric control. That is, the subject of the adjunct must be provided by the context: it can either be the same as the subject of the matrix clause, or it can refer to another entity altogether. The subject of the adjunct clause is specified to be PRED PRO and PRON-TYPE NULL, indicating that there is no overt pronoun form. This information is provided by the rule that introduces the clausal adjunct in the c-structure. An f-structure with simplified representations for the object pronouns is shown in (31).

(30) a. Toucher le bouton, [sans   le pousser].
       touch   the button without it push
      'Touch the button without pushing it.' (French)

    b. [To start the engine,] turn the key.

(31) a. To start it, turn it.

    b.

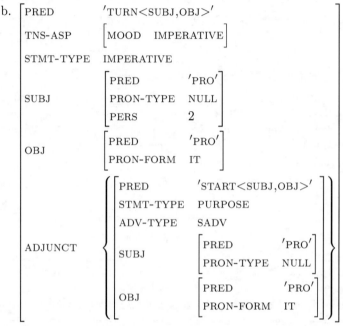

Note that bare infinitivals are not introduced by a subordinator so they have no COMP-FORM. In these cases, the infinitival adjunct denotes an imperative and is marked as such via the STMT-TYPE.

2.3.2 Participial

Passive and present/progressive participles can be used as clausal adverbials with and without subordinating conjunctions, as in (32)–(33). Again, as with the infinitival adjuncts, the nonovert PRO subject of the participial clause is introduced by a rule in the c-structure. This then accounts for the instances in which the subject of the participial is not necessarily related to that of the matrix clause, as in (32).

(32) The driver caught sight of the dog, turning the corner.

(33) a. [Turning the wheel,] press the brake gently.

b. [En   tournant,] le pousser.
   while turning   it push
   'While turning, push it.' (French)

c. [Supported by the struts,] it will remain open.

d. Im   Traktor sitzend, den   Schlüssel drehen.
   in.Dat tractor sitting the.Acc key   turn
   'Sitting in the tractor, turn the key.' (German)

(34) a. Touch the button without pushing it.

    b.

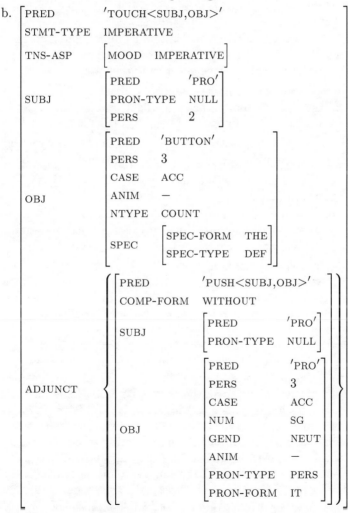

These participial clausal adjuncts have the same distribution as the other clausal adjuncts discussed here. When these participials are not introduced by an overt complementizer or conjunction, they also do not have a COMP-FORM.

2.3.3 Finite

Finite clausal adjuncts are generally introduced by a subordinator, dubbed a CONJsub in the grammars. These subordinators contribute a COMP-FORM and a STMT-TYPE to the f-structure analysis, but no predicate. Thus, the main predicate of the clausal adjunct is the verb, just as with embedded clauses introduced by *that*, for example. Many subordinators allow infinitives and participials as well as finite clauses in the clausal adjunct. As such, each subordinator must specify in its lexical entry which type of clausal complement it can occur with.

(35) Si le   moteur tourne, la   lampe s'allumera.
     if the motor   runs   the lamp   light up-Fut
     'If the motor is running, the lamp will light up.' (French)

There are some finite clausal adjuncts which do not have a subordinator, e.g., certain English and German conditionals, as in (36).

(36) a. Were I to go, I would need to leave immediately.
      b. Had I gone, I would have seen your cousin.
      c. Läuft der   Motor, (dann) leuchtet die   Lampe.
         runs the.Nom motor then   glows   the.Nom lamp
         'If the motor is running, then the lamp lights up.' (German)

These are also assigned a STMT-TYPE, but not a COMP-FORM since there is no subordinating conjunction. These constructions present an interesting case as they must be introduced by special rules which require the verb to appear in initial position. Furthermore, conditionals in the general form of *if-then* or *when-then* clauses can be identified as a particular kind of construction at the root level due to their syntactic properties. The presence of an *if*-clause, for example, always entails the presence of a *then*-clause. Even if the *if* or the *then* are not overt, the presence of a conditional can be deduced from the special word order within the *if* clause. This is exemplified by (36) above, where the English examples express the conditional via auxiliary inversion, while the German marks the conditional by instantiating a verb-initial clause.

A special c-structure rule encodes the particular structure of conditionals in all three grammars, taking into account the language particular word order and verb placement. Despite the crosslinguistic and language internal variation in the overt realization of conditionals, the special c-structure rules for conditionals in each case nevertheless correspond to basically identical f-structures. A sample f-structure for (36c) is shown in (37).

(37) a. Läuft der Motor, (dann) leuchtet die Lampe.
runs the.Nom motor then glows the.Nom lamp
'If the motor is running, then the lamp lights up.' (German)

b.

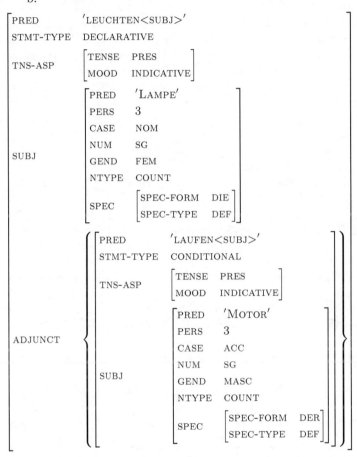

2.4 What about X′ Theory?

In this chapter we have presented our approach to basic clause types in French, German and English. In each case, the f-structures for each construction were similar across the languages. However, the c-structures differed based on language specific requirements. Note that while this is completely consonant with basic principles of LFG, which aims to represent the language particular variation at the level of c-structure, while capturing crosslinguistic generalizations at the level of f-structure, students of syntax who have been introduced to x′-Theory may be a little taken aback at the type and variety of c-structures introduced in this chapter alone.

We see two basic alternatives to the parsing of c-structure. One possibility is to implement a very strict x′-type approach which posits exactly two types of clauses, for example IP and CP, and then fits the differing clause types such as imperatives, conditionals, and questions within these two schemata, by allowing for large disjunctions of possibilities within them. A second approach is to posit specialized c-structure rules corresponding to the differing types of clauses, so that instead of there being a single CP rule with various disjunctions inside it, there are various c-structure rules corresponding to the subtypes of CP, such as CPrel (for relative clauses), CPint (for interrogatives), and so forth.[8]

While the first approach may seem somehow "cleaner" at first glance, this is in fact not the case. An approach which posits a single CP must necessarily cover exactly the same set of possible constructions that the sub-typed CP approach does, as the same set of differing constructions (imperatives, conditional, interrogatives, etc.) still remains to be accounted for. Within the single CP approach all of these constructions will not be labeled overtly as "imperative" or "interrogative", but properties of the CP in question will uniquely and implicitly determine the type of construction that has been analyzed, i.e., whether the complementizer position has been filled, whether the finite verb appears in first or second position (perhaps under I), etc.

Within our LFG approach we could have written rules which would have allowed for this superficially clean representation of the c-structure. The disjunctions needed to make the necessary distinctions would then have been expressed in the form of disjunctions over functional equations associated with c-structure rules. We did not choose to follow this latter alternative within ParGram, as we believe that those distinctions which are indeed language particular and which correspond to c-structure phe-

---

[8]Another possible approach, in particular with regard to German word order phenomena, is represented by an alternative feature unification-based theory, namely HPSG. For example, Kathol (1995, 1996) proposes to invest the descriptive generalizations made in terms of the German topological fields *Vorfeld*, *Mittelfeld* and *Nachfeld* with theoretical status and to encode linear order explicitly by means of features like VF, MF, NF, which are attached to lexical items and which ultimately determine the placement of that lexical item within the clause. This approach thus undertakes to encode linear precedence explicitly within a feature system, but must also rely on the notions of constructions (Kay and Fillmore 1994), in that differing construction types are recognized and organized within a type hierarchy.

nomena such as order and position should be modeled as such at the appropriate level. Within ParGram we have therefore adopted the approach of overt labeling of c-structures and take up the position that the particular distinctions we have made in terms of the formulation of the c-structure rules correspond to clear descriptive and typological distinctions found within and across languages. We have aimed to factor out what is common to all the subtypes of a given rule as much as possible, in order to preserve the relevant linguistic generalizations. Making use of these typological distinctions allows the development of a modular and logically well-organized grammar, without giving up the linguistic generalizations that motivated the analyses in the first place.

3

Verbal Elements

Verbal elements include predicates such as *drive*, which require one or more arguments, usually NPs, for a clause to be grammatical. These verbs can therefore be said to provide the essential backbone of a clause. As such the determination of a verb's *subcategorization frame* and the writing of verbal entries constitutes a central part of any grammar development effort. In this chapter we first go through verbal properties and subcategorization frames at some length, then present our treatment of further verbal elements such as the functional category of auxiliaries and the closed class of modals, and conclude with some particularly difficult constructions which we have not yet dealt with in the grammars.

3.1 Subcategorization

Subcategorized arguments are those arguments which are required by a verb or other predicate, i.e., if they do not appear the clause will either be ungrammatical or have a different meaning. There are a number of issues to be considered concerning the subcategorization of grammatical functions.

First, what are the possible grammatical functions which a predicate can subcategorize for? This in part depends on the linguistic theory. All versions of LFG assume the following functions: SUBJ, OBJ, COMP, XCOMP, OBL. Some versions subdivide OBL into different types, depending on their thematic role, usually indicated as OBL_θ, e.g., OBL_{loc} for locative obliques. Similarly, XCOMP can be divided into types depending on the head of the XCOMP, e.g., ones with verbal heads are VCOMPs, while ones with adjectival heads are ACOMPs (cf. Kaplan and Bresnan 1982). Most versions of the theory assume either OBJ2 (e.g., Kaplan and Bresnan 1982) or OBJ_θ for double object constructions in languages like English.[1] Other grammatical functions could be proposed if needed. For

---

[1] See also Bresnan and Moshi 1990 on double objects in Bantu.

example, a special function, here referred to as PREDLINK (section 3.8), has been posited for the second argument of copular (linking) verbs. In addition, other functions for nonverbal subcategorization might ultimately be needed. Note that a verb can only have one instance of a given grammatical function (section 1.2).

A second issue to consider is expletive vs. non expletive arguments. Most arguments are not expletives; that is, they are referential and must have a PRED value. This is indicated by placing the subcategorized feature within angled brackets in the entry for the predicate, as in (1).

(1) (↑PRED)='SEE<(↑SUBJ)(↑OBJ)>'

However, some verbs have expletive arguments; that is, arguments which function as so-called "dummy" expressions and which therefore need not, or must not, have a PRED value. In English the most common expletives are *it* and *there*, as in *There are cats in the garden* or as with weather verbs like *It is raining*. Expletive arguments are encoded by placing the expletive argument after the angled brackets, as in (2).

(2) (↑PRED)='RAIN<>(↑SUBJ)'

Note that most expletive arguments are direct arguments (either subjects or objects). In English expletive arguments are confined to the subject position, but this does not hold for German or French, as the German in (3) illustrates. Here the *es* is a dummy argument that may be analyzed as picking up the entire embedded clause. The expletive is subcategorized for by the verb as shown in (4), namely, as an expletive object.

(3) Er vermeidet [es], den   Drucker fallen zu lassen.
    he avoids   it   the.Acc printer fall   to let
    'He avoids letting the printer fall.'

(4) (↑PRED)='VERMEIDEN<(↑SUBJ) (↑XCOMP)>(↑OBJ)'

Another important issue is how to determine the subcategorization frame for a given verb. Intuitively, the subcategorized arguments of a predicate are those arguments which must always appear, as opposed to those which need not (see section 3.3.6 on adjuncts). However, it is often not easy to determine the precise status of a given NP or PP (cf. Grimshaw's (1990) notion of the *argument-adjunct*). While this remains an unresolved problem in linguistics, evidence from large corpora may serve to help resolve some of the problems (see section 14.1.1).

Once determined, subcategorization frames tend to vary over the type and number of arguments. Verbs which subcategorize for one argument are generally referred to as intransitives; ones with two arguments are transitives; and ones with three arguments are ditransitives. Additionally, many verbs have more than one subcategorization frame, as in (5), each of which must be part of the lexical entry of the verb.

(5) a. Il laisse jouer les enfants.
   he lets   play the children
   'He lets the children play.' (French)

   b. Elle laisse ses clefs dans son sac.
   she leaves her keys in   her bag
   'She leaves her keys in her bag.' (French)

   c. Il laisse   sa clef à la   gardienne.
   he entrusts his key to the door keeper
   'He entrusts his key to the door keeper.' (French)

Furthermore, lexical rules such as passive may affect whole classes of subcategorization frames (see section 3.4 for a general discussion and section 13.2.3 for a more formal description of lexical rules), systematically creating new ones. These two factors can make determining subcategorization frames less straightforward than it initially seems. A more detailed discussion on the ParGram efforts at building large lexicons is provided in Part II, section 14.1.1, which includes the semi-automatic extraction of subcategorization frames from corpora and the use of previously existing resources such as machine-readable dictionaries.

3.2   Nonverbal Subcategorization

Predicates other than verbs can subcategorize for arguments. Adjectives may subcategorize for OBL arguments, as in (6a). In addition, most prepositions subcategorize for an OBJ argument (Chapter 6), as in (6b).

(6) a. Die   Fahrerin ist stolz [auf ihren Traktor].
   the.Nom driver.F is proud of her   tractor
   'The driver is proud of her tractor.' (German)
   Adjective: $(\uparrow \text{PRED}) = \text{'stolz} < (\uparrow \text{OBL}) > \text{'}$

   b. The driver parked the tractor in [the garage].
   Preposition: $(\uparrow \text{PRED}) = \text{'in} < (\uparrow \text{OBJ}) > \text{'}$

Under some analyses, some subordinating conjunctions, e.g., *when, after*, subcategorize for either objects or sentential arguments, as in (7).

(7) The tractor started when [the red light flashed].
   Subordinating Conjunction: $(\uparrow \text{PRED}) = \text{'when} < (\uparrow \text{COMP}) > \text{'}$

Note that this is not the approach taken here. In our approach the subordinating conjunctions are treated as functional elements which serve to mark a subordinated clause (see section 2.2 in the previous chapter).

There is much debate in the linguistic literature as to the extent to which nominal elements subcategorize for arguments and, if they do, what type of grammatical functions these represent (e.g., Chomsky 1970, Grimshaw 1990). The issue arises largely due to pairs like those in (8) in which the modifiers of the noun correspond to arguments in the verbal construction.

(8) a. NP: the Romans' destruction of the city
     b. S: the Romans destroyed the city

In many cases, it is possible to simply treat these as ADJUNCTs (section 3.3.6) in the case of the *of the city* and a specifier (SPEC, see section 5.1.1 for a discussion of specifiers) and leave the task of connecting the semantic relatedness of adjuncts to the noun to a semantic module. However, it is also possible to develop an analysis whereby nouns derived from verbs, such as *destruction* in (8) above, would retain the verb's subcategorization frame. The syntactic rules for NPs would then have to ensure that modificatory NPs such as *of the city* and *The Romans'* fill the right grammatical function slots. Within our approach, we have chosen to represent these modificatory NPs as adjuncts to the main noun because we believe that the proper level of analysis for the dependency relations between the main noun and its modifiers in this case is at the level of thematic argument structure, not at the level of grammatical functions. That is, the generalization that unifies the common dependencies between (8a) and (8b) is that in both cases the *Romans* and the *city* function as *agent* and *patient*, respectively, of the main predicate (cf. Grimshaw 1990). In the verbal manifestation in (8b) these thematic arguments are realized in terms of the grammatical functions SUBJ and OBJ, while in the nominal case in (8a) the arguments are realized as adjuncts or specifiers. Sample analyses showing how NPs are analyzed within our approach can be found in Chapter 4.

3.3 Types of Grammatical Functions

3.3.1 Subjects

Many linguistic theories, including LFG, assume a *Subject Condition* (Baker 1983, Alsina 1996:20), which requires that all verbs subcategorize for a subject. However, this condition has been challenged by researchers working on languages such as Hindi (Mohanan 1994) and Dutch (Zaenen 1989). German also provides a case in point as it displays constructions which do not appear to have subjects. Consider the example in (9a), which ostensibly is a passivized version of the intransitive verb *tanzen* 'dance'. An active version is shown in (9b), in which the NP *die Leute* functions as the SUBJ.

(9) a. Hier wird   getanzt.
      here be.Pass.Pres.3.Sg dance.PerfP
      'Dancing takes place here.' (German)
      Lit.: 'Here is danced.'
   b. Die   Leute tanzen.
      the.Nom people dance
      'The people are dancing.' (German)

Given that there is no overt subject in (9a) and that German is not a pro-drop language because it does not freely allow the omission of arguments, the conclusion one is forced to draw is that there is no subject in (9a). This is precisely the analysis we have adopted in the German grammar, as illustrated by the f-structure in (10). Here the verb *tanzen* 'dance' is represented as normally subcategorizing for one argument. However, under passivization this one SUBJ argument has been suppressed to NULL via the application of a lexical rule (see section 3.4).

(10) a. Hier wird   getanzt.
      here be.Pass.Pres.3.Sg dance.PerfP
      'Dancing takes place here.' (German)

   b.
$$\begin{bmatrix} \text{PRED} & \text{'TANZEN<NULL>'} \\ \text{TNS-ASP} & \begin{bmatrix} \text{TENSE} & \text{PRES} \\ \text{MOOD} & \text{INDICATIVE} \end{bmatrix} \\ \text{ADJUNCT} & \left\{ \begin{bmatrix} \text{PRED} & \text{'HIER'} \\ \text{PRON-TYPE} & \text{LOC} \end{bmatrix} \right\} \end{bmatrix}$$

In general, however, clauses do have subjects. The question then is how to identify the subject in a given language. In German, French and English verb agreement is a very good indication: if an NP agrees with the verb, then that NP is the subject. In German, furthermore, case morphology provides another very strong test: if an NP is inflected with nominative case marking, then it is the subject. In French and English case morphology only helps with pronominal forms, e.g., *il* (subject) vs. *le* (French), *he* (subject) vs. *him*. However, properties of subjects vary from language to language and therefore a catalog of subject tests must be established independently for each language. Often further good tests are properties such as which NP is bound by a reflexive, as in (11).

(11) John gave himself to Mary.

Here the *himself* must be bound by the subject *John*, and not by any other arguments in the clause. For a catalog of sample subject tests see Mohanan 1994 on Hindi.

3.3.2 Objects

Transitive verbs have a SUBJ and a second argument. This second argument is usually an OBJ. An example of a transitive verb which subcategorizes for a SUBJ and an OBJ is shown in (12).

(12) They saw the box. (↑PRED)='SEE<(↑SUBJ)(↑OBJ)>'

Objects can again be identified by a cluster of properties which may vary from language to language. In English, position is a good indication since the object must follow the verb and be adjacent to it (be a sister to the verb). Example (13) can only be good under a special intonation pattern which extracts the object out of the clause, and (14b), in which an adverb attempts to intervene between the verb and its object is illformed.

(13) The box they saw.

(14) a. They saw the box yesterday.
       b. *They saw yesterday the box.

In German, however, position is not such a good indicator since arguments may be scrambled around in the sentence, as in (15). Instead, case marking is a very good indicator of objecthood: noun phrases marked with the accusative can be analyzed as objects.

(15) a. Der   Fahrer startet den   Traktor.
         the.Nom driver starts the.Acc tractor
         'The driver is starting the tractor.' (German)
       b. Den   Traktor startet der   Fahrer.
         the.Acc tractor starts the.Nom driver
         'The driver is starting the tractor.' (German)

In both English and French case marking can only serve as a test on pronouns such as *he* vs. *him* (object) and *il* vs. *le* (object) (French).

Crosslinguistically a very good test for objects is passivization. Under passivization the NP that is the object in the active sentence corresponds to the subject in the passive sentence. The active subject is realized as NULL in the passive sentence (this is often referred to as *argument suppression*). An English example is given in (16).

(16) a. They saw the box. (↑PRED)='SEE<(↑SUBJ)(↑OBJ)>'
       b. The box was seen. (↑PRED)='SEE<NULL(↑SUBJ)>'

3.3.3 Secondary Objects (OBJ2)

Ditransitive verbs subcategorize for three arguments. The typical ditransitive verb, such as the German *geben* 'give' will subcategorize for a subject, and object and a secondary, indirect object.

(17) Der   Chef gab dem   Fahrer den   Schlüssel.
the.Nom boss gave the.Dat driver the.Acc key
'The boss gave the driver the key.' (German)

In German, the dative case on the NP is an indicator of its status as an indirect object. However, note that dative case can also be found in so-called "psych-constructions" as in (18) and on the objects of certain transitive verbs as in (19).

(18) Ihr   wurde mulmig.
her.Dat became uneasy
'She started feeling uneasy.' (German)

(19) Der   Fahrer hilft dem   Chef.
the.Nom driver helps the.Dat boss
'The driver is helping the boss.' (German)

In German the secondary object (OBJ2) can thus be identified as a dative NP that co-occurs with another (primary) object in the clause. The dative NP in (17) is therefore an OBJ2, while the dative NPs in (18) and (19) are not (in (19) the dative NP is an OBJ). Note also that one can only passivize the direct object in German, as shown in (20).

(20) a. Der   Chef gab dem   Fahrer den   Schlüssel.
the.Nom boss gave the.Dat driver the.Acc key
'The boss gave the driver the key.' (German)

b. Der   Schlüssel wurde dem   Fahrer gegeben.
the.Nom key   was   the.Dat driver given
'The key was given to the driver.' (German)

c. *Der   Fahrer wurde den   Schlüssel gegeben.
the.Nom driver was   the.Acc key   given
'The driver was given the key.' (German)

This is not the case in many dialects of English, where either one of the objects may be subject to passivization, as is illustrated in (21).

(21) a. She gave him the book.
$(\uparrow\text{PRED})=\text{'GIVE}<(\uparrow\text{SUBJ})(\uparrow\text{OBJ2})(\uparrow\text{OBJ})>'$

b. He was given the book.
$(\uparrow\text{PRED})=\text{'GIVE}<\text{NULL}(\uparrow\text{SUBJ})(\uparrow\text{OBJ})>'$

c. The book was given him.
$(\uparrow\text{PRED})=\text{'GIVE}<\text{NULL}(\uparrow\text{OBJ2})(\uparrow\text{SUBJ})>'$

Also note that in English the indirect (secondary) object must be adjacent to the verb, followed by the direct object. Position is thus the major test for distinguishing direct from indirect objects.

Finally, in French all NPs which may be replaced by a dative clitic are treated as OBJ2, as illustrated in (22). Note that these are not simply all NPs marked by *à*, as illustrated in (23), in which the *à* marked NP cannot be replaced by a dative clitic.[2]

(22) a. Jean a   donné un livre à Marie.
        Jean has given a   book to Marie
        'Jean has given a book to Marie.' (French)

    b. Jean lui   a   donné un livre.
        Jean her/him has given a   book
        'Jean has given her a book.' (French)

(23) a. Jean pense à Marie.
        Jean thinks to Marie
        'John is thinking of Marie.' (French)

    b. *Jean lui pense.

    c. Jean pense à elle.

3.3.4 Obliques

In English the ditransitive subcategorization frame for verbs of giving alternates (*the dative alternation*) with a ditransitive frame whose third argument is an oblique, as in (24).

(24) a. She gave the book to him.
        $(\uparrow\text{PRED})='\text{GIVE}<(\uparrow\text{SUBJ})(\uparrow\text{OBJ})(\uparrow\text{OBL})>'$

    b. The book was given to him.
        $(\uparrow\text{PRED})='\text{GIVE}<\text{NULL}(\uparrow\text{SUBJ})(\uparrow\text{OBL})>'$

The *to him* is analyzed as an OBL in English rather than as a secondary object (OBJ2) because it cannot undergo passivization in English.

Obliques are a difficult class of arguments to define. In general, they are nonsubject arguments which are not of the appropriate morphosyntactic form to be objects and which do not undergo syntactic processes which affect objects, such as passivization in English. Obliques are generally PPs. Some verbs subcategorize for a very specific oblique, i.e., one with a given preposition or case, as in (25).

(25) Der   Fahrer denkt [an] seinen Traktor.
     the.Nom driver thinks at his.Acc tractor
     'The driver is thinking about his tractor.' (German)

---

[2]These sentences were provided by Anette Frank who also implemented the analysis of OBJ2s in the French grammar after one of our co-authors had already left the project.

Other verbs subcategorize for a semantic class of obliques, e.g., *put* requires a locative PP, but any preposition is allowable as long as the meaning is appropriate, as in (26).

(26) She put the box on the shelf/in the truck/under the bed.

Obliques often resemble adjuncts in form and can be distinguished from them only by whether they are required by the predicate. An additional complicating factor is that arguments which look like obliques, may in fact be objects. This occurs with certain English verbs where the object is preceded by a preposition, as in (27); the fact that it is an object and not an oblique is seen by its ability to passivize, a process which only affects objects in English.

(27) a. Our employees frequently refer to this document.

b. This document is frequently referred to by our employees.

Certain adjectives also subcategorize for obliques. One type of these involve idiosyncratic subcategorization for OBL, similar to that of many verbs. For example, *clear* in English can subcategorize for an OBL in the form *clear of X*. Lexical entries of such adjectives must specify that they allow, or require, an OBL and the particular preposition or case required on it. Adjectives can systematically subcategorize for an OBL in their comparative form (5.2.5.1); in this case the OBL corresponds to the *than* phrase which serves as the overt basis of comparison for the adjective.

3.3.5   XCOMP and COMP

Arguments of a verb are not confined to being either an NP or PP. Entire clauses may also serve as the complement of a verb, and in some cases may alternate with NP arguments, as shown in (28).

(28) a. I know [this story].   (NP object)

b. I know [that this tractor is red].   (*that*-clause object)

Within LFG two different types of clausal arguments are distinguished: XCOMP and COMP. An XCOMP is a complement whose subject is obligatorily functionally controlled from outside the clause, as in (29a), while a COMP is a closed complement with its own subject which is not functionally controlled, as in (29b). For an in-depth discussion of control and complementation see Bresnan 1982a.

(29) a. The woman wants to drive the tractor.
XCOMP=to drive the tractor
(↑XCOMP SUBJ)=(↑SUBJ)

b. The driver thinks that the tractor will start.
COMP=that the tractor will start

    c. Il empêche le   moteur de chauffer.
       it prevents the motor of heat
       'It prevents the motor from heating.' (French)
       XCOMP=de chauffer (↑XCOMP SUBJ)=(↑SUBJ)

In general, this means that COMPs will have overt subjects, while XCOMPs will not. This may be more clearly illustrated by sample f-structure analyses for (29a) and (29b), shown in (30) and (31), respectively. The matrix subject controls the embedded subject in (30), as indicated by the connecting line and the absence of a separate bundle of information in the embedded subject.

(30) a. The woman wants to drive the tractor.

      b.

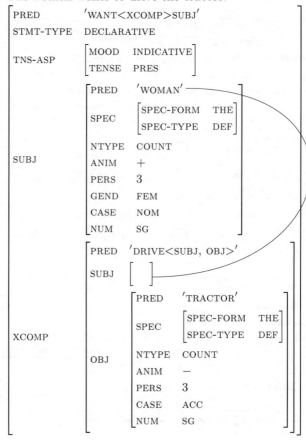

(31) a. The driver thinks that the tractor will start.

b.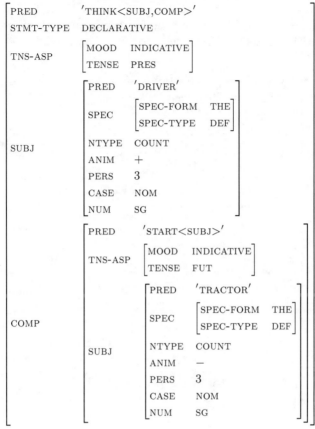

In the example with the COMP in (31), on the other hand, the matrix subject does not control the embedded subject: each of the subjects is independent of each other. Also note that the finite COMP in (31) has its own TNS-ASP specification.

In many languages the difference between open complements (XCOMP) and closed complements (COMP) correlates with a difference between finite and nonfinite clauses. However, this seeming correlation is misleading. Although it is rare, finite clauses can appear with controlled subjects and must thus be analyzed as XCOMPs. More frequently, nonfinite clauses may have a nonovert subject which is not functionally controlled, as in (32). These clausal arguments are analyzed as closed categories (in (32) as a SUBJ) and are assumed to be *anaphorically controlled* (see Bresnan 1982a): that is, the subject of the clausal complement must be determined from the context of the utterance, as in (32), where it is not clear who pinched the elephants when the sentence is uttered in isolation. Note that these discourse considerations cannot be part of a syntactic analysis. As shown in (32b), all the f-structure analysis encodes is the fact that the subject is a noncontrolled PRO whose referent is yet to be determined.

(32) a. Pinching those elephants was foolish.

b.

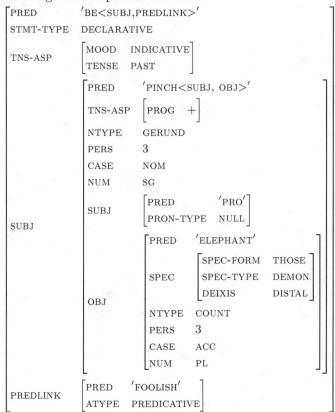

The example in (32) also illustrates another fact that may not be obvious: clausal complements are not restricted to the object role. In (32) the gerundive clause functions as the subject of the sentence, as is the case for the German *that*-clause in (33).

(33) Daß die   Erde rund ist, hat ihn gewundert.
     that the.Nom earth round is   has him surprised
     'That the world is round surprised him.' (German)

A good discussion of the properties of German COMPs and further examples of usage in which the clausal complement stands in alternation with with genitive NPs and differing types of PPs can be found in Berman 1996.

3.3.6   Adjuncts

Adjuncts are grammatical functions which are not subcategorized for by the verb. Adjuncts include a large number of disparate items, including adverbs (Chapter 7), prepositional phrases (Chapter 6), and certain embedded clauses (section 2.3). Examples of all three kinds are found in (34a). Adjuncts are analyzed as belonging to a set, which can occur with any PRED, i.e., they are not subcategorized for. So, (34a) would have the simplified f-structure in (34b).

(34)   a.   When the light flashes, quickly push the lever towards the seat.

   b.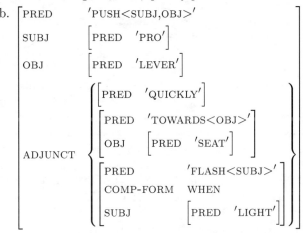

As adjuncts are collected in a set, their relative scope to one another is not encoded at f-structure. The determination of the scope of the adjuncts is left to the s(emantic)-structure, since it is not simply a matter of the linear order in which the adjuncts occur.

While treatment of adjuncts as a collection of items in a set can thus be motivated linguistically, technical problems with this treatment did arise within our project. In some cases, for example, a particular adjunct within the set of adjuncts needs to be accessed in order to check for wellformedness conditions. This occurs regularly when there is a discontinuous constituent: extraposed relative clauses, as in (35a) for example; or comparatives, as in (35b); or questions, as in (35c).

(35) a. In der   Kabine leuchtet die   Lampe immer auf
in the.Dat cabin   lights the.Nom lamp   always on
[dem   Schalter] auf, [der defekt   ist].
the.Dat switch   up that defective is
'In the cabin the light always lights up on the switch that is
defective.' (German)

    b. A diesel engine runs [more efficiently] in the winter [than a gas
one (does)].

    c. [Which hammer] did he hit the nail [with] after lining it up?

In these situations, a requirement is made on a member of the ADJUNCT
set. For example, in the German (35a) the relative clause *der defekt ist*
needs to be attached to the appropriate constituent. Given the fact that
relative pronouns exhibit gender agreement with their head nouns, the
only correct attachment possibility for the masculine relative pronoun is
the masculine *Schalter* 'switch'. However, as the relative clause could in
principle attach to any of the adjuncts, each member of the adjunct set
must be checked for the property of masculine gender (number agreement must also be checked, see 4.4 for a discussion of relative clauses).
This is difficult to do under the standard LFG approach to adjuncts,
which holds that if you have collected individuals as members of a set
then a given property is taken to be true of all members of the set, and is
distributed over the set. This approach is useful in handling coordination
phenomena, which are described in more detail in Chapter 8, but does
not yield the right results with regard to phenomena like the German
extraposed relative clause.

A more differentiated approach to sets was therefore introduced to
the formalism in the course of the project: the grammar can now nonde-
terministically choose an element from a set and check a given feature
specification against each member. This results in the f-structure analysis of (35a) shown in (36). Note that for reasons of space some of the
nonessential features such as NTYPE have been left out; in addition,
ADJUNCT-REL has been abbreviated to ADJ-REL.[3]

---

[3] Other features of (36) such as the treatment of particle verbs and the analysis of
prepositions will be discussed in section 3.7 and Chapter 6, respectively.

(36) a. In der   Kabine leuchtet die   Lampe immer auf
in the.Dat cabin   lights   the.Nom lamp   always on
[dem   Schalter] auf, [der defekt   ist].
the.Dat switch   up that defective is
'In the cabin the light always lights up on the switch that is
defective.' (German)

b.

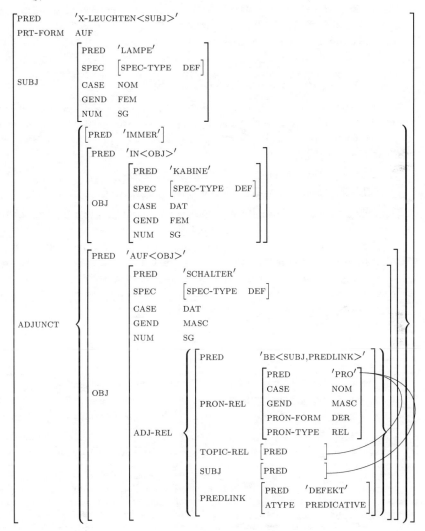

Another problem with the collection of adjuncts into one and the same set is that adjuncts may differ systematically with regard to their syntactic properties and that it would therefore be more convenient to be able to identify the type of adjunct one is dealing with in a more obvious manner than to go check each of the members of the set of all adjuncts for a particular feature. For example, if we wanted to check whether a given adjunct was a relative clause, the grammar could check for the presence of the feature PRON-REL.

Another way to go about this is to define different types of adjuncts according to systematic syntactic criteria. In our grammars, for example, relative clauses are encoded as ADJUNCT-REL, as illustrated by (36), parentheticals are ADJUNCT-PAREN, and comparatives are ADJUNCT-COMP.

3.4 Altering Subcategorization Frames

There are a number of relationships between the possible subcategorization frames of a given verb that linguists have analyzed as *alternations* between subcategorization frames. One such example is the passive, as illustrated for English in (37).

(37) a. The tractor pushed the trailer. (active)
      b. The trailer was pushed by the tractor. (passive)

Passivization systematically applies to all subcategorization frames of a given type. In the case of English and French, all transitive verbs which have an OBJ as the second argument may be passivized. Here (and generally), passivization involves demotion of a SUBJ to either an unexpressed argument or an ADJUNCT or OBL.[4] Within our grammars, passivization is accomplished by means of a lexical rule, as in (38).

(38) PASS(SCHEMATA) = SCHEMATA
$$(\uparrow\text{OBJ}) \longrightarrow (\uparrow\text{SUBJ})$$
$$(\uparrow\text{SUBJ}) \longrightarrow \text{NULL}$$
$$(\uparrow\text{PASSIVE}) =_c +$$

This lexical rule is called by verbs which can passivize, e.g., by transitive verbs. The lexical rule has the OBJ become the SUBJ and the old SUBJ become NULL. In addition, it requires a passive form of the verb

---

[4]In passive constructions, the demoted agent is often assumed to be an OBL with a restricted form, e.g., with the preposition *by* in English. This analysis has the advantage that it captures the fact that the OBL plays a special role with respect to the verb, i.e., that it is the logical subject. However, this analysis also has the disadvantage that the OBL is not obligatory since the demoted subject need not be overtly expressed. This means that every passive occuring with an argument of the appropriate form will have two analyses, one in which the argument is the OBL and one in which it is an adjunct. In our grammars passives do not subcategorize for an OBL, meaning that the demoted agent is always an adjunct; the semantics can then determine whether a member of the adjunct set is the agent of the verb.

to be used. SCHEMATA refers to the subcategorization frame of the verb which is provided by verbs calling PASS.

Different languages may require variations of the passive lexical rule. For example, German allows passivization of certain intransitive verbs, as in (39), and hence needs a variant of passivization which does not require the OBJ to become the SUBJ.

(39) Gestern   wurde viel   gelacht.
     yesterday was   much laughed
     'There was much laughter yesterday.' (German)

The lexical rule for these cases looks as in (40) and is called by the set of verbs which undergo this type of passivization.[5]

(40) NOSUBJ-PASS(SCHEMATA) = SCHEMATA
                                $(\uparrow$SUBJ$) \longrightarrow$NULL
                                $(\uparrow$PASSIVE$)=_c$ +

The ability to passivize and the type of passivization must thus be specified in the lexical entry of each verb. The lexical rules not only serve as a useful tool for encoding the same generalization over a subset of the verbs in a given language, but also encode precisely the fact that a linguistically relevant generalization can and must be made over the lexicon of a given language.

A second example of a productive alternation is the formation of medial passives in French. These are signalled by the reflexive pronoun *se* and are illustrated in (41).

(41) a. Cette chemise se   porte avec une cravate rouge.
         this   shirt   REFL wears with a   tie   red
         'This shirt is worn with a red tie.' (French)

      b. Ces   livres se   vendent bien.
         these books REFL sell   well
         'These books sell well.' (French)

The lexical rule for this construction is similar to that of the regular passive with the additional restriction that REFL have the value +. This value is provided by the reflexive pronoun, which provides no other information to the f-structure (see section 4.1.4 on reflexives).

It should be noted, however, that despite the apparent usefulness of lexical rules, only five lexical rules were being used in the French (one rule), English (two rules) and German (two rules) grammars at the point

---

[5]This lexical rule also applies to transitive verbs in German which have a dative object, as in *Ihm wurde geholfen* 'Him was helped.' In these cases the object remains a dative rather than becoming a nominative subject.

that this book went to press.

One reason for this is that lexical rules have the effect of changing one grammatical function into another. In more recent work within LFG, the emphasis has shifted from lexical rules such as the passive shown above to a more general theory of *linking* or *mapping* between the predicate-argument structure and the grammatical functions (Bresnan and Kanerva 1989, Bresnan and Moshi 1990, Bresnan and Zaenen 1990, etc.; for an overview of the issues at stake and the relevant literature, see Alsina 1996). Within *Mapping Theory* subcategorization frame alternations such as the passive or the English dative alternation discussed in the section on indirect objects and obliques (sections 3.3.3 and 3.3.4) are seen as different possibilities of mapping from the predicate-argument structure to the grammatical functions of a predicate (also see Butt, Dalrymple and Frank 1997 on this issue). The effect of passivization under this view is that the *agent* argument of a verb is suppressed and that the other argument, usually a *theme*, then mapped to a SUBJ. This differs markedly from first rendering an already existing SUBJ null and void, and then changing the already existing OBJ into a SUBJ.

Within the ParGram project we did not implement a separate encoding of predicate-argument structures. However, we followed the general spirit of Mapping Theory by assuming it and by then grouping related subcategorization possibilities together by means of templates (discussed in more detail in Part II in section 13.2.1). A template basically serves as a shorthand in which to state generalizations that need to apply to large sections of the lexicon. The template for the dative alternation in (42), for example, specifies that a given predicate P (the English verb *give*, for example) may have one of two subcategorization frames that alternate freely.

(42) DATIVE-ALT(P)= { (↑PRED)='P<(↑SUBJ)(↑OBJ)(↑OBL) >'
                        |(↑PRED)='P<(↑SUBJ)(↑OBJ2)(↑OBJ) >' }

Templates can also be thought of as reusable blocks which express a generalization about the language. As such, they are made wide use of in each of the ParGram grammars.

3.5 Auxiliaries

Auxiliaries crosslinguistically are a closed class of verbal elements. They generally have developed from main verbs such as *be, stay, have* or *go*. In terms of subcategorization frames, there are two main ways to analyze auxiliaries. On the one hand, an auxiliary can be treated as a special type of raising verb, which takes two arguments, a SUBJ and an XCOMP (e.g., Pollard and Sag 1994, Bresnan 1982a). On the other hand, auxiliaries can simply be considered as feature carrying elements, which contribute tense/aspect or voice information to the clause, but which do not have a PRED or subcategorization frame (e.g., Bresnan 1998a, King 1995).

We have adopted the second approach, so that the auxiliary systems of the three languages are analyzed as having a hierarchical c-structure and a "flat" f-structure, which combines tense and aspectual information from all of the auxiliaries. This allows for the invariant contribution of auxiliaries to (complex) tenses to be modelled crosslinguistically in the f-structure, while language particular, idiosyncratic syntactic properties (e.g., VP-deletion, VP-fronting, the number of auxiliaries involved in the expression of a given complex tense) are handled in the c-structure.

3.5.1 Brief Introduction to the Auxiliary Systems

English, French and German all make use of auxiliaries which can be treated as morphological markers of tense, aspect, and voice. The basic features of the three auxiliary systems are as follows: all auxiliaries require their following auxiliary or verb to have a particular form. For example, in English, the basic order is: (perfective *have*) — (progressive *be*) — (passive *be*) — main verb. Perfective *have* requires a following past participle form; progressive *be* a present participle form; and passive *be* a passive participle form, as shown in (43).

(43) It might have been being driven.

German and French additionally exhibit auxiliary selection for the perfective auxiliary: verbs select either *être* 'be' or *avoir* 'have' in French, or *sein* 'be' or *haben* 'have' in German. If the main verb is (di)transitive or an *unergative* intransitive as in (44b), the auxiliary selected is 'have'. If the main verb is an intransitive *unaccusative* as in (44a), the auxiliary must be 'be'.[6] Note that the participle agrees with *elle* 'she' in (44a) but not in (44b).

(44) a. Elle est   arrivée.
        she be.Pres arrived.F
        'She has arrived.'   unaccusative verb (French)

     b. Elle a   marché.
        she have.Pres walked
        'She has walked.'   unergative verb (French)

---

[6]The distinction between unergatives and unaccusatives goes back to work in Relational Grammar by Perlmutter (1978). The way it is now commonly understood is that unaccusative verbs have an underlying object or theme that then must surface as a subject due to the fact that it is the only argument (examples are 'fall', 'sit'). Unergative verbs in contrast are assumed to have an underlying subject or agent that is realized as a subject by default (examples are 'sneeze', 'run', 'cough').

In addition, subject to certain constraints, German allows scrambling of the various auxiliaries with respect to one another, e.g., when the VP is topicalized, as in (45b). Even in the VP topicalization example, each auxiliary still determines the form of the next auxiliary or verb.

(45) a. Der   Fahrer wird den   Hebel gedreht haben.
     the.Nom driver will the.Acc lever turned have
     'The driver will have turned the lever.' (German)

    b. [Den   Hebel gedreht haben] wird der   Fahrer.
     the.Acc lever turned have   will the.Nom driver
     'The driver will have turned the lever.' (German)

3.5.2 Previous Analyses

As mentioned above, there is a family of analyses which have treated auxiliaries as raising verbs. Under this view, auxiliaries are predicates which take a SUBJ and an XCOMP complement. Their subject is identified with the subject of their XCOMP. The f-structure correspondingly reflects as many levels of embedding as there are auxiliaries in the c-structure, as shown in (46). In particular, in the f-structure, the top level predicate does not correspond to what is intuitively the main predicate of the sentence.

(46) a. She has appeared.

    b.

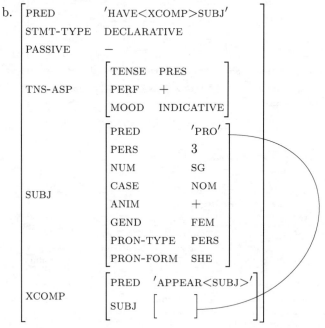

3.5.3 Flat F-structure Analysis

The analysis proposed here abstracts away from the particular realization of tense and aspect in the c-structure, and provides a "flat" f-structure, where the main verb is the main predicate. The auxiliaries are simply feature carrying elements, which do not have their own argument structure, but which provide information about tense, aspect, and voice.

(47)   a. He will have driven the tractor.

   b.

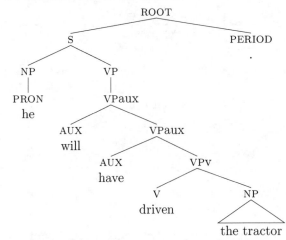

c.
$$
\begin{bmatrix}
\text{PRED} & \text{'DRIVE<SUBJ,OBJ>'} \\
\text{STMT-TYPE} & \text{DECLARATIVE} \\
\text{TNS-ASP} & \begin{bmatrix} \text{TENSE} & \text{FUT} \\ \text{PERF} & + \\ \text{MOOD} & \text{INDICATIVE} \end{bmatrix} \\
\text{SUBJ} & \begin{bmatrix} \text{PRED} & \text{'PRO'} \\ \text{PERS} & 3 \\ \text{ANIM} & + \\ \text{GEND} & \text{MASC} \\ \text{PRON-TYPE} & \text{PERS} \\ \text{PRON-FORM} & \text{HE} \\ \text{NUM} & \text{SG} \\ \text{CASE} & \text{NOM} \end{bmatrix} \\
\text{OBJ} & \begin{bmatrix} \text{PRED} & \text{'TRACTOR'} \\ \text{SPEC} & \begin{bmatrix} \text{SPEC-FORM} & \text{THE} \\ \text{SPEC-TYPE} & \text{DEF} \end{bmatrix} \\ \text{PERS} & 3 \\ \text{ANIM} & - \\ \text{NUM} & \text{SG} \\ \text{CASE} & \text{ACC} \end{bmatrix}
\end{bmatrix}
$$

Under this analysis the parallelism between the examples in (48) can be captured at a functional level as each of the sentences receives the same f-structure analysis in each of the grammars.

(48) a. He [will have] driven the tractor.

     b. Il [aura]   conduit le   tracteur.
       he have.Fut driven   the tractor
       'He will have driven the tractor.' (French)

     c. Er [wird] den   Traktor gefahren [haben].
       he will   the.Acc tractor driven   have
       'He will have driven the tractor.' (German)

At the level of c-structure the analyses mirror the difference in the level of embedding: French expresses the future perfective morphologically by means of the auxiliary *aura*, while German and English use two auxiliaries. The parallel f-structure analyses reflect the fact that this difference in surface realization does not have any consequences for the interpretation of the auxiliaries and that the top level predicate in all three sentences is 'drive'.

3.5.4 Morphosyntactic Structure

For both generation and parsing purposes, we need to ensure that each auxiliary can only be followed by an auxiliary or verb of the proper form, e.g., in English a perfective *have* is always followed by a past participle. In the XCOMP hierarchical approach, these morphological wellformedness conditions are easy to state, since each auxiliary states in its lexical entry that its XCOMP must be of a particular form. However, under the flat f-structure approach, there is no place in the f-structure in which to state the hierarchically organized wellformedness restrictions, since all of the information contributed by the auxiliaries is mapped to the same level of f-structure, i.e., to the f-structure of the main verb (see (47b) above).

In order to solve this problem, we implemented a m(orphosyntactic)-structure. This functions as a projection from the c-structure and is used to encodes only morphosyntactic wellformedness conditions, such as the form that a particular auxiliary requires on the verb heading its verbal complement. The m-structure is a hierarchical projection, mirroring the c-structure. So, in addition to its c- and f-structures, (47b) will also have the m-structure in (49).

$$(49) \quad \begin{bmatrix} \text{FIN} & + \\ \text{DEP} & \begin{bmatrix} \text{VFORM} & \text{BASE} \\ \text{DEP} & \begin{bmatrix} \text{VFORM} & \text{PERFP} \end{bmatrix} \end{bmatrix} \end{bmatrix}$$

The introduction of m-structure is described in more detail in Butt, Niño and Segond 1996 and is originally due to a suggestion by Ron Kaplan. Formally, the projection works similarly to the projection from c-structure to f-structure that was described in the introductory chapter. The projection is realized in terms of annotations on c-structure rules, as illustrated in (50), and as information in lexical entries, as in the entry for *will* in (51). The notation "$m*$" refers to the m-structure of the current node, this is similar to the functional notation of $\downarrow$ which is an abbreviation for "$f*$". The notation "$mM*$" refers to the mother node, again in parallel to the functional notation $\uparrow$, which is an abbreviation for "$fM*$".

(50)   VPaux $\longrightarrow$ AUX: $\uparrow=\downarrow$
                              $mM* = m*$
                              VPaux: $\uparrow=\downarrow$
                              $(mM* \text{ DEP})=m*$

(51)   will   AUX $(\uparrow\text{TNS-ASP TENSE}) = \text{FUT}$
                             $(mM* \text{ DEP VFORM}) =_c \text{BASE}$
                             $(mM* \text{ FIN}) = +$

3.5.5 The Treatment of Tense/Aspect

As described in Butt, Niño and Segond 1996, the grammars originally combined the contribution of the auxiliaries in a given clause into a complex tense value. For example, the value for the combination *will have driven* would have been TENSE FUTPERF. This treatment of tense/aspect information was found to be inadequate as it was difficult to devise a standardized system that properly reflected the interplay between tense and aspect in all three languages. It was therefore decided to separate the dimensions of tense and aspect. The feature TENSE now encodes the simple distinctions present (PRES), past (PAST) and future (FUT). The aspectual dimension is now recorded by the features PERF and PROG, whose values are either '+' or '−', whereby PROG is only used in the English grammar. In the f-structures shown in this book, we have only displayed the feature when it has a positive value.

The f-structure thus now encodes exactly those distinctions which are made overtly in each of the languages without attempting to second guess a semantic analysis by providing complex tense features. The idea is that the information recorded at f-structure should serve as input for a further semantic analysis of tense/aspect.

3.6 Modals

Unlike auxiliaries which are analyzed as having a flat f-structure and no PRED, modals have a PRED and subcategorize for XCOMP complements. Some languages, such as English, are restricted to a single modal per clause; others, like German, allow modals to take other modals as their complements and also allow scrambling that does not respect the hierarchy of embedding. An example is shown in (52).
Again, we do not attempt to provide a semantic analysis. On the other hand, the scrambling phenomena of German can be treated very simply under the application of functional uncertainty whereby arguments and adjuncts can be base generated in any of the positions they might be found in and connected to the clause they belong in via a functional uncertainty path such as (↑XCOMP XCOMP OBJ). For an introduction and discussion of functional uncertainty, see Johnson 1986, Kaplan and Zaenen 1989, Zaenen and Kaplan, and Kaplan and Maxwell 1996.

(52) a. Einen raschen Erfolg müßte   er erzielen können.
          a.Acc rapid   success should.Subj he achieve can
          'He should be able to achieve a rapid success.' (German)

b.

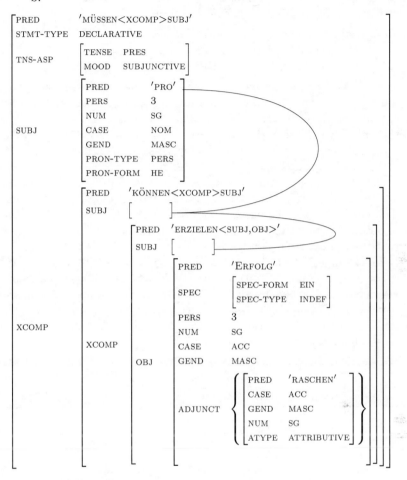

3.7 Particle Verbs

Some languages, such as English and German, have particles which occur
with a subset of verbs and have an effect on the meaning. As illustrated
in (53), most particles are homophonous with prepositions; however,
unlike prepositions, they need not be followed by an NP complement.

(53) a. The light came [on].
  b. They locked themselves [out].
  c. Diese rote Kontrolleuchte leuchtet [auf].
    this red warning light lights   up
    'This red warning light lights up.' (German)

German differs from English in that the German particles must be analyzed as separable prefixes, as shown in (54).

(54) Weil   diese rote Kontrolleuchte [auf]leuchtet, ...
     because this   red warning light   up lights
     'Because this red warning light lights up...' (German)

The German prefix becomes separated from the verb when the verb is finite and hence must appear in clause second position, as in (53c). When the finite verb is restricted to the clause final position, as is the case in the embedded clause in (54), the particle serves as a verbal prefix. Given these differences between the two languages, the treatments of particle verbs within our grammars also differ slightly.

In both languages, verbs which can appear with particles are assigned a special subcategorization frame. This frame not only reflects possible differences between the number and type of arguments of the base verb as opposed to the verb in combination with a prefix, but also makes sure that the right particle is required.

For example, the entry for the verb in (53a) will state: $(\uparrow\text{PRED})=\,'\text{COME-ON}<(\uparrow\text{SUBJ})>'$ and $(\uparrow\text{PRT-FORM})=\text{c ON}$. The value of PRT-FORM is provided by the particle and thus satisfies the constraining equation. The particle itself has a special c-structure category, PART, to capture its limited c-structure distribution. The complete f-structure analysis for the sentence in (53a) is as shown in (55b).

(55) a. The light came on.

   b.
$$\begin{bmatrix} \text{PRED} & '\text{COME-ON}<\text{SUBJ}>' \\ \text{STMT-TYPE} & \text{DECLARATIVE} \\ \text{PRT-FORM} & \text{ON} \\ \text{TNS-ASP} & \begin{bmatrix} \text{TENSE} & \text{PAST} \\ \text{MOOD} & \text{INDICATIVE} \end{bmatrix} \\ \text{SUBJ} & \begin{bmatrix} \text{PRED} & '\text{LIGHT}' \\ \text{SPEC} & \begin{bmatrix} \text{SPEC-FORM} & \text{THE} \\ \text{SPEC-TYPE} & \text{DEF} \end{bmatrix} \\ \text{PERS} & 3 \\ \text{NUM} & \text{SG} \\ \text{CASE} & \text{NOM} \\ \text{ANIM} & - \\ \text{NTYPE} & \text{COUNT} \end{bmatrix} \end{bmatrix}$$

An f-structure containing a German particle verb was already seen in (36). Note that here the particle is not listed as part of the predicate.

The predicate appears as 'X-LEUCHTEN<SUBJ>'. The constraint on the particle is stated as in the English grammar: (↑PRT-FORM)=c AUF. The difference reflects the fact that German uses separable prefixes and that the use of this type of particle is much more wide spread in German than in English. As such, it is more general and efficient to list one subcategorization frame such as 'X-LEUCHTEN<SUBJ>' for the many prefixes that appear with *leuchten* 'light' as an intransitive verb and combine this entry with a disjunctive list of the prefixes that go with the intransitive *leuchten*.

3.8 Predicatives

Predicative constructions involve a linking or *copular* verb which has a subject and another argument, as in (56). The postverbal argument can be of a number of categories, e.g., NP, PP, AP.

(56) a. John is a professor.

　　 b. Le gyrophare est sur le   toit.
　　　　the beacon   is on the roof
　　　　'The beacon is on the roof.' (French)

　　 c. Der   Traktor ist rot.
　　　　the.Nom tractor is red
　　　　'The tractor is red.' (German)

Due to the semantic relationship between the subject and the phrase after the linking verb, these verbs are given special subcategorization frames. Traditionally, this has been done by having the postverbal phrase be an XCOMP whose subject is controlled by the linking verb's subject. However, a new analysis, termed the PREDLINK analysis, is used by the ParGram grammars.

Under both approaches, linking verbs may have their own c-structure category and their own VP rule which allows the postverbal NP, AP, and PP to be assigned the appropriate grammatical function; note that most verbs do not allow these c-structure categories to have such grammatical functions.

3.8.1 Controlled Subject Analysis

Under the controlled subject analysis, the subcategorization frame of a verb like linking *be* is as in (57).

(57) (↑PRED)='BE<(↑XCOMP)>(↑SUBJ)'
　　 (↑SUBJ)=(↑XCOMP SUBJ)

The main drawback of this approach is that the postverbal constituent must have a SUBJ to be filled by the control equation of the verb. However, as NPs, APs, and especially PPs do not generally have an overt subject, we believe the representation of the relationship between the noun and thing predicated of it should either be encoded at the level of argument structure, or of semantic structure. Note that if one does implement the controlled subject analysis, it becomes necessary to provide two subcategorization frames for each of these categories: one without a SUBJ argument for simple NPs such as the *a cat* in *A cat ate my food*, and one for predicatively used NPs such as *a cat* in *Harry is a cat*.

3.8.2 Predlink Analysis

The PREDLINK analysis avoids these difficulties by positing a grammatical function PREDLINK. Under this analysis the subcategorization frame of a verb like the copula *be* is shown in (58). This representation for predicative constructions models the fact that a particular property is predicated of the subject in a syntactically reasonable way and provides enough information for subsequent semantic analysis. As PREDLINK is a closed category, there is no control equation between the SUBJ and the PREDLINK and hence no need for NPs, APs, and PPs to have subject arguments.

(58) $(\uparrow\text{PRED})='\text{BE}<(\uparrow\text{SUBJ})(\uparrow\text{PREDLINK})>'$

The f-structure for (59a) using the PREDLINK analysis is shown in (59b). It is interpreted as there being a subject *the tractor* of which a certain property, namely that of being *red*, is predicated, as indicated by the grammatical function PREDLINK.

(59) a. The tractor is red.

b.
$$
\begin{bmatrix}
\text{PRED} & '\text{BE}<\text{SUBJ,PREDLINK}>' \\
\text{STMT-TYPE} & \text{DECLARATIVE} \\
\text{TNS-ASP} & \begin{bmatrix} \text{MOOD} & \text{INDICATIVE} \\ \text{TENSE} & \text{PRES} \end{bmatrix} \\
\text{SUBJ} & \begin{bmatrix} \text{PRED} & '\text{TRACTOR}' \\ \text{SPEC} & \begin{bmatrix} \text{SPEC-FORM} & \text{THE} \\ \text{SPEC-TYPE} & \text{DEF} \end{bmatrix} \\ \text{ANIM} & - \\ \text{CASE} & \text{NOM} \\ \text{NTYPE} & \text{COUNT} \\ \text{PERS} & 3 \\ \text{NUM} & \text{SG} \end{bmatrix} \\
\text{PREDLINK} & \begin{bmatrix} \text{PRED} & '\text{RED}' \\ \text{ATYPE} & \text{PREDICATIVE} \end{bmatrix}
\end{bmatrix}
$$

3.9 Bridge Verbs

Bridge verbs are verbs which allow extraction out of their sentential complements. For example, extraction out of the embedded complement of *think*, a bridge verb, is acceptable, as shown in (60), but not out of the embedded complement of *whisper*, a nonbridge verb, as shown in (61).

(60) What does Mary think that John drives?

(61) *What did Mary whisper that John said?

In order to capture these facts for English and German, our grammars have two different verbal templates for verbs which take sentential complements. In the bridge verb template, the sentential complement bears the grammatical function COMP-EX, indicating that extraction is permitted, while in the nonbridge verb template, the sentential complement bears the grammatical function COMP. Then in the functional uncertainty equations in questions and other extraction constructions, only COMP-EX appears as a possible path, so that a question where the *wh*-word corresponds to an argument of the embedded clause of a nonbridge verb will fail.

3.10 Verbal Complexes

In addition to the verbal elements listed above, each of the three languages also contains verbal complexes which are not only difficult to implement, but whose particular linguistic analysis is still subject to debate. For some of these constructions, we have achieved a rudimentary implementation. However, as the current implementation does not cover the data adequately and must be considered work in progress, we do not present any analyses here and merely point out the problematic areas in each language.

3.10.1 German Coherent Verbs

As discussed in the section on embedded complements (sections 2.2 and 3.3.5) verbs may embed another verb in an embedded complement, as in (62). In German, however, there is a set of verbs, dubbed *coherent* by Bech (1983) which do not appear to embed the other verb, but instead appear to combine with it to form a verbal complex. An example of the coherent verb *lassen* 'let' is shown in (63).

(62) a. Der   Fahrer hat [den   Traktor zu reparieren] versucht.
          the.Nom driver has the.Acc tractor to repair   tried
          'The driver tried to repair the tractor.' (German)

      b. Der Fahrer hat versucht, den Traktor zu reparieren. (noncoherent)

(63) a. Der   Fahrer hat den   Traktor [reparieren lassen].
          the.Nom driver has the.Acc tractor repair   let
          'The driver had the tractor repaired.' (German)

      b. *Der Fahrer hat lassen, den Traktor reparieren. (coherent)

Note that this coherent verbal complex differs from the notion of a *complex predicate*, discussed in section 3.10.2 below in that the two verbs do not actually form a single domain of predication. Instead, the coherent verbs differ from the noncoherent verbs with regard to syntactic factors such as the placement of negation, scambling possibilites (the verbal complex in coherent constructions cannot be separated, as shown in (63b) above) and long-distance extraction of arguments (coherent verbs allow it). For an overview of the phenomenon see Bech 1983 and von Stechow and Sternefeld 1988:406–410. For a comparison of coherent verbs to complex predicates see Rambow 1996.

3.10.2 French Causatives

Like most of the Romance languages, French has complex predicates. The French causative complex predicate in (64) is characterized by the fact that the two verbs 'make' and 'repair' appear to act as a single predicate with respect to phenomena such as clitic climbing. As illustrated in (64), the clitic *lui* may appear in the domain of the verb *fait* 'make' even though it is actually an argument of the verb *réparer* 'repair'.

(64) Marie lui a   fait   réparer la   voiture.
      Marie him has made repair the.F car
      'Marie made him repair the car.' (French)

Such clitic climbing is not possible in the usual verb-complement constructions and as such a different analysis, involving neither COMP or XCOMP, must be posited. Recent argumentation about two different approaches within LFG may be found in Frank 1996 and Alsina 1996. Pointers to previous work and to differing analyses within various frameworks may be found in the references therein.

3.10.3 Noun-Verb Constructions

Finally, there are a number of noun-verb constructions which also appear to act as a single predicate in German. These constructions, illustrated here by (65), are referred to as *Funktionsverbgefüge* (see Helbig 1984 for a description).

(65) Der Fahrer traf eine   Entscheidung.
     the driver hit a.Acc decision
     'The driver made a decision.' (German)

In these constructions the main predicational force comes from the noun, while the verb serves to encode aspectual, Aktionsart, or other semantic information that has only been vaguely defined in the literature. As can be seen from the translation in (65), English has a similar construction, as in *make a decision, make a claim, take a shower*, etc.

These constructions, along with the French complex predicates and the German coherent constructions, currently receive treatments in our grammars; however, the current state of the implementation represents work in progress.

4

Nominal Elements

Nominal elements include NPs, free relative clauses, pronouns and clitics, and other elements which can sometimes act as nominals, such as gerunds. Relative clauses are also discussed here due to their similarities with free relatives.

A full NP may include a determiner, modifiers, such as adjectives, prepositional phrases, relative clauses, and pre- and post-nominal verbal modifiers (see section 4.2). All NPs have case, but the manner in which case is assigned varies in the three grammars. In English, for example, NPs are not case marked morphologically. Case is assigned by the c-structure rules, according to the position in which the NP appears. This is in contrast to German, where the verbs specify the case of the arguments they subcategorize for (i.e., they assign case), and any overt morphological case marking on a noun or a determiner plus noun (see Chapter 5) must be compatible with the case assigned by the verb.

4.1 Pronouns

There are a number of different types of pronouns. Some of these share c-structure categories, such as English expletives and personal pronouns, and have differing f-structures, while others have specific c-structure categories as well, such as the interrogative and relative pronouns. The French clitic pronouns are dicussed in section 4.1.5.

4.1.1 Personal and Demonstrative Pronouns

Personal pronouns supply information about person, number, gender, and case. In English, they also supply information about animacy. Pronouns, like proper nouns, generally cannot appear with determiners or prenominal modification.[1] They are thus instantiated directly under NP. However, pronouns do allow relative clauses, as in (1). In English, these

---

[1] Exceptions are fixed expressions like *lucky me, poor you,* or *a certain someone.*

pronouns form a restricted set and are treated as full nouns within the
c-structure. At f-structure they are given an analysis which is in accord
with other pronouns. In German, the ability to take relative clauses is
part and parcel of being a pronoun, so no special rules are needed.

(1) a. someone that I know

   b. Ihn, den   ich kenne
      him whom I   know
      'him, who I know' (German)

As can be seen in (2), pronouns are analyzed as having a PRED value
of PRO, indicating that these are anaphors awaiting resolution within
the semantic component. In order to provide such a component with as
much information as possible, the surface form of the pronoun is encoded
in the PRON-FORM feature. Also encoded are the gender, number, person
and animacy features which are needed for a semantic evaluation of the
pronoun.

(2) a.   NP
           |
          PRON
           he

   b. $\begin{bmatrix} \text{PRED} & '\text{PRO}' \\ \text{PERS} & 3 \\ \text{NUM} & \text{SG} \\ \text{GEND} & \text{MASC} \\ \text{CASE} & \text{NOM} \\ \text{PRON-TYPE} & \text{PERS} \\ \text{PRON-FORM} & \text{HE} \\ \text{ANIM} & + \end{bmatrix}$

Finally, the feature PRON-TYPE is used to distinguish between various
types of pronouns. Demonstrative pronouns such as *this* or *those* are
assigned PRON-TYPE DEMON, and have an attribute DEIXIS, whose value
may be DISTAL or PROXIMAL (this latter feature is identical to that which
appears with demonstratives in their determiner use, e.g., *this book*).
Otherwise, demonstratives function just like personal pronouns.

4.1.2 Interrogative and Relative Pronouns

Personal pronouns are taken as the default type of pronoun which can
appear anywhere an NP can. Interrogative and relative pronouns are
distinguished at c-structure from the default PRON by being assigned the
c-structure categories PRONint and PRONrel, respectively. This allows a

simple formulation of constraints on their distribution in terms of the c-structure, as PRONint and PRONrel are only called in the NPint and NPrel rules.

(3)   NPrel
         |
       PRONrel
       which

They are assigned a PRON-TYPE of INT or REL, respectively. In addition, they also contribute a PRON-FORM attribute, whose value registers the actual form of the pronoun.

(4) $\begin{bmatrix} \text{PRED} & '\text{PRO}' \\ \text{PRON-TYPE} & \text{REL} \\ \text{PRON-FORM} & \text{WHICH} \\ \text{ANIM} & - \end{bmatrix}$

4.1.3   Expletive Pronouns

Expletive pronouns are distinct in that they do not refer to an actual entity. That is, they are not anaphoric and as such need not undergo semantic resolution. These form a restrictive class, and in many languages only appear in subject position. English and French are examples of such languages. In German, however, the expletive *es* 'it' may also appear in object position.[2] Expletives are encoded by not being assigned a PRED value: they are predicationally empty (Kaplan and Bresnan 1982). They are encoded with a PRON-TYPE EXPLETIVE, and their surface form is registered in PRON-FORM.

(5) a. There is a light in the tractor.

   b. Il est possible de démonter   le   tracteur.
       it is   possible of disassemble the tractor
       'It is possible to disassemble the tractor.' (French)

   c. Es regnet.
       it rains
       'It is raining.' (German)

   d. Er hat es nicht gewußt, daß die   Lampe kaputt ist.
       he has it not   known   that the.Nom lamp   broken is
       'He didn't know that the lamp is broken.' (German)

Within LFG, such nonpredicational, or nonthematic, arguments of a verb are encoded by writing the appropriate argument outside the angle

---

[2]English may also have object expletive pronouns in constructions like *I prefer it when it is cold.*

brackets of the subcategorization frame.. To avoid overgeneration, the lexical entry of the verb may specify that a PRON-TYPE EXPLETIVE is required, as shown in (6). To cover cases as in English, where there may be more than one expletive (*it* and *there*), the overt form of the pronoun is encoded in PRON-FORM. As an example, the f-structure for (5c) is shown in (7).

(6) $(\uparrow\text{PRED})='\text{REGNET}<>(\uparrow\text{SUBJ})'$
     $(\uparrow\text{SUBJ PRON-TYPE})=_c \text{EXPLETIVE}$

(7)
$$
\begin{bmatrix}
\text{PRED} & '\text{REGNEN}< \ >\text{SUBJ}' \\
\text{STMT-TYPE} & \text{DECLARATIVE} \\
\text{TNS-ASP} & \begin{bmatrix} \text{TENSE} & \text{PRES} \\ \text{MOOD} & \text{INDICATIVE} \end{bmatrix} \\
\text{SUBJ} & \begin{bmatrix} \text{PERS} & 3 \\ \text{CASE} & \text{NOM} \\ \text{NUM} & \text{SG} \\ \text{GEND} & \text{NEUT} \\ \text{PRON-TYPE} & \text{EXPLETIVE} \\ \text{PRON-FORM} & \text{ES} \end{bmatrix}
\end{bmatrix}
$$

4.1.4   Reflexives

Many languages have two types of reflexives: one with a PRED value and one without. The type with a PRED value is predicational, as in (8) (for a comprehensive discussion on anaphoric relations, including reflexives, see Dalrymple 1993). The second type is found with inherent reflexive verbs, such as the French and German verbs in (9). Here, the reflexive has been incorporated into the lexical meaning of the verb so that the reflexive itself does not perform a predicational function anymore; instead, it merely functions as a morphosyntactic requirement of the verb. This second type also occurs as the result of certain argument changing processes, such as the medio-passive in (10a) and the intransitivization of certain causatives, as in (10b).

(8) a. She saw herself.
     b. *She saw myself.

(9) a. Marie s'   est évanouie.
       Marie REFL is   fainted
       'Marie fainted.' (French)

    b. Maria befindet   sich in Kalifornien.
       Maria located at REFL in California
       'Maria is in California.' (German)

(10) a. La branche s'   est cassée.
        the branch REFL is   broken
        'The branch broke.' (French)

    b. Der   Hebel bewegt sich.
       the.Nom lever move   REFL
       'The lever is moving/moves.' (German)

Reflexives agree with their antecedents in person, number, and gender. Ideally, this requirement should be stated via inside-out functional uncertainty (cf. Dalrymple 1993) which allows the lexical entry of the reflexive to require that its antecedent be of a particular gender, number, and person. Unfortunately, inside-out functional uncertainty is not implemented in either Medley or XLE; so, the treatment of such reflexives has taken the following provisional form within ParGram.

Reflexives with PRED values, such as those found in English,[3] are treated as arguments and have a c-structure distribution similar to that of personal pronouns. The f-structure of *himself* is shown in (11); it differs from that of personal pronouns only in that the PRON-TYPE is encoded as REFL.

(11) $\begin{bmatrix} \text{PRED} & '\text{PRO}' \\ \text{ANIM} & + \\ \text{CASE} & \text{ACC} \\ \text{PRON-FORM} & \text{HE} \\ \text{GEND} & \text{MASC} \\ \text{PRON-TYPE} & \text{REFL} \\ \text{PERS} & 3 \\ \text{NUM} & \text{SG} \end{bmatrix}$

The reflexives which do not have PRED values are treated as morphological marking in French, and as predicationally empty in German. In both languages, the reflexives contribute features that match require-

---

[3]There are a few inherently reflexive verbs in English such as *behave oneself* and *perjure oneself*; whether the reflexive in these verbs is an argument remains an open question.

ments stipulated by a given verb (PRON-TYPE REFL). The person, number, and gender features are checked against those of the subject in order to ensure wellformedness. In addition, there is an f-structure feature REFL whose value indicates whether the verb is semantically reflexive or not. For example, an inherently reflexive verb like the French *s'évanouir* 'faint' ((9a)) is not semantically reflexive, while a derived reflexive verb like the French *se voir* 'see oneself' is semantically reflexive, even though neither type of verb has a reflexive OBJ in French.

Some verb classes, such as inherently reflexive verbs, are designated as reflexive verbs in their lexical entries, while others are derived from nonreflexive verbs via lexical rules (section 3.4). For example, the formation of French reflexive middles (e.g.,(10a)) changes the OBJ to the SUBJ, and the SUBJ to NULL, in addition to requiring the presence of features provided by the reflexive pronoun.

With inherently reflexive verbs, the reflexive is not a semantic argument of the verb.

(12) a. Il se   trouve dans un tracteur.
          it REFL finds   in   a   tractor
          'It is located in a tractor.' (French)

      b. Er beruhigt sich.
          he calm   REFL
          'He calms down.' (German)

There are two basic approaches to inherently reflexive verbs. The first is to have the reflexive function as an expletive argument of the verb. So, a verb like *beruhigen* 'calm' in (12b) would have a subcategorization frame as in (13) with a requirement that ($\uparrow$OBJ PRON-TYPE)=c REFL.

(13) ($\uparrow$PRED)='BERUHIGEN<($\uparrow$SUBJ)>($\uparrow$OBJ)'

The OBJ argument is satisfied by a reflexive pronoun which has no PRED value. The gender, person, and number of the reflexive OBJ are constrained to match that of the subject. This can be done in the reflexive verb template or in the c-structure for languages such as French which have fixed positions for reflexives (see section 13.2.1 on templates).

The second approach is to have the reflexive not be an argument of the verb. Instead, it just contributes a feature to the f-structure to indicate the presence of the reflexive. In this case, a verb like *beruhigen* 'calm' in (12b) would have a subcategorization frame as in (14) with a requirement that there be a reflexive attribute in the f-structure. This reflexive attribute can only be provided by the reflexive pronoun.

(14) ($\uparrow$PRED)='BERUHIGEN<($\uparrow$SUBJ)>'

As with the expletive argument approach, this requires there to be two entries for reflexive pronouns: one with a PRED and one without. In the latter case the pronoun simply supplies the (↑REFL)=+ feature and constraining equations on the gender, number, and person of the subject. This second approach is linguistically justified in that verbs like *trouver* 'find' and *beruhigen* 'calm' behave as if they were intransitives, not as transitives.

4.1.5 Clitics

In French there are a special class of pronouns referred to as clitics. These pronouns are interesting because their phrase structure position is distinct from that of their nonpronominal counterparts:[4]

(15) a. Il a vu   la boîte.
         he has saw.Part.M the box.F
         'He saw the box.' (French)

     b. Il l'   a vue.
         he it.Clitic has saw.Part.F
         'He saw it.' (French)

In (15a) the nonpronominal object occurs after the verb; note that it does not trigger agreement of the past participle. However, if the object is pronominalized, as in (15b), then it occurs before the verb and triggers agreement on the participle.

In addition to their special verb adjacent positioning, clitics also have a set order amongst themselves. That is, if there is more than one clitic, they must appear in a particular order:

(16) a. Il nous   les   y   donne.
         he us.Clitic them.Clitic there.Clitic gives
         'He gives them to us there.' (French)

     b. *Il les y nous donne.

Given the restricted behavior of the clitic pronouns, special c-structure categories and rules are introduced for them. These are called in the relevant position (preverbal in declaratives, postverbal in imperatives, etc.). The c-structure rules require the order and placement of the clitics seen in (17). As with nonclitic pronominals, each clitic pronoun provides a PRED PRO as well as information as to person, number, gender, etc. Note that the pronoun *y* provides f-structure information similar to that of a PP, reflecting the fact that it corresponds not to an NP argument, but to an adverbial PP meaning. That is, the pronoun *y* itself is embedded un-

---

[4]Clitics have special prosodic properties which are not discussed here.

der an assumed preposition *à* 'to'. The grammatical function is provided, as with nonclitic pronominals, by annotations on the c-structure.

In sum, clitic pronouns are similar to nonclitic pronouns in the f-structure. However, their restricted c-structure positioning, both in their fixed order relative to one another and their strict verb adjacent position, is captured by specific c-structure categories and rules. That is, unlike in English and German, clitic pronouns in French are not a subtype of N. We particularly recommend Grimshaw 1982, Andrews 1990 and Berman and Frank 1995 for further detailed reading on LFG analyses of Romance clitics.

(17) a. Il nous   les   y   donne.
        he us.Clitic them.Clitic there.Clitic gives
        'He gives them to us there.' (French)

b.

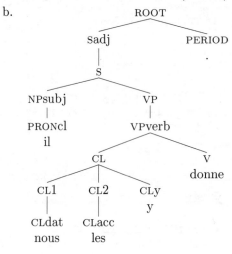

$$
(18) \begin{bmatrix}
\text{PRED} & \text{'DONNER<SUBJ,OBJ,OBJ2>'} \\
\text{STMT-TYPE} & \text{DECLARATIVE} \\
\text{TNS-ASP} & \begin{bmatrix} \text{MOOD} & \text{INDICATIVE} \\ \text{TENSE} & \text{PRES} \end{bmatrix} \\
\text{SUBJ} & \begin{bmatrix} \text{PRED} & \text{'PRO'} \\ \text{PRON-FORM} & \text{IL} \\ \text{GEND} & \text{MASC} \\ \text{CASE} & \text{NOM} \\ \text{PRON-TYPE} & \text{PERS} \\ \text{PERS} & 3 \\ \text{NUM} & \text{SG} \end{bmatrix} \\
\text{OBJ} & \begin{bmatrix} \text{PRED} & \text{'PRO'} \\ \text{PRON-FORM} & \text{LE} \\ \text{CASE} & \text{ACC} \\ \text{PRON-TYPE} & \text{PERS} \\ \text{PERS} & 3 \\ \text{NUM} & \text{PL} \end{bmatrix} \\
\text{OBJ2} & \begin{bmatrix} \text{PRED} & \text{'PRO'} \\ \text{PRON-FORM} & \text{NOUS} \\ \text{CASE} & \text{DAT} \\ \text{PRON-TYPE} & \text{PERS} \\ \text{PERS} & 1 \\ \text{NUM} & \text{PL} \end{bmatrix} \\
\text{ADJUNCT} & \left\{ \begin{bmatrix} \text{PRED} & \text{'À<OBJ>'} \\ \text{PSEM} & \text{LOC} \\ \text{OBJ} & \begin{bmatrix} \text{PRED} & \text{'PRO'} \\ \text{PRON-FORM} & \text{Y} \\ \text{PCASE} & \text{À} \\ \text{PRON-TYPE} & \text{PERS} \end{bmatrix} \end{bmatrix} \right\}
\end{bmatrix}
$$

4.2 Full Noun Phrases

In German and French, simple nouns encode gender and number features. In English they encode number, but not gender, since English has no grammatical gender with the possible exception of its pronominal system.

All nouns are encoded with a particular NTYPE in the f-structure. Most common nouns such as *dog* or *tractor* are encoded as NTYPE COUNT. This distinguishes them from mass nouns such as WATER, which are given NTYPE MASS. This distinction is syntactically necessary as mass nouns can appear without a determiner and may occur in constructions such as *a liter of water*.

Proper names also display a syntactic behavior which differs from that of count and mass nouns. They are therefore distinguished by an NTYPE PROPER. Proper names normally cannot be modified with determiners, adjectives, prepositional phrases, etc. A further distinction made through the NTYPE feature is to set titles like *Professor, Ms.*, or *Herr* off from other nouns.

The c-structure treatment of NPs differs considerably in the three grammars as the internal structure of NPs in German, English and French is characterized by different syntactic properties.

4.2.1 English

The relative order of determiners, adjectives, PPs and relative clauses is fixed in English; so, the English grammar provides a heavily structured analysis. As can be seen in (19), an explicit level of attachment is provided for PPs and APs, compounding (Nmod), determiners, and postnominal modifiers (i.e., the relative clause). This strict hierarchical structure in terms of NP constituents like NPap is motivated by coordination, as each of these levels of attachments may be coordinated as constituents (see Chapter 8).

(19)

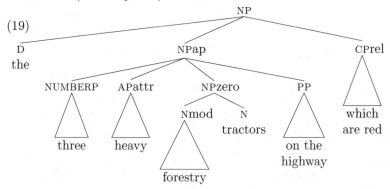

4.2.2 German

The internal structure of the German NP is as complex as that of its English counterpart; however, in keeping with the general flexible word order of German, the prenominal elements within the NP are not amenable to the rigid analysis presented for English. The basic structure of the NP is similar to that of English: a determiner followed by modifiers, followed by the head noun, which may in turn be followed by a number of modifiers. As an illustration of the similarities and differences, the counterpart to the English (19) is provided in (20).

(20) a. die   drei   schweren Forsttraktoren   auf der
     the.Nom three heavy   forestry.tractors on   the.Dat
     Autobahn, die   rot sind.
     highway   which red are
     'the three heavy forestry tractors on the highway which are red'
     relative clause (German)
    b.

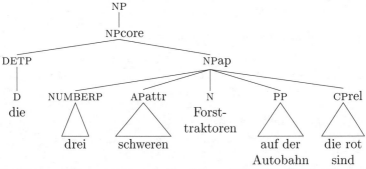

The major difference between English and German lies in the nature and distribution of pre- and postnominal modifiers. German may have prenominal modifiers, like those in (21), which can only be expressed as (reduced) relative clauses in English.

(21) Der   auf der   Mauer sitzende Hund bellt.
     the.Nom on the.Dat wall   sitting   dog   barks
     'The dog sitting on the wall barks.' (German)

Prenominal modifiers in German include numbers, participials with their arguments and modifiers, and simple adjectives with modifying adverbs. These may appear in any order, although the arguments and modifiers of a participial must precede it, and an adverb must precede the adjective.

Postnominal modifiers include comparatives (*a cat bigger than a dog*), participials with their arguments and modifiers, finite *daß* 'that' or infinitival clauses as in (22a) and (22b), adjectives as in (22c), appositions as in (22d), genitives as in (22e), PPs, and relative clauses, as in (19).

(22) a. die   Tatsache, daß er lacht
     the.Nom fact   that he laughs
     'the fact that he laughs' finite clause (German)

b. der   Versuch zu gewinnen
   the.Nom attempt to win
   'the attempt to win' infinitival clause (German)

c. ein   Mann nicht besonders klug
   a.Nom man   not   very   intelligent
   'a not very intelligent man' adjective (German)

d. Montag, zehnter August
   Monday tenth   August
   'Monday, the tenth of August' apposition (German)

e. die   Katze der   Frau
   the.Nom cat   the.Gen woman
   'the cat of the woman' genitive (German)

The order of these postnominal modifiers is fairly fixed. Genitives must appear immediately after the noun. PPs and comparatives come next, interchangeably, followed by participials, appositions, finite and nonfinite clauses, and finally, relative clauses. Given this distribution of modifiers, the German grammar employs a general grouping of prenominal and postnominal modifiers under different macros (but not constituents) in which the linear order described above is imposed (section 13.2). Since there is no evidence for a particular constituency within these modifiers, a hierarchy of constituents is not implemented in the c-structure.

4.2.3 French

The basic French NP is similar in spirit to that of English in that the order of constituents is relatively fixed and the internal structure of the NP is hierarchical. The most obvious difference is that pronouns in French are not called by the NP rule since they pattern differently (see section 4.1.5 on clitic pronouns).

As seen in (23), French allows adjectives to appear both before and after the head noun. This is lexically determined, i.e., some adjectives can appear in only one of these positions and some can appear in either position but with a difference in meaning. This distribution is constrained by a feature APOS. In addition, adjectives agree in gender and number with their head noun. This is constrained by annotations on the phrase structure rules which introduce APs.

(23) a. le   grand filtre rouge dans le   tracteur que   je vois
        the big   filter red   in   the tractor which I see
        'the big red filter in the tractor which I see' (French)

b.

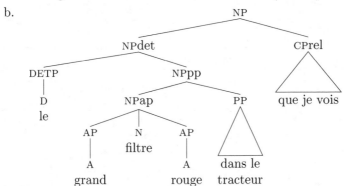

4.2.4 F-structure

Despite the differences in the analyses of NPs at c-structure, the analyses in terms of f-structures are very similar across the languages. This is because the c-structures shown in the previous sections just represent different ways of putting together essentially the same information, as demonstrated by the f-structures in (24) and (25). These correspond to the NPs in (18) and (19) above. Not all the pieces of NPs can be treated in parallel. Structures which have no analog in another language, such as certain types of appositions or participial prenominal modifiers in German, are given an f-structure analysis which does not have a parallel counterpart in English or French.

Note that despite the fact that the German *Forsttraktoren* 'forestry tractor' appears as a single lexical item at c-structure, it is decomposed into its components at f-structure and thus corresponds almost exactly to its English counterpart (see section 4.3 on compounds). This decomposition is done as part of the morphological analysis. Not all lexical vs. syntactic compounds will have exact correspondences. In the structures below, for example, the English *highway* is not a compound, while its German counterpart *Auto-bahn* 'car track' is.

(24) a. the three heavy forestry tractors on the highway which are red

b.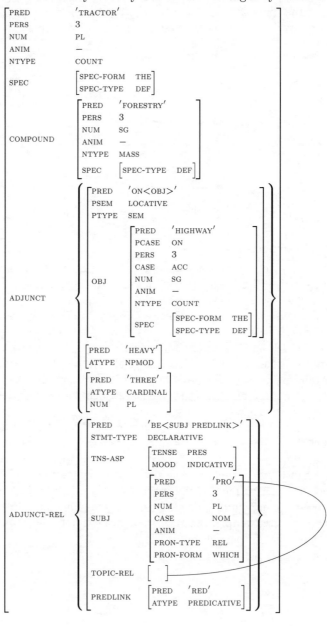

(25) a. die drei schweren Forsttraktoren auf der Autobahn, die rot sind.
'the three heavy forestry tractors on the highway which are red'

b.

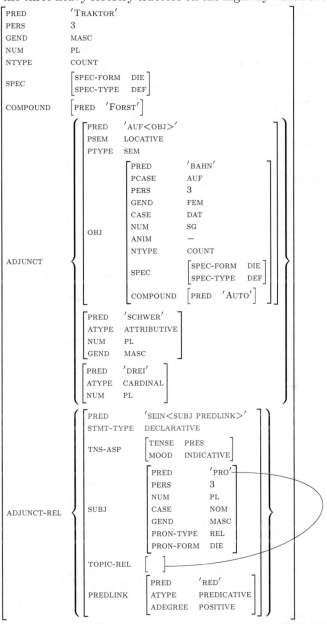

4.3   Compounds and N-N Sequences

Titles like *Professor John Smith* and names like *the linguistics depart-ment* are treated as N-N sequences and are parsed by a specialized subset of c-structure rules within the NP rule system. While German is well-known for its lexical noun compounding, English employs a nonlexical compounding strategy and French uses PPs, as illustrated by (26).

(26)   a. Hydraulikölfilter (German)
       b. hydraulic oil filter
       c. le filtre à huile hydraulique (French)

In English and French, these nonlexical compounds are dealt with by means of a special c-structure rule which analyses N-N sequences that are not titles or names as compounds in the f-structure.

(27)   a.   English:

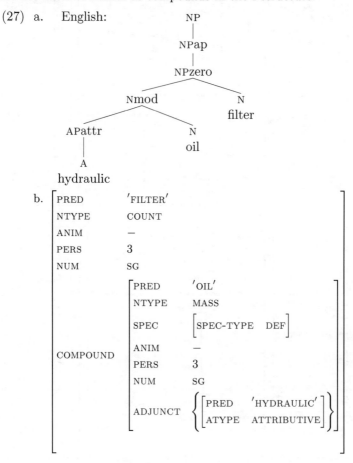

(28) a. French:

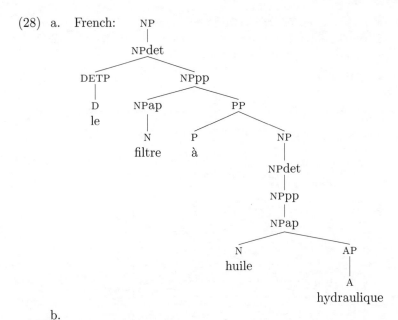

b.

$$
\begin{bmatrix}
\text{PRED} & \text{'FILTRE'} \\
\text{NTYPE} & \text{COUNT} \\
\text{GENDER} & \text{MASC} \\
\text{PERS} & 3 \\
\text{NUM} & \text{SG} \\
\text{SPEC} & \begin{bmatrix} \text{SPEC-FORM} & \text{LE} \\ \text{SPEC-TYPE} & \text{DEF} \end{bmatrix} \\
\text{ADJUNCT} & \left\{ \begin{bmatrix} \text{PRED} & \text{'Á<OBJ>'} \\ \text{OBJ} & \begin{bmatrix} \text{PRED} & \text{'HUILE'} \\ \text{NTYPE} & \text{COUNT} \\ \text{GENDER} & \text{FEM} \\ \text{PERS} & 3 \\ \text{PCASE} & \text{À} \\ \text{NUM} & \text{SG} \\ \text{ADJUNCT} & \left\{ \begin{bmatrix} \text{PRED} & \text{'HYDRAULIQUE'} \\ \text{ATYPE} & \text{ATTRIBUTIVE} \\ \text{GEND} & \text{FEM} \\ \text{NUM} & \text{SG} \end{bmatrix} \right\} \end{bmatrix} \end{bmatrix} \right\}
\end{bmatrix}
$$

In German, the lexical compounding is dealt with at the level of the morphological analyzer, a finite state machine which encodes German rules of compounding (section 11.3.2).

(29) a. German:

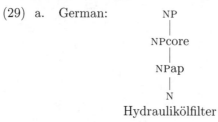

$$
\begin{array}{c}
\text{NP} \\
| \\
\text{NPcore} \\
| \\
\text{NPap} \\
| \\
\text{N} \\
\text{Hydraulikölfilter}
\end{array}
$$

b.
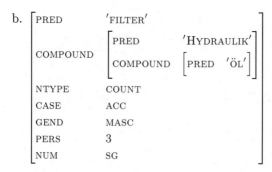

$$
\begin{bmatrix}
\text{PRED} & \text{'FILTER'} \\
\text{COMPOUND} & \begin{bmatrix} \text{PRED} & \text{'HYDRAULIK'} \\ \text{COMPOUND} & \begin{bmatrix} \text{PRED} & \text{'ÖL'} \end{bmatrix} \end{bmatrix} \\
\text{NTYPE} & \text{COUNT} \\
\text{CASE} & \text{ACC} \\
\text{GEND} & \text{MASC} \\
\text{PERS} & 3 \\
\text{NUM} & \text{SG}
\end{bmatrix}
$$

While the rules necessary to treat most N-N sequences found in the languages are in place, a problem remains. Almost any noun can be turned into a "title", as in *grammar writer John*, or a name, as in the German *Tankstelle Greifenberg* 'gas station Greifenberg'.[5] Hand coding each nominal lexical entry for precise information is unfeasible, and loosening the c-structure rules to allow for new creations of N-N sequences can lead to overgeneration. Thus, while the grammars can parse most N-N sequences, the issue has not as yet been completely resolved.

4.4   Relative Clauses

Relative clauses modify NPs. In accordance with differences in syntactic distribution, a c-structure difference is made between free and bound relative clauses. Both types are treated as full clauses in the sense that a STMT-TYPE and tense/aspect information are provided, and that the subcategorization requirements of the embedded verb must be satisfied. The relative pronoun is treated as an argument of the embedded verb. Additionally, motivated by the English preposing of the relative pro-

---

[5]These are not to be confused with appositions which are extremely productive and whose analysis is also not finalized at this point.

noun, the relative pronoun is encoded as the TOPIC-REL of the relative clause. This treatment satisfies traditional filler-gap analyses without resorting to an overt movement analysis.

4.4.1 Bound Relatives

Relative clauses are analyzed as being of category CPrel. The notation is meant to indicate that it is a clause which is akin to standard notions of a CP: a node dominating a tensed clause that allows an extra position for items like complementizers, or, in this case, relative pronouns. The category of the fronted constituent varies, but it is always labeled as a relative, e.g., NPrel (30a) or PPrel (30b).

(30) a. the light [**which** flashes on the console]
       b. the console [**on which** the light flashes]

Various functional equations on the c-structure rules within NPrel and PPrel guarantee that there will be agreement in number (English) and number and gender (French and German) between the head noun and the relative clause.

(31) a. the light which flashes
       b. the lights which flash

(32) a. das   Licht, das   neben dem
          the.N.Sg.Nom light   that.N.Sg.Nom next   the.M.Sg.Dat
          Fahrersitz   aufleuchtet
          driver's seat uplights
          'the light which lights up next to the driver's seat' (German)
       b. die   Katze, die   miaut
          the.F.Sg.Nom cat   that.F.Sg.Nom meows
          'the cat that meows' (German)

(33) la   lampe qui   est allumée
     the.F light.F which is   lit.F
     'the light which is lit' (French)

The f-structure of (30b) is shown in (34b).

(34) a. the console on which the light flashes

b.

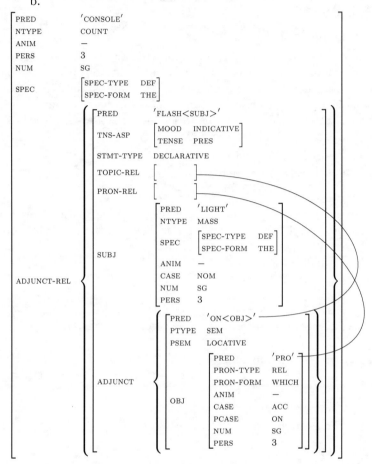

4.4.2 Free Relatives

English free relatives, as in (35) are treated as NPs because they have the distribution of an NP. Pronouns heading free relatives in English are instantiated by special lexical items like *whoever* or *whatever*.

The analog of free relatives in German, also shown in (35), cannot be treated as NPs since they distribute more like finite clauses, i.e., they may appear clause initially or clause finally, but not clause internally. Free relative clauses are thus treated in German not as NPs, but rather as CPs in analogy to relative clauses, and are distinguished by a special category name (CPfreerel). Finally, the free relative pronouns are supplied by the

set of interrogative pronouns in German: free relative pronouns are thus
not lexically distinguished from their interrogative counterparts.

(35) a. She will drive whatever is available.

   b. Wer den   Traktor fährt, lacht.
       who the.M.Sg.Acc tractor drives laughs
       'Whoever drives the tractor laughs.' (German)

Despite these c-structure differences, the f-structure analysis is again
held parallel across languages. As a representative analysis, the f-structure
for the English free relative in (35a) is shown below.

(36) a. Whoever drives the tractor laughs.

   b.

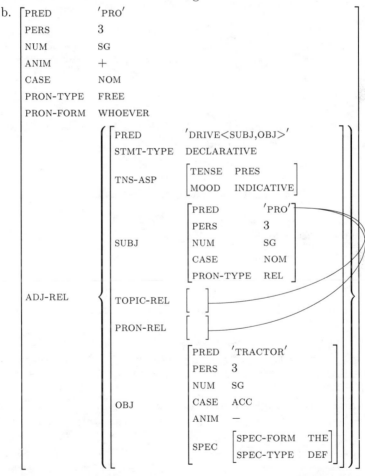

The free relative pronoun is taken to fulfill a double function both as the head of the free relative and as an argument of the root verb (*laugh* in (35a)). From either the construction (German) or the lexical information provided by the free pronoun (English), the existence of an empty argument of the root verb is deduced and registered at f-structure, along with appropriate features gleaned from the lexical entry of the free pronoun.

Just as with bound relatives, the relative VP is represented in an ADJUNCT-REL,[6] with the TOPIC-REL feature registering the fronted constituent as a topic.

4.5 NPs without a Head Noun

4.5.1 Nominalized Adjectives

Some languages, such as French and German, allow adjectives to be heads of NPs, as in (37). That these are NPs can be seen by their syntactic distribution, including the fact that they can be preceded by a determiner.

(37) a. Il y a   deux leviers dont   un petit.
         there are two   levers of them a little
         'There are two levers one of which is little.' (French)

      b. Die   Kleinen   lachen.
         the.M.Pl.Nom little.M.Pl.Nom laugh
         'The little ones are laughing.' (German)

Contrast these constructions with their English counterparts in which there is a nominal head, as in (38).

(38) the little one(s)

In both French and German, this construction is very productive. In German the nominalized adjectives are identified by the fact that they are capitalized. They are thus identified as nominalized adjectives by the morphological analyzer and pose no further problem for analysis. In French, however, these adjectives are not offset from noun modifying adjectives in any way; so, it is impractical to have separate N lexical entries for every adjective. Instead, a separate option in the c-structure of the NP is provided whereby an adjective can be the head, instead of a noun, as in (39). In addition, NPs with adjectival heads may have different syntactic properties, e.g., French NPs of this type do not require determiners, which can be accounted for by different annotations on the adjectival c-structure rule.

---

[6] In (37b) ADJUNCT-REL has been abbreviated to ADJ-REL.

(39)

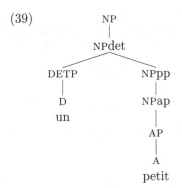

4.5.2 Headless NPs

In contrast with the nominalized adjectives above, German also has true headless constructions, as shown in (40a) for adjectives and (40b) for PPs.

(40) a. Der   Fahrer kauft neue Reifen, die   [alten]
          the.M.Sg.Nom driver buys new tires   the.F.Pl.Acc old
          wirft   er weg.
          throws he away
          'The driver is buying new tires, he will throw away the old
          ones.' (German)

      b. Der   [aus Berlin] lacht.
          the.M.Sg.Nom from Berlin laughs
          'The one from Berlin laughs.' (German)

In order to deal with these constructions, a version of the NP rules (NPheadless) supplies an empty head only when either a determiner or an adjective is present. Though this implementation can easily lead to overgeneration unless suitably constrained, we do not see another viable alternative at present.

English has a similar construction for certain possessives, as in (41).

(41) I am going to the dentist's.

The English construction is more constrained due to its more limited distribution, but the basic approach is identical to that of the German. The English rule is shown in (42). The annotations provide the head of the f-structure, while the possessive is parsed by NPposs and hence analyzed as a specifier (section 5.1.1); this is shown in (43).

(42) NPheadless $\longrightarrow$ NPposs
$\qquad\qquad\qquad\qquad$ ($\uparrow$NUM)=SG
$\qquad\qquad\qquad\qquad$ ($\uparrow$PERS)=3
$\qquad\qquad\qquad\qquad$ ($\uparrow$PRED)='PRO'
$\qquad\qquad\qquad\qquad$ ($\uparrow$PRON-TYPE)=NULL

(43) a. the dentist's

b.
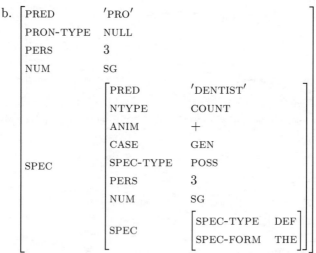

4.6 The NP Squish

4.6.1 Gerunds

Gerunds are ubiquitous in English, but do not occur in German or French. In keeping with general practice (Milsark 1988), they are analyzed externally as NPs in that they receive case, are assigned person and number for verb agreement, and may appear in NP positions in the c-structure. Internally, however, they are clausal. They either occur with a null pronominal subject (44a) or a genitive pronoun or possessive subject NP (44b).[7]

(44) a. [Driving the tractor] is good.

b. [His/John's driving] the tractor amazes me.

The c-structure in (45) corresponds to (44a).

---

[7]Constructions of the type 'the driving of the tractor' are treated as standard NPs, not as gerunds. That is, these are deverbal nouns, which are provided as nouns by the morphology and as such receive no special treatment either morphologically or syntactically. Whether their semantics warrants special treatment is not examined here.

(45) a. Driving the tractor is good.

b.

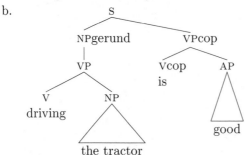

4.6.2   Sentential Subjects

In all three languages, a class of verbs and predicate adjectives can occur with sentential subjects, as in (46). Note that these must be constrained appropriately since not all verbs allow sentential subjects.

(46) a. That the tractor started immediately astounded me.

b. Que tu viennes   ne changera   rien   à la   situation
that you come.Subj not change.Fut nothing to the situation
'That you come will change nothing about the situation.'
(French)

c. Daß der   Traktor startet, hat mich gewundert.
that the.M.Sg.Nom tractor starts   has me   surprised
'That the tractor started surprised me.' (German)

While sentential complements are usually analyzed in f-structure as COMP, this is not the case for sentential subjects (see Bresnan 1982b). Instead, they are assigned the role SUBJ. One argument for this rather different approach to sentential subjects vs. sentential objects is that they appear in the c-structure position reserved for subjects in languages like English. A fresh look at German and some of the English data has recently led to some discussion (Berman 1996) questioning the validity of the original analysis. A valid alternative analysis may involve a structural topic position for sentential subjects. However, as the development of such an alternative analysis presupposes a large amount of linguistic research outside the scope of ParGram collaboration, we have chosen to implement the traditional analysis of sentential subjects presented in Bresnan (1982b). For sample f-structure analyses see section 3.3.5.

5

Determiners and Adjectives

5.1 Determiners

5.1.1 Types of Specifiers

Articles (determiners), quantifiers and prenominal genitives pattern similarly in English in that they appear in the first position in an NP: they precede any modifiers, as in (1), and cannot be preceded by another article or quantifier which modifies the noun, as in (2).

(1) The/a/every/Kim's small dog barks.

(2) *The a/every/Kim's dog barks.

The intuition that has guided most of the modern syntactic approaches to these constructions is that they serve to "specify" the head noun rather than simply "modify" it.[1]

Although most specifiers are introduced through a category D or DETP (determiner phrase), the analysis of specifiers differs slightly at the level of c-structure.[2] Articles, quantifiers and prenominal genitives are treated uniformly in all three grammars in that they are represented under a SPEC feature in the f-structure, as in (3).

---

[1]The special properties of these specifiers have prompted a reanalysis of the traditional notion of NPs (the one implemented here) in which the N is considered to be the head of the NP. The alternative DP-hypothesis (Abney 1987) maintains that the specifiers are the heads of the constituents we used to think of as NPs, and that in keeping with the requirements of x′ theory, a DP should be posited. We have not implemented the DP hypothesis within ParGram, though we do use a determiner phrase (DETP).

[2]For example, the English grammar introduces genitive names such as *John's* through a specialized rule within the NP, while the German grammar treats genitives on a par with other determiners and generates them within a DETP.

(3) a. the dog

　　 b.
$$
\begin{bmatrix}
\text{PRED} & \text{'DOG'} \\
\text{PERS} & 3 \\
\text{NUM} & \text{SG} \\
\text{CASE} & \text{NOM} \\
\text{NTYPE} & \text{COUNT} \\
\text{ANIM} & + \\
\text{SPEC} & \begin{bmatrix} \text{SPEC-TYPE} & \text{DEF} \\ \text{SPEC-FORM} & \text{THE} \end{bmatrix}
\end{bmatrix}
$$

The precise semantics of specifiers are difficult to capture and continue to be the subject of much linguistic investigation (see Kamp and Reyle 1993 for a good overview). Our implementation reflects the syntactic characteristics of specifiers, though the grammars also provide a rough classification of specifier types in addition to recording their surface form in a SPEC-FORM feature. Some SPEC-TYPES are given here as examples, for the full range of types used, see the Appendix.

(4)

SPEC-TYPE	Example
DEF	the dog
INDEF	a dog
QUANT	every dog
NEG	no dog
POSS	my/John's dog

It should be noted that most of the German equivalents of English quantifiers (SPEC-TYPE QUANT) such as *every, some,* and *many* are not treated as specifiers in the German grammar. Rather, with the exception of *alle* 'all', they are analyzed as quantifying adjectives. The reason for this is that they may appear with a determiner before them, as in (5), and that they show the same kind of morphological inflection as adjectives (see section 5.2.1.2).[3]

(5) Ein　　　　　jeder　　　　　Traktor ist rot.
　　a.M.Sg.Nom.W every.M.Sg.Nom.S tractor is red
　　'Every tractor is red.'

Although prenominal genitives pattern like articles and quantifiers as

---

[3]Note that (5) is the first German example which contains a complete close gloss for determiners and adjectives. For the sake of greater perspicuity, we left out information as to the strong/weak (s/w) declension in previous chapters, and only gradually introduced information about case, number and gender, as it became relevant in each chapter.

far as the syntax is concerned, they do differ in terms of complexity. Genitives give rise to more complex specifiers, as illustrated in (6).

(6) a. the driver's dog

b.
$$\begin{bmatrix} \text{PRED} & \text{'DOG'} \\ \text{PERS} & 3 \\ \text{NUM} & \text{SG} \\ \text{CASE} & \text{NOM} \\ \text{ANIM} & + \\ \text{NTYPE} & \text{COUNT} \\ \\ \text{SPEC} & \begin{bmatrix} \text{PRED} & \text{'DRIVER'} \\ \text{PERS} & 3 \\ \text{ANIM} & + \\ \text{CASE} & \text{GEN} \\ \text{SPEC} & \begin{bmatrix} \text{SPEC-TYPE} & \text{DEF} \\ \text{SPEC-FORM} & \text{THE} \end{bmatrix} \\ \text{SPEC-TYPE} & \text{POSS} \end{bmatrix} \end{bmatrix}$$

The genitive NP *the driver's* is embedded under the SPEC feature of *dog*, indicating that the entire NP serves as a specifier of *dog*. Since *the driver's* is itself an NP with a specifier (the article *the*), a SPEC feature is embedded under the higher one. Note that any further material in the genitive NP would also be embedded under the SPEC feature of *dog*. For example, with *the nice driver's dog*, the adjective *nice* would be analyzed as an adjunct modifying *driver* and be placed inside the SPEC feature modifying *dog*.

5.1.2   Morphosyntactic Considerations

The German determiner system encodes grammatical case, number and gender, thus presenting the grammar writer with a complicated inflectional paradigm.[4] An example for *der* 'the' and *ein* 'a' with the feminine *Katze* 'cat' and the masculine *Hund* 'dog' is given below.

(7)

CASE	FEM	MASC
Nominative	die Katze	der Hund
Genitive	der Katze	des Hundes
Dative	der Katze	dem Hund
Accusative	die Katze	den Hund

---

[4]French determiners show number and gender agreement, but not case agreement. With the prepositions *de* and *à*, the plural and masculine singular definite determiners have special forms (*des, du, aux, au*).

The gender, number and case agreement requirements can be dealt with straightforwardly under LFG's unification-based approach: the morphosyntactic specifications of the determiners are simply required to unify with those of the head noun.

However, there is a further complication which characterizes the German determiner system. Determiners are classified as inflecting according to either a weak or a strong paradigm. So, for example, the definite article *der* 'the' inflects according to the strong paradigm, but the indefinite *ein* 'a' follows the weak paradigm. This interacts with adjectival inflections, as shown in (8).

(8) a. der   [kleine]   Hund
     the.M.Sg.Nom.S small.M.Sg.Nom.W dog
     'the small dog' (German)

   b. ein   [kleiner]   Hund
     a.M.Sg.Nom.W small.M.Sg.Nom.S dog
     'a small dog' (German)

Adjectives in German are also inflected for gender, number, case and the weak/strong distinction (section 5.2.1.2). The generalization which emerges is that strong determiners require weak adjectives and weak determiners require strong adjectives. In the German grammar, this requirement has also been implemented via unification by inverting the traditional descriptive value that is assigned to the determiners: weak determiners are thus given a STRONG value for the feature ADJ-AGR (adjective agreement), while strong determiners are given a WEAK value. Given that this division into strong vs. weak inflection does not seem to reflect any functional or semantic information, the feature ADJ-AGR is projected into the m-projection (see the discussion in section 3.5 for the motivation of this projection), where it can fulfill its purpose of checking for wellformedness without cluttering up the f-structure.

The effect is that a weak determiner will only be compatible with a strong adjective (which also carries the feature ADJ-AGR STRONG), and vice versa. Note that not all determiners pattern exactly according to this generalization: *etliche* 'several' and *einige* 'some', for example, inflect differently (most probably due to their special *-ig/-ich* forms (A. Schiller, p.c.)). These determiners are therefore treated as exceptions to the general rule and are captured by specialized lexical entries.

5.2 Adjectives

Adjectives are characterized by the fact that they modify nouns and, in some languages including French and German, inflect for agreement.

English adjectives do not inflect to show gender or number agreement with the head noun. However, it is possible to form comparative and superlative forms of English adjectives, as in (9); so, in a sense adjectives inflect even in the morphologically impoverished English.

(9) green/greener/greenest

Furthermore adjectives may be modified by a small set of adverbs such as *very*. Some adjectives subcategorize for arguments (section 5.2.4), but the majority do not.

At c-structure, adjectives form APs (adjective phrases) which contain the adjective and any adverbial modifiers, e.g., *very red, trés rouge* (French), *sehr rot* (German). The AP also contains any NP or clausal arguments, and PP modifiers or arguments. In German, all of these constituents may appear in a prenominal AP, as in (10). Note that (10b) is an example of a deverbal adjective.

(10) a. Die   ihrer   Firma   treue
         the.F.Sg.Nom.S her.F.Sg.Dat.S company loyal.F.Sg.Nom.W
         Frau   lacht.
         woman laughs
         'The woman loyal to her company laughs.' (German)

      b. Die   im   Garten den
         the.F.Sg.Nom.S in.the.M.Sg.Dat.W garden the.M.Sg.Acc.S
         Tee schnell trinkende   Frau   lacht.
         tea quickly drinking.F.Sg.Nom.W woman laughs
         'The woman drinking tea quickly in the garden laughs.' (German)

These German constructions must be analyzed as instances of APs, and not, for example, the equivalent of English reduced relative clauses because the adjectives *treue* 'loyal' and *trinkende* 'drinking' inflect to agree with the head noun and otherwise pattern like adjectives.

At f-structure, adjectives are analyzed as ADJUNCTs when encountered prenominally (section 5.2.1), and as PREDLINKs when used predicatively (section 5.2.3). All adjectives are marked with an ATYPE at f-structure in order to distinguish the various uses and types of adjectives.

5.2.1   Prenominal Adjectives

Prenominal adjectives come in several different varieties: simple adjectives, comparatives/superlatives, deverbal adjectives, and cardinals/ordinals. Degree adjectives (comparatives/superlatives) are described in section 5.2.5. The other types of adjectives are simply analyzed as adjuncts at f-structure, as illustrated in (11).

(11) a. the small dog

b.
$$
\begin{bmatrix}
\text{PRED} & \text{'DOG'} \\
\text{PERS} & 3 \\
\text{NUM} & \text{SG} \\
\text{CASE} & \text{NOM} \\
\text{NTYPE} & \text{COUNT} \\
\text{SPEC} & \begin{bmatrix} \text{SPEC-FORM} & \text{THE} \\ \text{SPEC-TYPE} & \text{DEF} \end{bmatrix} \\
\text{ADJUNCT} & \left\{ \begin{bmatrix} \text{PRED} & \text{'SMALL'} \\ \text{ATYPE} & \text{ATTRIBUTIVE} \end{bmatrix} \right\}
\end{bmatrix}
$$

5.2.1.1   Deverbal Adjectives

Deverbal adjectives as in (12) appear prenominally in English and German and inflect just like the attributive adjectives discussed below.

(12) the barking dog

These adjectives are therefore analyzed as being ATYPE ATTRIBUTIVE and obey the inflectional constraints introduced in the section above.

5.2.1.2   Attributive Adjectives

The prototypical adjective for French, German and English is a prenominal attributive adjective. This type of adjective is encoded has having the ATYPE ATTRIBUTIVE, as was illustrated in (12). There may be several attributive adjectives separated by commas or coordinated. In German and French, but not in English, due to its sparse morphology, adjectives agree with the head noun they modify in gender and number. German additionally requires agreement in terms of case and the weak/strong features, which depend on the type of determiner and its particular gender, number and case features (section 5.1.2).

(13) a. der   graue   Hund
         the.M.Sg.Nom.S grey.M.Sg.Nom.W dog
         'the grey dog' (German)

      b. den   grauen   Hund
         the.M.Sg.Acc.S grey.M.Sg.Acc.W dog
         'the grey dog' (German)

The full paradigm for *grau* 'grey' is given in (14) in conjunction with the definite article *der*, the masculine noun *Hund* 'dog', and the feminine noun *Katze* 'cat'.

(14)	NUM	CASE	FEM	MASC
	Sg	Nom	die graue Katze	der graue Hund
		Gen	der grauen Katze	des grauen Hundes
		Dat	der grauen Katze	dem grauen Hund
		Acc	die graue Katze	den grauen Hund
	Pl	Nom	die grauen Katzen	die grauen Hunde
		Gen	der grauen Katzen	der grauen Hunde
		Dat	den grauen Katzen	den grauen Hunden
		Acc	die grauen Katzen	die grauen Hunde

These agreement requirements are enforced via functional equations on the c-structure rules wherever an attributive AP is called. A simplified rule is given in (15). Where German requires agreement in four dimensions: gender, case, number and weak/strong (ADJ-AGR), French only requires that gender and number agreement be enforced. Note that the strong/weak requirement is checked at m-structure via the ADJ-AGR feature.

(15) $\quad$ NP $\longrightarrow$ $\quad$ AP $\qquad\qquad\qquad\qquad\qquad$ N

$\qquad\qquad\qquad\quad$ $\downarrow\in$ ($\uparrow$ADJUNCT) $\qquad\qquad\qquad$ $\uparrow=\downarrow$

$\qquad\qquad\qquad\quad$ ($\uparrow$GEND)=($\downarrow$GEND)

$\qquad\qquad\qquad\quad$ ($\uparrow$NUM)=($\downarrow$NUM)

$\qquad\qquad\qquad\quad$ ($\uparrow$CASE)=($\downarrow$CASE)

$\qquad\qquad\qquad\quad$ ($mM*$ ADJ-AGR)=($m*$ ADJ-AGR)

The rule in (15) essentially looks inside ($\downarrow/m*$) the AP and requires that the value of the specified feature (GEND, NUM, CASE, ADJ-AGR) be the same as the value of the feature in the mother node ($\uparrow/mM*$). A clash in one of these features will lead to an illformed structure. A representative (wellformed) f-structure is given in (16).

(16) a. die   graue   Katze
the.F.Sg.Nom.S grey.F.Sg.Nom.W cat
'the grey cat' (German)

b.
$$
\begin{bmatrix}
\text{PRED} & \text{'KATZE'} \\
\text{PERS} & 3 \\
\text{NUM} & \text{SG} \\
\text{CASE} & \text{NOM} \\
\text{GEND} & \text{FEM} \\
\text{NTYPE} & \text{COUNT} \\
\text{SPEC} & \begin{bmatrix} \text{SPEC-FORM} & \text{DIE} \\ \text{SPEC-TYPE} & \text{DEF} \end{bmatrix} \\
\text{ADJUNCT} & \left\{ \begin{bmatrix} \text{PRED} & \text{'GRAU'} \\ \text{ATYPE} & \text{ATTRIBUTIVE} \\ \text{NUM} & \text{SG} \\ \text{CASE} & \text{NOM} \\ \text{GEND} & \text{FEM} \end{bmatrix} \right\}
\end{bmatrix}
$$

5.2.1.3 Cardinals and Ordinals

Ordinals as in (17) also behave just like simple attributive adjectives with regard to inflection.

(17) a. the third tractor

     b. . der   dritte   Traktor
the.Sg.M.Nom.S third.Sg.M.Nom.W tractor
'the third tractor' (German)

     c. le   troisième   tracteur
the.M.Sg third.M.Sg tractor
'the third tractor' (French)

However, in English these have a different c-structure distribution and so are assigned the syntactic category NUMBERP. They are also distinguished at f-structure in terms of the ATYPE that is assigned: ORDINAL. An example is given in (18).

(18) a. the third tractor

b.
$$
\begin{bmatrix}
\text{PRED} & \text{'TRACTOR'} \\
\text{PERS} & 3 \\
\text{NUM} & \text{SG} \\
\text{CASE} & \text{NOM} \\
\text{ANIM} & - \\
\text{NTYPE} & \text{COUNT} \\
\text{SPEC} & \begin{bmatrix} \text{SPEC-FORM} & \text{THE} \\ \text{SPEC-TYPE} & \text{DEF} \end{bmatrix} \\
\text{ADJUNCT} & \left\{ \begin{bmatrix} \text{PRED} & \text{'THREE'} \\ \text{ATYPE} & \text{ORDINAL} \\ \text{NUM} & \text{SG} \end{bmatrix} \right\}
\end{bmatrix}
$$

Cardinals, on the other hand, do not inflect, but do require the noun to be plural (unless the cardinal is *one*), and exhibit a slightly different syntactic pattern at c-structure, as shown by the contrast given in (19).

(19) a. The three brown dogs bark.

b. The *brown three dogs bark.

Cardinals are thus also introduced by a special rule at c-structure (NUM-BERP), and are distinguished at f-structure by being assigned ATYPE CARDINAL, as in (20).

(20) a. the three dogs

b.
$$
\begin{bmatrix}
\text{PRED} & \text{'DOG'} \\
\text{PERS} & 3 \\
\text{NUM} & \text{PL} \\
\text{CASE} & \text{NOM} \\
\text{ANIM} & + \\
\text{NTYPE} & \text{COUNT} \\
\text{SPEC} & \begin{bmatrix} \text{SPEC-FORM} & \text{THE} \\ \text{SPEC-TYPE} & \text{DEF} \end{bmatrix} \\
\text{ADJUNCT} & \left\{ \begin{bmatrix} \text{PRED} & \text{'THREE'} \\ \text{ATYPE} & \text{CARDINAL} \\ \text{NUM} & \text{PL} \end{bmatrix} \right\}
\end{bmatrix}
$$

5.2.2 Postnominal Adjectives

In German and French, but not in English, adjectives may appear post-nominally. The German and French postnominal adjectives fulfill different functions in the languages and therefore cannot be given parallel analyses. In the following subsections, each of these language particular constructions is described.

5.2.2.1 German

Postnominal adjectives in German allow for at least three different general constructions, illustrated in (21). They may either be separated from the head noun by a comma, as in (21a-b), or not, as in (21c). Arguments or modifiers of adjectives may appear either before the adjective, as in (21b), or follow it, as in (21a,c). The adjectival form (participial, comparative, or simple) behaves like a predicative adjective in that it never inflects to show number, person or gender agreement with the head noun.

(21) a. Der   Hund, müde vom Bellen, schläft.
         the.M.Sg.Nom.S dog   tired from barking sleeps
         'Tired from barking, the dog sleeps.' (German)

      b. Die   Frau,   langsam den   Tee
         the.F.Sg.Nom.W woman slowly   the.M.Sg.Acc.W tea
         trinkend, lacht.
         drinking laughs
         'The woman laughs while slowly drinking the tea.' (German)

      c. eine   Katze schneller als   der
         a.F.Sg.Nom.W cat   faster   than the.M.Sg.Nom.S
         Hund
         dog
         'a cat faster than the dog' (German)

Each of these constructions, the simple adjective in (21a), the deverbal adjectival participle in (21b) and the comparative in (21c), are analyzed as appositions (APP) in keeping with traditional descriptive grammars. At c-structure, these constructions are treated via specialized AP rules, whereby the rules for the deverbal adjectives borrow very heavily from the VP rules in order to account for the argument positions of the deverbal adjective.

A sample f-structure is shown below for (21b) (for a treatment of comparatives see section 5.2.5).[5]

---

[5]Note that the adverb *langsam* also receives an ATYPE. Most adjectives in predicative (uninflected) form can serve as adverbs in German. See Chapter 7 for discussion.

(22) a. Die   Frau,   langsam den   Tee
the.F.Sg.Nom.W woman slowly   the.M.Sg.Acc.W tea
trinkend, lacht.
drinking laughs
'The woman laughs while slowly drinking the tea.' (German)

b.

$$
\begin{bmatrix}
\text{PRED} & \text{'LACHEN<SUBJ>'} \\
\text{STMT-TYPE} & \text{DECLARATIVE} \\
\text{TNS-ASP} & \begin{bmatrix} \text{TENSE} & \text{PRES} \\ \text{MOOD} & \text{INDICATIVE} \end{bmatrix} \\
\text{SUBJ} & \begin{bmatrix}
\text{PRED} & \text{'FRAU'} \\
\text{PERS} & 3 \\
\text{NUM} & \text{SG} \\
\text{CASE} & \text{NOM} \\
\text{GEND} & \text{FEM} \\
\text{NTYPE} & \text{COUNT} \\
\text{SPEC} & \begin{bmatrix} \text{SPEC-FORM} & \text{DIE} \\ \text{SPEC-TYPE} & \text{DEF} \end{bmatrix} \\
\text{APP} & \begin{bmatrix}
\text{PRED} & \text{'TRINKEN<OBJ>'} \\
\text{ATYPE} & \text{PREDICATIVE} \\
\text{OBJ} & \begin{bmatrix}
\text{PRED} & \text{'TEE'} \\
\text{PERS} & 3 \\
\text{NUM} & \text{SG} \\
\text{CASE} & \text{ACC} \\
\text{GEND} & \text{MASC} \\
\text{NTYPE} & \text{COUNT} \\
\text{SPEC} & \begin{bmatrix} \text{SPEC-FORM} & \text{DIE} \\ \text{SPEC-TYPE} & \text{DEF} \end{bmatrix}
\end{bmatrix} \\
\text{ADJUNCT} & \left\{ \begin{bmatrix} \text{PRED} & \text{'LANGSAM'} \\ \text{ATYPE} & \text{ADVERBIAL} \\ \text{ADEGREE} & \text{POSITIVE} \end{bmatrix} \right\}
\end{bmatrix}
\end{bmatrix}
\end{bmatrix}
$$

5.2.2.2 French

French postnominal adjectives are basically equivalent to their prenominal counterparts, though some adjectives must be interpreted slightly differently in accordance with the position they appear in (see Nølke and Korzen 1996 and references therein on the order of adjectives in French). This is illustrated in (23).

(23) a. un ancien élève
          a   former pupil
          'a former/ex pupil' (French)

      b. un élève ancien
          a   pupil old
          'an old/elderly pupil' (French)

However, not all adjectives may appear freely in either position. Those adjectives which are restricted to one position or another are assigned an m-structure attribute APOS with a value of PRE or POST in the lexicon. The pre- and postnominal calls to AP then check for the appropriate value of APOS. As long as there is no clash, the structure is licit. This can be seen in (25) which shows the c-structure, f-structure, and m-structure of (24).

(24) le   grand témoin   rouge
     the big   warning light red
     'the big red warning light' (French)

(25) a.

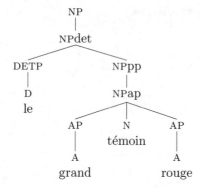

b.
$$\begin{bmatrix} \text{PRED} & \text{'TÉMOIN'} \\ \text{GEND} & \text{MASC} \\ \text{PERS} & 3 \\ \text{NUM} & \text{SG} \\ \text{SPEC} & \begin{bmatrix} \text{SPEC-TYPE} & \text{DEF} \\ \text{SPEC-FORM} & \text{LE} \end{bmatrix} \\ \text{ADJUNCT} & \left\{ \begin{bmatrix} \text{PRED} & \text{'GRAND'} \\ \text{ATYPE} & \text{ATTRIBUTIVE} \\ \text{GEND} & \text{MASC} \\ \text{NUM} & \text{SG} \end{bmatrix} \begin{bmatrix} \text{PRED} & \text{'ROUGE'} \\ \text{ATYPE} & \text{ATTRIBUTIVE} \\ \text{GEND} & \text{MASC} \\ \text{NUM} & \text{SG} \end{bmatrix} \right\} \end{bmatrix}$$

c.
$$\begin{bmatrix} \text{NON-DEP} & \left\{ \begin{bmatrix} \text{APOS} & \text{PRE} \end{bmatrix} \begin{bmatrix} \text{APOS} & \text{POST} \end{bmatrix} \right\} \end{bmatrix}$$

As with prenominal adjectives in French, postnominal adjectives must agree in gender and number with the noun that they modify. This is accomplished just as for prenominal adjectives by requiring that gender and number be identical when the AP is called in the NP rule.

5.2.3 Predicative Adjectives

All adjectives in predicative position are marked with the feature ATYPE PREDICATIVE to indicate the contrast to attributive adjectives. Both German and English adjectives show no inflection in predicative position. For German, this constitutes a contrast to prenominal attributive adjectives, which do inflect for gender, number, case, and the weak/strong distinction.

(26) a. The cat is grey.

    b. Die   Katze ist grau.
      the.F.Sg.Nom.S cat is grey
      'The cat is grey.' (German)

In French, on the other hand, both predicative and attributive adjectives inflect. Agreement via inflections is obligatory in French, as seen in (27).

(27) a. La boîte   est grise.
          the box.F.Sg.Nom is   grey.F.Sg
          'The box is grey.' (French)

     b. *La boîte   est gris.
          the box.F.Sg.Nom is   grey.M.Sg
          'The box is grey.' (French)

     c. *La boîte   est grises.
          the box.F.Sg.Nom is   grey.F.Pl
          'The box is grey.' (French)

The agreement facts are taken care of by equating the subject's person and gender values with the values of the predicate adjective in the AP rule that introduces predicatives.

5.2.4   Arguments of Adjectives

5.2.4.1   The General Approach

In the above examples, adjectives do not themselves subcategorize for an argument. However, adjectives function as semantic predicates in the sense that they predicate a certain property to hold for some arguments. The semantic contribution of adjectives is difficult to characterize (Siegel 1976), giving rise to debates as to the right semantic interpretation of NPs like *false money* or as to the right crosslinguistic analysis for resultatives like *paint the fence red*.

In keeping with our general grammar writing strategy, we have only modeled those cases where adjectives impose syntactic wellformedness requirements. Section 5.2.1.2 illustrated such requirements in terms of inflectional restrictions. The examples in (28) illustrate that some adjectives further require the syntactic realization of an argument.

(28) a. The driver is proud of the tractor.   (PP argument)
     b. The tractor is hard to push.   (VP argument)
     c. It is important that the dog does not bark.   (CP argument)

A comparison with (29) shows that in these cases the adjectives are responsible for the introduction of the PP, VP or CP argument.

(29) a. *The driver is red of the tractor.   (PP argument)
     b. *The tractor is red to push.   (VP argument)
     c. *It is red that the dog does not bark.   (CP argument)

Those adjectives which subcategorize for arguments are given special lexical entries which indicate their subcategorization frame,[6] thus allow-

---

[6] For the German grammar, adjective entries were produced semi-automatically

ing for the fact that an adjective can require an OBJ, OBL, XCOMP or COMP at the level of f-structure, as in (30).[7]

(30) a. The driver is proud of the tractor.   (OBL argument)

b.

$$
\begin{bmatrix}
\text{PRED} & \text{'BE<SUBJ,PREDLINK>'} \\
\text{STMT-TYPE} & \text{DECLARATIVE} \\
\text{TNS-ASP} & \begin{bmatrix} \text{TENSE} & \text{PRES} \\ \text{MOOD} & \text{INDICATIVE} \end{bmatrix} \\
\text{SUBJ} & \begin{bmatrix} \text{PRED} & \text{'DRIVER'} \\ \text{PERS} & 3 \\ \text{NUM} & \text{SG} \\ \text{CASE} & \text{NOM} \\ \text{ANIM} & + \\ \text{NTYPE} & \text{COUNT} \\ \text{SPEC} & \begin{bmatrix} \text{SPEC-FORM} & \text{THE} \\ \text{SPEC-TYPE} & \text{DEF} \end{bmatrix} \end{bmatrix} \\
\text{PREDLINK} & \begin{bmatrix} \text{PRED} & \text{'PROUD<OBL>'} \\ \text{ATYPE} & \text{PREDICATIVE} \\ \text{OBL} & \begin{bmatrix} \text{PRED} & \text{'OF<OBJ>'} \\ \text{PTYPE} & \text{SEM} \\ \text{OBJ} & \begin{bmatrix} \text{PRED} & \text{'TRACTOR'} \\ \text{PERS} & 3 \\ \text{NUM} & \text{SG} \\ \text{CASE} & \text{ACC} \\ \text{PCASE} & \text{OF} \\ \text{ANIM} & - \\ \text{NTYPE} & \text{COUNT} \\ \text{SPEC} & \begin{bmatrix} \text{SPEC-FORM} & \text{THE} \\ \text{SPEC-TYPE} & \text{DEF} \end{bmatrix} \end{bmatrix} \end{bmatrix} \end{bmatrix}
\end{bmatrix}
$$

based on data extraction from very large corpora. Similarly, the subcategorization frames of deverbal adjectives are derived from the subcategorization frames of the verbs, which were also produced semi-automatically from data extraction over large corpora and various other resources (see section 14.1.1 for some more discussion).

[7]The grammatical function PREDLINK in (31) indicates that the construction is PREDicational and that the material in the PREDLINK is being predicated of the subject of the sentence (section 3.8). Other LFG analyses of adjectives (e.g., Bresnan 1982b) assume that adjectives also subcategorize for a subject (i.e., *tractor* in *red tractor*).

The c-structure adjective rules are augmented to allow for the possibility of an NP (German only), PP, VP or CP either following or preceding (German only) an adjective as its argument.

5.2.4.2 Extraction

As mentioned previously, one of the possible arguments of an adjective is a COMP. As also discussed previously in section 3.3.5, a COMP can be either a nonfinite VP as in (31), or a *that*-clause as in (32). As an example, the f-structure for (31b) is shown in (33).

(31) a. It is important to laugh.

b. It is important that the dogs bark.

(32) a. It is important that the dogs bark.

b.
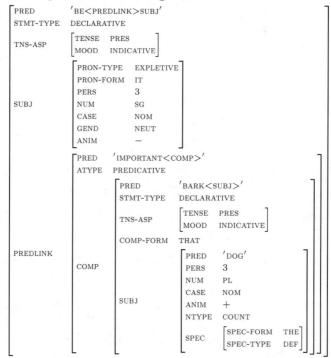

In all three languages, these COMPs can be preposed and thus extracted from the local subcategorization domain of the adjective, as shown for English in (33).

(33) a. To laugh is important.

b. That the dogs bark is important.

The adjectives which subcategorize for COMPs and allow the extraction in (34) are specially marked in the lexicon. In the nonextraction cases, the expletive *it* (*es* in German, *il* in French) is treated as a subject SUBJ of the copula *be* (see section 3.8 for a more detailed discussion of copula constructions).

(34) a. That the dog barks is important.

b.

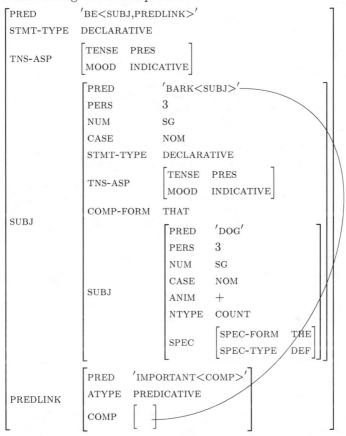

In the extraposed cases, as in (34), where there is no expletive which can function as the subject, the clause fulfills a double role: it serves both as the COMP argument of the adjective, and as the SUBJ argument of the copula. In English, in fact, the *that*-clause is in canonical subject position, so that such an analysis is explicitly motivated. As German does not encode subjects by position, this motivation does not carry over to German. Neither is it contradicted by any other language internal facts, however; so, the German grammar adopts the English analysis as well. Note that PERS and NUM features of the extraposed clause must be written since *that*-clauses are not inherently marked for person and number; if these features were not provided, improper verb forms such as in *That the dog barks are important* could not be ruled out.

5.2.5 Degrees of Comparison

Adjectives in all three of these languages have morphological markers which allow the formation of comparatives or superlatives from a base form.

(35) a. a heavier truck   (comparative)
    b. the heaviest truck   (superlative)

In addition, the base form of the adjective can occur in equatives and with periphrastic comparative constructions.

(36) a. That dog is as heavy as a truck.   (equative)
    b. more pleasant   (periphrastic comparative)
    c. le plus rouge   (periphrastic superlative)
     the more red
     'reddest' (French)

Although these differ in terms of how they are realized at c-structure, the f-structures corresponding to both the periphrastic and the morphological comparatives receive the same analysis (see section 5.2.5.1 for sample f-structures).

The degree of comparison and the positive or negative force (e.g., the difference between *more pleasant* and *less pleasant*) are represented at f-structure in terms of the features ADEGREE and ADEG-TYPE, respectively.

In terms of grammatical functions at f-structure, we analyze comparatives as consisting of two main parts: the degree (comparative, equative, or superlative) of the adjective (e.g., *heavier*) and the further (often optional) comparative phrase it can license (e.g., *than a truck*). The degree adjective is treated as an adjunct, like all other adjectives. However, it is treated as a special kind of adjunct which has special syntactic properties, and is therefore encoded as an ADJUNCT-COMP at f-structure. This indicates that it is an adjunct, but that it specifies a degree of comparison. The comparative phrase (e.g., *than a truck*) is analyzed as an oblique argument of the adjective. Again, in order to indicate that a degree of comparison is indicated, a special grammatical function OBJ-COMP is posited for comparative phrases. The intuition behind this is that the *than*-phrases appear to function somewhat like PPs which are subcategorized for by a predicate, and which have traditionally been analyzed as obliques (OBL) at f-structure (cf. Bresnan 1982a). The lexical item *than* (*que* in French, *als* in German) is treated as a special type of conjunction since it may head complete clauses, as in (38).

In addition to prenominal constructions as in (35), comparatives can also appear postnominally, as in (37), and predicatively, as in (38). Post-nominal comparatives are analyzed at f-structure strictly in parallel to prenominal comparatives, i.e., an ADJUNCT-COMP is introduced as a modifier of the head noun. Predicatives, on the other hand, receive a differing analysis, discussed in section 5.2.5.2.

(37) A dog heavier than a tractor barked.

(38) She is taller than I am.

Note that at c-structure the comparative adjectives occupy exactly the same position as simple adjectives. The *than*-phrase, however, is introduced through a special c-structure node CONJPcomp in all three grammars. Additionally, in some degree constructions, as in (39), the adjective phrase forms a constituent with the than-phrase. This constituent is introduced at c-structure via a specialized rule called APcomp.

(39) a. It is [more comfortable than a tractor].

    b.

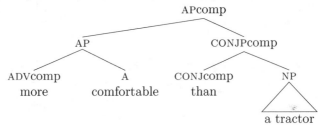

Note that regardless of their syntactic position, *than*-clauses always correspond to the OBL-COMP argument of a comparative. As such, a sentence like (40) is syntactically three-ways ambiguous in English because the *than*-clause could in principle be associated with any of the comparatives (*more tractors, redder lights, more quickly*).

(40) More tractors flash redder lights more quickly than would be expected.

The interpretation of the *than*-clause is related to the semantics of ellipsis. Whether a clause can be felicitously interpreted with a given comparative is part of the semantics and pragmatics, not the syntax. As such, we have not implemented a treatment for the resolution of *than*-clauses within our grammars. Some relevant examples are given below.

(41) The light flashes more quickly than the beacon.
=The light flashes more quickly than the beacon flashes.

(42) a. John drove the tractor faster than Bill.
=John drove the tractor faster than Bill drove the tractor.

b. John drove the tractor faster than the car.
=John drove the tractor faster than he drove the car.

5.2.5.1 Comparatives

A representative f-structure for the German NP in (43a) is given in (43b). There is no *than*-phrase and the comparative adjective is encoded under the ADJUNCT-COMP within the SUBJ.

(43) a. eine   schnellere   Katze
a.F.Sg.Nom.S quick.Comp.F.Sg.Nom.W cat
'a quicker cat' (German)

b.
$$
\begin{bmatrix}
\text{PRED} & \text{'KATZE'} \\
\text{PERS} & 3 \\
\text{NUM} & \text{SG} \\
\text{CASE} & \text{NOM} \\
\text{GEND} & \text{FEM} \\
\text{NTYPE} & \text{COUNT} \\
\text{SPEC} & \begin{bmatrix} \text{SPEC-FORM} & \text{EIN} \\ \text{SPEC-TYPE} & \text{INDEF} \end{bmatrix} \\
\text{ADJUNCT-COMP} & \begin{bmatrix} \text{PRED} & \text{'SCHNELL'} \\ \text{ADEGREE} & \text{COMPARATIVE} \\ \text{ADEG-TYPE} & \text{POSITIVE} \\ \text{NUM} & \text{SG} \\ \text{CASE} & \text{NOM} \\ \text{GEND} & \text{FEM} \end{bmatrix}
\end{bmatrix}
$$

The f-structure in (44b) illustrates a comparative adjective in conjunction with a *than*-clause. Again, the comparative adjective is encoded under the ADJUNCT-COMP. The *than*-phrase is represented as the OBL-COMP argument of the comparative adjective. The *als* 'than' is encoded in terms of the feature CONJ-FORM-COMP, indicating that while the *als* 'than' functions like a conjunction, it is a special kind of comparative conjunction.[8]

---

[8]In the interest of space, ADJUNCT-COMP has been abbreviated to ADJ-COMP in (44b).

(44) a. Eine   schnellere   Katze als
     a.F.Sg.Nom.S quick.Comp.F.Sg.Nom.W cat   than
     der   Hund erscheint.
     the.M.Sg.Nom.S dog   appear.3.Sg.Pres
     'A quicker cat than the dog appears.' (German)

b.

$$
\begin{bmatrix}
\text{PRED} & \text{'ERSCHEINEN<SUBJ>'} \\
\text{TNS-ASP} & \begin{bmatrix} \text{TENSE} & \text{PRES} \\ \text{MOOD} & \text{INDICATIVE} \end{bmatrix} \\
\text{STMT-TYPE} & \text{DECLARATIVE} \\
\text{VSEM} & \text{UNACC} \\
\text{SUBJ} & \begin{bmatrix}
\text{PRED} & \text{'KATZE'} \\
\text{PERS} & 3 \\
\text{NUM} & \text{SG} \\
\text{CASE} & \text{NOM} \\
\text{GEND} & \text{FEM} \\
\text{NTYPE} & \text{COUNT} \\
\text{SPEC} & \begin{bmatrix} \text{SPEC-FORM} & \text{EIN} \\ \text{SPEC-TYPE} & \text{INDEF} \end{bmatrix} \\
\text{ADJ-COMP} & \begin{bmatrix}
\text{PRED} & \text{'SCHNELL<OBL-COMP>'} \\
\text{ADEGREE} & \text{COMPARATIVE} \\
\text{ADEG-TYPE} & \text{POSITIVE} \\
\text{NUM} & \text{SG} \\
\text{CASE} & \text{NOM} \\
\text{GEND} & \text{FEM} \\
\text{OBL-COMP} & \begin{bmatrix}
\text{PRED} & \text{'HUND'} \\
\text{CONJ-FORM-COMP} & \text{ALS} \\
\text{PERS} & 3 \\
\text{NUM} & \text{SG} \\
\text{CASE} & \text{NOM} \\
\text{GEND} & \text{MASC} \\
\text{NTYPE} & \text{COUNT} \\
\text{SPEC} & \begin{bmatrix} \text{SPEC-FORM} & \text{DER} \\ \text{SPEC-TYPE} & \text{DEF} \end{bmatrix}
\end{bmatrix}
\end{bmatrix}
\end{bmatrix}
\end{bmatrix}
$$

5.2.5.2 Predicatives

In predicative constructions as in (45) the degree adjective is not treated as an adjective which modifies a head noun. Rather, it is seen as an argument of the copula *be*, a PREDLINK (section 3.8). Other than this difference, the analysis of degree adjectives parallels that of the prenominal cases above: the degree adjective may introduce an argument (OBL-COMP), which corresponds to the *than*-clause. An example, which also incidentally illustrates a periphrastic comparative, is given below.

(45) a. It is more comfortable than a tractor.

b.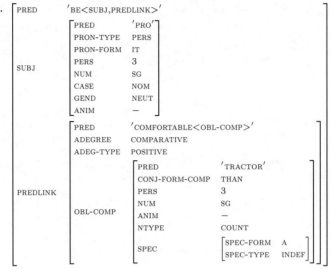

5.2.5.3 Equatives

Equatives compare two entities and indicate that they are equivalent in terms of one of their properties. Unlike comparatives, equatives do not appear without a comparative phrase (e.g., *as big as a tractor*).[9] This requirement is ensured by a constraint in the lexical entry of the equative that requires the existence of a comparative phrase. Equative adjectival constructions also do not appear prenominally, but surface either postnominally as in (46), or predicatively as in (47).

(46) A dog as heavy as a truck barked.

Other than a difference in the ADEGREE and the ADEG-TYPE (which is not specified for equatives), the f-structures for comparatives and equatives do not differ in these constructions. An example of a predicative construction is illustrated below.

---

[9]In both French and German one may find colloquial examples such as *Moi, je ne suis pas aussi libre* 'Me, I'm not as free', which have an equative but no comparative (thanks to Anette Frank for pointing these out). However, in these cases, the equative may also be analyzed as an adverb without comparative function.

(47) a. That dog is as heavy as a truck.

b.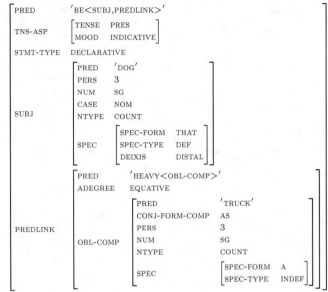

5.2.5.4   Superlatives

Superlatives indicate that a given entity is the extreme and unique instantiation of that kind. In these constructions it is thus not the case
that two entities are being compared, but rather that one entity is being
singled out as special. As such, superlatives cannot occur with *than*-
clauses. This generalization is ensured by a combination of constraints
in the c-structure rules, and in the lexical entries of the superlatives.

(48) a. The best driver owns the heaviest tractor.

b. a better/*best driver than the owner

In the f-structure, superlatives are treated just as comparatives and
equatives, with the exception that they never subcategorize for an OBL-
COMP (i.e., a *than*- or *as*-phrase), and that the values for ADEGREE differ.
The f-structure for (48a) is given in (49b).

(49) a. The best driver owns the heaviest tractor.

b.
$$
\begin{bmatrix}
\text{PRED} & \text{'OWN<SUBJ,OBJ>'} \\
\text{TNS-ASP} & \begin{bmatrix} \text{TENSE} & \text{PRES} \\ \text{MOOD} & \text{INDICATIVE} \end{bmatrix} \\
\text{STMT-TYPE} & \text{DECLARATIVE} \\
\text{SUBJ} & \begin{bmatrix}
\text{PRED} & \text{'DRIVER'} \\
\text{PERS} & 3 \\
\text{NUM} & \text{SG} \\
\text{CASE} & \text{NOM} \\
\text{ANIM} & + \\
\text{NTYPE} & \text{COUNT} \\
\text{SPEC} & \begin{bmatrix} \text{SPEC-FORM} & \text{THE} \\ \text{SPEC-TYPE} & \text{DEF} \end{bmatrix} \\
\text{ADJUNCT-COMP} & \begin{bmatrix} \text{PRED} & \text{'GOOD'} \\ \text{ADEGREE} & \text{SUPERLATIVE} \\ \text{ATYPE} & \text{ATTRIBUTIVE} \end{bmatrix}
\end{bmatrix} \\
\text{OBJ} & \begin{bmatrix}
\text{PRED} & \text{'TRACTOR'} \\
\text{PERS} & 3 \\
\text{NUM} & \text{SG} \\
\text{CASE} & \text{ACC} \\
\text{ANIM} & - \\
\text{NTYPE} & \text{COUNT} \\
\text{SPEC} & \begin{bmatrix} \text{SPEC-FORM} & \text{THE} \\ \text{SPEC-TYPE} & \text{DEF} \end{bmatrix} \\
\text{ADJUNCT-COMP} & \begin{bmatrix} \text{PRED} & \text{'HEAVY'} \\ \text{ADEGREE} & \text{SUPERLATIVE} \\ \text{ATYPE} & \text{ATTRIBUTIVE} \end{bmatrix}
\end{bmatrix}
\end{bmatrix}
$$

6

Prepositional Phrases

This chapter discusses prepositions which appear with both nominal and clausal complements. Prepositions in German may appear both before and after an NP. In English and French, the prepositions more truly live up to their name in that they must appear before their complement (as opposed to *postpositions*, which appear after the complement). Additionally, English allows preposition stranding in contexts such as question-formation, relativization and passivization.

Prepositions are usually subdivided into two major classes: semantic and nonsemantic. Semantic prepositions usually (but not always) give rise to adjunct PPs, as in *the book on the table*. Nonsemantic prepositions, on the other hand, mark argument PPs such as *I referred to the book*. In some cases, a particular preposition is also required by the verb in one of its particular meanings, as in *wait on somebody* in a restaurant. Our treatment of these and other phenomena is presented in the following sections.

6.1   Semantic Prepositions

The most common type of PP involves a preposition which has a clear semantic content of its own, such as the locatives *on, in, under*, etc., the instrumental *with*, and the directionals *into, onto*, etc. In our grammars, these prepositions are endowed with a PRED value and a subcategorization frame which indicates that the preposition requires an object. This object is usually an NP, as in (1). In addition, semantic prepositions are marked with PTYPE SEM in order to distinguish them from nonsemantic prepositions.

(1) a. on the panel
    b. dans le   tracteur
      in   the tractor
      'in the tractor' (French)

A sample f-structure is shown in (2). Note that the feature PCASE encodes the form of the preposition. This feature is located in the f-structure of the object of the preposition and reflects the intuition that prepositions have a somewhat verbal character in that they both license an object and assign case to it (e.g., Baker 1988 on preposition incorporation and Kaplan and Bresnan 1982 on the treatment of prepositions within LFG).

(2) a. on the panel

b.
$$\begin{bmatrix} \text{PRED} & \text{'ON<OBJ>'} \\ \text{PSEM} & \text{LOCATIVE} \\ \text{PTYPE} & \text{SEM} \\ \text{OBJ} & \begin{bmatrix} \text{PRED} & \text{'PANEL'} \\ \text{PCASE} & \text{ON} \end{bmatrix} \end{bmatrix}$$

In German, prepositions impose morphological case requirements on their objects. Objects of prepositions may appear with dative, accusative, or genitive case. Sometimes the particular case required is a purely idiosyncratic property of the preposition. Many of the German prepositions, however, display a systematic alternation with regard to the morphological case required on the object. If the PP has a directional force, as in (3a), then the object must be accusative. On the other hand, if the PP describes a location, then the object must be dative, as in (3b).

(3) a. Sie geht in den   Garten.
      she goes in the.M.Sg.Acc.S garden
      'She is going in(to) the garden.' (German)
    b. Sie hat im   Garten Tee getrunken.
      she has in.the.M.Sg.Dat.W garden tea drunk
      'She drank tea in the garden.' (German)

We therefore posit a feature PSEM, which encodes the semantic class of each preposition. Thus, the PSEM in the English locative example in (2) is LOCATIVE. In the German example in (3a) the PSEM is DIRECTIONAL, as shown in the sample f-structure analysis in (4).

(4) a. Sie geht in den   Garten.
      she goes in the.M.Sg.Acc.S garden
      'She is going in(to) the garden.' (German)

b.

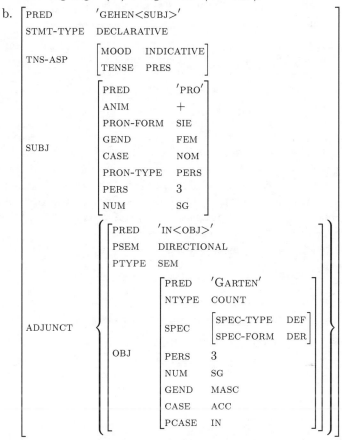

The PSEM value is additionally used for tasks such as determining which phrases can occur in English locative inversion constructions, what type of adjunct a PP is, and whether the subcategorization requirements of verbs like *put* have been met.

6.2   Nonsemantic Prepositions

In certain constructions, a particular preposition is required by the verb in one of its particular meanings. In these cases, the preposition makes no or very little semantic contribution of its own (see section 3.7 on particles, which are distinct from nonsemantic prepositions). As such, these

PPs are treated as arguments of the verb and are encoded with a PTYPE NOSEM to mark the difference from the semantic adjunct PPs discussed in the previous section. An alternation from German, which illustrates the contrast between the semantic and nonsemantic prepositional use of one and the same preposition, is shown in (5).

(5) a. Der   Fahrer wartet auf das   Buch.
     the.M.Sg.Nom.S driver waits on the.N.Sg.Acc.W book
     'The driver is waiting for the book.' (German)

    b. Der   Fahrer wartet auf dem   Traktor.
     the.M.Sg.Nom.S driver waits on the.M.Sg.Dat.S tractor
     'The driver is waiting on (top of) the tractor.' (German)

Note that again a difference in object casemarking accompanies the difference in meaning. In (5b) the preposition has a clear semantic force and indicates a locative adjunct to the verb. In (5a), on the other hand, this particular usage of *warten* requires a nonsemantic (i.e., nonlocational and nondirectional) usage of *on*. In this case, the PP *auf das Buch* is analyzed as an argument of the verb.

One reason for positing this analysis is that the NP can be passivized out of the PP, as is illustrated for English in (6) and (7), and for German in (8).

(6) a. The driver must comply with these regulations.

    b. These regulations must be complied with.

(7) a. He relies on this book.

    b. This book is (often) relied on.

(8) Auf das   Buch wird gewartet.
   on the.N.Sg.Acc.W book is   waited
   'This book is being waited for.' (German)

Prepositions which occur in these constructions are analyzed as not having a PRED (thus encoding their lack of semantic force). They therefore do not subcategorize for an object, which means that the PP arguments such as *on this book* are treated as objects of the verb. A sample f-structure for this construction is shown for (7a) in (9b).

(9) a. He relies on this book.

b.
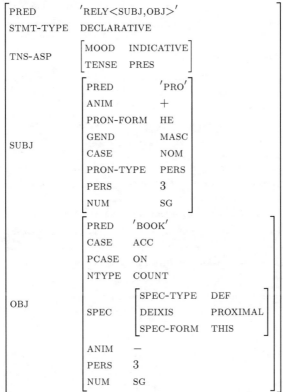

$$\begin{bmatrix} \text{PRED} & \text{'RELY<SUBJ,OBJ>'} \\ \text{STMT-TYPE} & \text{DECLARATIVE} \\ \text{TNS-ASP} & \begin{bmatrix} \text{MOOD} & \text{INDICATIVE} \\ \text{TENSE} & \text{PRES} \end{bmatrix} \\ \text{SUBJ} & \begin{bmatrix} \text{PRED} & \text{'PRO'} \\ \text{ANIM} & + \\ \text{PRON-FORM} & \text{HE} \\ \text{GEND} & \text{MASC} \\ \text{CASE} & \text{NOM} \\ \text{PRON-TYPE} & \text{PERS} \\ \text{PERS} & 3 \\ \text{NUM} & \text{SG} \end{bmatrix} \\ \text{OBJ} & \begin{bmatrix} \text{PRED} & \text{'BOOK'} \\ \text{CASE} & \text{ACC} \\ \text{PCASE} & \text{ON} \\ \text{NTYPE} & \text{COUNT} \\ \text{SPEC} & \begin{bmatrix} \text{SPEC-TYPE} & \text{DEF} \\ \text{DEIXIS} & \text{PROXIMAL} \\ \text{SPEC-FORM} & \text{THIS} \end{bmatrix} \\ \text{ANIM} & - \\ \text{PERS} & 3 \\ \text{NUM} & \text{SG} \end{bmatrix} \end{bmatrix}$$

The preposition now merely serves to assign PCASE to an argument of the verb. Note that the presence of this PCASE feature is important, as it must be matched with a requirement by the verb. For example, in German (as in English) *warten* 'wait' is normally intransitive. When it subcategorizes for a *for*-phrase, however, it is transitive. Thus, the transitive subcategorization frame can only be chosen in the presence of the feature PCASE AUF (German) or PCASE ON (English).

6.3 Interrogatives and Relatives

In all three languages, prepositional phrases may also appear in interrogative and relative clause constructions, as in (10).

(10) a. [From where] did the driver appear?   (interrogative)

b. The tractor, [on which] you will find a beacon ...   (relative)

Both semantic and nonsemantic PPs may appear in these constructions. As such, the treatment of these constructions does not differ from the PPs described above, except that the prepositions take an interrogative or relative prounoun as a complement, rather than a full NP.

6.4 Clause-Taking Prepositions

In addition to nominal elements, prepositions may also take clausal elements as a complement in the three languages. Examples for English are given in (11).

(11) a. [Irrespective of whether it is switched on], the lamp lights up.
    b. Turn the lever [with the engine running].

Again, the analysis does not differ markedly from the semantic and nonsemantic prepositions discussed above, other than the fact that the object of the preposition is a clause. A sample analysis is given below. Note that *irrespective of* is treated as a multiword (see section 12.2) whose semantic type (PSEM) is unspecified. The value UNSPECIFIED is assigned to those prepositions which do not appear to form a useful semantic class as far as the grammars are concerned. The *whether* is analyzed as an interrogative complementizer.

(12) a. irrespective of whether it is switched on

    b.
$$
\begin{bmatrix}
\text{PRED} & \text{'IRRESPECTIVE-OF<OBJ>'} \\
\text{PSEM} & \text{UNSPECIFIED} \\
\text{PTYPE} & \text{SEM} \\
\text{OBJ} & \begin{bmatrix}
\text{PRED} & \text{'SWITCH-ON<NULL,SUBJ>'} \\
\text{STMT-TYPE} & \text{INTERROGATIVE} \\
\text{TNS-ASP} & \begin{bmatrix} \text{MOOD} & \text{INDICATIVE} \\ \text{TENSE} & \text{PRES} \end{bmatrix} \\
\text{COMP-FORM} & \text{WHETHER} \\
\text{PRT-FORM} & \text{ON} \\
\text{PCASE} & \text{IRRESPECTIVE-OF} \\
\text{SUBJ} & \begin{bmatrix}
\text{PRED} & \text{'PRO'} \\
\text{ANIM} & - \\
\text{PERS} & 3 \\
\text{PRON-FORM} & \text{IT} \\
\text{PRON-TYPE} & \text{PERS} \\
\text{GEND} & \text{NEUT} \\
\text{CASE} & \text{NOM} \\
\text{NUM} & \text{SG}
\end{bmatrix}
\end{bmatrix}
\end{bmatrix}
$$

6.5   Multiple Prepositions

In addition to appearing singly, prepositions may also be nested, as in
the English example in (13a), or circumscribe the complement, as in
the German examples in (13b–c). Multiply occuring prepositions are
semantic in nature, and as such receive the same general treatment as
simple semantic prepositions.

(13)   a. next to the tractor

   b. vom   Fahrersitz   aus
      from.the.M.Sg.Dat.S driver's seat out
      'from the driver's seat' (German)

   c. um   den   Traktor herum
      around the.M.Sg.Acc.S tractor around
      'around the tractor (making a complete round)' (German)

In English, multiply occuring prepositions are analyzed as corresponding to a series of nested embeddings: *next* is analyzed as a PP which takes
another PP in the c-structure and in the f-structure.

However, this approach does not work well for the German examples
since it does not capture the intuition that the prepositions are forming
a semantic complex in these cases. It also does not reflect the fact that
the German prepositions circumscribe their common complement. In the
German grammar, an alternative approach is therefore adopted. Under
this approach, the c-structure rule that generates PPs allows for two P
daughters, as shown in (14).

(14)

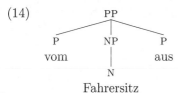

The second P daughter is restricted to co-occur with the first P daughter, reflecting that German does not allow postpositions, but does allow
circumpositions. The first P daughter is always a semantic preposition
and is analyzed in the same way as the semantic prepositions discussed
above. The second preposition may only occur when appropriately li-
censed. The *herum* in (13c), for example, may only co-occur with *um* in
German. This restriction is enforced by checking for *um* via the PCASE
feature. The second preposition (i.e., *herum*) is not encoded in terms of
a PCASE, but its form and type are encoded in the f-structure within
separate features, leaving the precise semantic analysis of these circumpositions to a further semantic module.

7

Adverbial Elements

Adverbial elements comprise a large, disparate class of constituents which serve as nonsubcategorized modifiers (adjuncts). Adverbs vary so considerably with regard to syntactic distribution and semantic content that the grammatical category of adverb is often used as a kind of catch-all category for lexical items that one is at a loss to define.

However, adverbs do have some properties which characterize the class as a whole. Unlike adjectives and verbs, adverbs never inflect (though they may bear casemarking). Adverbs serve to modify either the clause or a constituent: they never stand alone. From a semantic perspective, adverbs may encode the manner of motion, the location in time of a given event (temporal adverbs), intentionality (*purposely* vs. *accidentally*), they may serve to intensify a modifier (e.g., *very*) or negate a clause or constituent (negation). There is as yet no good syntactic or semantic overview of the properties and types of adverbs; readers are instead referred to the grammars of a particular language (e.g., Quirk et al. 1985 for English) for an overview.

7.1 Adverbs

Adverbs can be loosely divided into three types: adverbs which modify adjectives and other adverbs, as in (1a), adverbs which modify VPs, as in (1b), adverbs which modify clauses, as in (1c).

(1) a. der   [sehr] graue   Hund
       the.M.Sg.Nom.S very grey.M.Sg.Nom.W dog
       'the very grey dog' (German)

    b. Elle l' a   fait [doucement].
       she it has done gently
       'She did it gently.' (French)

    c. She [usually] drives home.

These types can be further subdivided as needed, depending on the language. In English, the type of adverb correlates strongly with a restriction on which syntactic position it may appear in. For example, any adverb which appears in the AP rules must be of the type that can modify adjectives and other adverbs, e.g., its ADV-TYPE must be AD-JADVMOD. Similar distinctions can be made within the VP and S so that only adverbs of a certain type (e.g., SMOD, VPMOD) can appear in a particular position. However, adverb placement is notoriously difficult to determine, in part because the semantics of a given adverb may shift in certain contexts, thus allowing it to appear in a different position than usual. Because of the general free word nature of German, the placement of adverbs is particularly hard to describe and constrain in this language. Ideally, a grammar might parse a given adverb in virtually any adverb position, but only generate it in a very restricted set of positions.

German provides an interesting morphological situation since there is no difference in form between the uninflected form of the adjective and its adverbial counterpart, e.g., *schnell* can either mean 'fast' or 'quickly'. One approach to this property of the language is to encode it via a systematic ambiguity in the lexicon, and have both an A and ADV entry for each of these items. Another approach, which is the one taken in the German grammar, is to postulate only one c-structure category as the base, namely A. This category may then be called by c-structure rules which produce adverbial phrases (ADVP), as shown in (2).

(2)   ADVP
          |
        APbase
          |
          A
        schnell

The rule for ADVP requires that the adjectival form be uninflected, and that it be assigned an ADV-TYPE feature so that it can be identified as an adverb at the level of the f-structure analysis.

Note that as in English and French there is a closed class of items such as *sehr* 'very' which do not lead such a double life. They are simply treated as being of the c-structure type ADV, as shown in (3), and receive the appropriate ADV-TYPE feature in the lexicon.

(3)   ADVP
          |
         ADV
        sehr

German furthermore sports a subset of adverbs which are generally referred to as *discourse particles*, such as *ja* 'yes', *doch*, 'really'. An example is given in (4).

(4) Ich geh ja schon.
  I go yes already
  'I'm already going (don't worry).' (German)

The *ja* in (4) does not mean 'yes' but instead serves to intensify the other adverb *schon* 'already'. The precise semantics and syntactic distribution of these German discourse particles is not well understood, but see König 1991a,b for some discussion and analyses.

7.2 PPs as Adverbials

As was already discussed in Chapter 6 on prepositions, many PPs act as adjuncts. A subset of those PPs, namely those which overlap in distribution and semantics with simple adverbs may also be analyzed as adverbials. Example (5) shows a manner of motion PP adverbial coordinated with a simple adverb, which indicates that the two should be given parallel analyses as manner of motion adverbials.

(5) They left noisily and with unusual haste.

7.3 NPs as Adverbials

A limited number of NPs act as adverbials, as in (6); these are often time and frequency adverbs, including dates.

(6) a. [Tuesday mornings] he goes to the store.
  b. Clean the tape head [every time you use it].
  c. Fast forward the tape [every ten plays].
  d. [Le matin], je lave les mains.
    the morning I wash the hands
    'In the morning, I wash my hands.' (French)

  The difficulty with these constructions is to make sure that only certain NPs, namely the ones with the correct semantics, will distribute as adverbials. One possibility is to have nouns which frequently occur in these constructions, such as dates and times of day, provide a feature which the NP adverbial construction requires. However, constructions like that in (6c) make this difficult to do completely.

7.4 Negation

Negation particles such as the English *not*, German *nicht*, or French *ne ... pas* are usually analyzed as a subtype of adverb because negation serves to modify a clause or a constituent, as the other adverbials do.

However, the distribution and semantics of negative elements is often very different from that of other adverbials. As such, in our grammars negative particles are given a different c-structure category, NEG, which serves to constrain its appearance and distinguish it from the other adverbs.

7.4.1 Clausal Negation

First consider simple clausal negation. In English and French, there is only one position in the sentence where negation can appear and have sentential scope. For example, in finite clauses negation appears before the finite verb in French and immediately after the finite auxiliary in English. This restriction in syntactic distribution is encoded in the c-structure rules.

(7) a. They should not have been eating.
    They should have not been eating. (* on sentential reading)
    They should have been not eating. (* on sentential reading)
  b. They have not been eating.
  c. They are not eating.

In German, the negative marker *nicht* distributes with the sentential adverbs, as in (8), and as such may appear almost anywhere. The c-structure rules are therefore not coded as restrictively as for English and French.

(8) Ich bin gestern   nicht mit   meinem Bruder in die Stadt
    I   am yesterday NEG   with my   brother in the city
    gegangen.
    went
    'I did not go to the city with my brother yesterday.' (German)

In keeping with general ParGram policy, we do not encode much of the semantics of negation. As negation does not have a fixed position in German, the scope of negation is difficult to determine from c-structure information alone. We therefore do not attempt to represent the scope of negation at f-structure and instead simply register the presence of clausal negation with a NEG + feature at the same level as the clausal PRED in the f-structure (in (7) this would be the PRED 'eat').

Note that some languages divide negation into two parts. An example is French, as illustrated in (9).

(9) a. Elle n'   a   pas   mangé de soupe.
       she NEG have POSTNEG eaten of soup
       'She did not eat any soup.' (French)

   b. Elle ne   mange jamais   de soupe.
       she NEG eat   POSTNEG.never of soup
       'She never eats soup.' (French)

In these cases, one of the markers is analyzed as being of the c-structure
category NEG. This marker provides the NEG + feature at f-structure.
Furthermore, this category may only appear if another negative particle
is found in the clause. This constraint is achieved via a feature NEG-
FORM, which must be contributed by the other negative particle. The
feature NEG-FORM also serves to differentiate different possible post-
posed negative particles from one another, e.g., *pas* 'not' from *jamais*
'never' (French).

7.4.2 Constituent Negation

Constituent negation is used to negate constituents other than the entire clause. An example is given in (10). In many cases the negated
constituent is contrasted with another one within the same clause.

(10) a. They found the ball not in its box, but on the floor.

   b. Ils   ont trouvé la   balle non pas dans la   boîte, mais
       they have found the ball NEG   in the box   but
       sur le   plancher.
       on the floor
       'They found the ball not in the box, but on the floor.' (French)

   c. Er hat mir nicht das Buch gegeben, sondern die Zeitschrift.
       he has me NEG the book given   but   the magazine
       'He did not give me the book, but the magazine.' (German)

As with clausal negation, the negative marker provides a feature NEG
+ to the f-structure. Note that the one difficulty with the approach
to negation that we have chosen is that in the f-structure constituent
negation of a verb looks identical to clausal negation of the entire VP,
as in both cases the feature NEG + will be at the same f-structure level.
In fact, this is a problem for all heads, e.g., constituent negation of a
preposition is f-structure identical to negation of a PP.

7.4.3 Pleonastic Negation

Some languages have pleonastic negation in certain contexts. Pleonastic negation occurs when there is a negative marker, but no negative
meaning.

(11) Je crains qu' il ne   vienne.
    I   fear   that he NEG come
    'I am afraid that he will come.' (French)

In our analyses, pleonastic negation crucially does not provide a NEG + feature to the f-structure, thus indicating that a real semantic negation is not at hand. However, the type of the negation is encoded by means of a feature NEG-TYPE PLEONASTIC, and this feature may then be used to constrain pleonastic negation to occur in more restricted environments than true clausal negation, e.g., to constrain it to appear only in the complements of specific verbs.

8

Coordination

8.1 Basic Approach

The basic approach to constituent coordination in LFG (Bresnan, Kaplan and Peterson 1985, Kaplan and Maxwell 1988b; see also Andrews 1983) is as follows.[1] A c-structure rule such as that in (1) allows any category, e.g., S, VP, PP, to be coordinated. The conjuncts form a set via the $\downarrow \in \uparrow$ annotation. The conjunction contributes a CONJ-FORM, which appears as an attribute of the coordination as a whole, as shown in (2).

$$(1) \quad \text{SCCOORD(CAT)} \quad = \quad \begin{matrix} \text{CAT} & \text{CONJ} & \text{CAT} \\ \downarrow \in \uparrow & \uparrow = \downarrow & \downarrow \in \uparrow \end{matrix}$$

There are two different mechanisms in LFG which regulate the flow of information between the coordination set and its element f-structures: *generalization* and *distribution*.[2] These are described below. Distribution yields the more linguistically intuitive results, and is therefore the mechanism we have adopted for the ParGram grammars.

Generalization asserts information about a set as a whole when all of its elements have in common a feature and its value. For instance, if the members of a set of NPs all have CASE NOM, then the set has CASE NOM. If some of the NPs have CASE NOM and some have CASE ACC, then the set does not have a CASE attribute.

Distribution differs from generalization with respect to the behavior of nondefining or existential constraints, such as ($\uparrow$CASE), which states that case must exist, or ($\uparrow$CASE)=c NOM, which constrains case to be nominative, and ($\uparrow$CASE)≠NOM which disallows nominative case. Unlike gen-

---

[1] We do not discuss the problem of nonconstituent coordination here. For a recent proposal on how to deal with nonconstituent coordination within LFG, see Maxwell and Manning 1996. For a more general discussion see Sag, Gazdar, Wasow and Weisler 1985.

[2] See Kehler, Dalrymple, Lamping and Saraswat 1995 on the topic of information flow.

eralization, distribution distributes nondefining constraints across the set elements, much like defining constraints such as ($\uparrow$CASE)=NOM are distributed across the set elements by plain set distribution.

(2) a. [[in the tractor]$_{PP}$ [and]$_{CONJ}$ [on the trailer]$_{PP}$]$_{PP}$

b.
$$
\left[\left\{
\begin{array}{ll}
\text{PRED} & '\text{IN}<(\uparrow\text{OBJ})>' \\
\text{OBJ} & \left[
\begin{array}{ll}
\text{PRED} & '\text{TRACTOR}' \\
\text{SPEC} & \left[\begin{array}{ll}\text{SPEC-TYPE} & \text{DEF} \\ \text{SPEC-FORM} & \text{THE}\end{array}\right] \\
\text{NTYPE} & \text{COUNT} \\
\text{PERS} & 3 \\
\text{NUM} & \text{SG} \\
\text{ANIM} & - \\
\text{CASE} & \text{ACC} \\
\text{PCASE} & \text{IN}
\end{array}\right] \\
\text{PSEM} & \text{LOCATIVE} \\
\text{PTYPE} & \text{SEM}
\end{array}
\right., \\
\begin{array}{ll}
\text{PRED} & '\text{ON}<(\uparrow\text{OBJ})>' \\
\text{OBJ} & \left[
\begin{array}{ll}
\text{PRED} & '\text{TRAILER}' \\
\text{SPEC} & \left[\begin{array}{ll}\text{SPEC-TYPE} & \text{DEF} \\ \text{SPEC-FORM} & \text{THE}\end{array}\right] \\
\text{NTYPE} & \text{COUNT} \\
\text{PERS} & 3 \\
\text{NUM} & \text{SG} \\
\text{ANIM} & - \\
\text{CASE} & \text{ACC} \\
\text{PCASE} & \text{ON}
\end{array}\right] \\
\text{PSEM} & \text{LOCATIVE} \\
\text{PTYPE} & \text{SEM}
\end{array}
\right\} \\
\text{CONJ-FORM} \quad \text{AND}
\right]
$$

There are two situations in which the difference between generalization and distribution is crucial. One such situation is when the conjuncts differ with regard to a certain feature, but may still be coordinated. For example, if the first conjunct has the feature CASE NOM, but the second conjunct has CASE ACC, then the treatment of coordination will differ as follows. Imagine that an existential constraint such as ($\uparrow$CASE) is asserted of the coordinated structure in order to make sure that the conjunct as a whole will be marked for case. But as each of the elements of the conjunct have different values for case, the generalization of the case attribute is empty: the CASE attribute could not be generalized over the whole conjunct since each of the elements has a different value for it. However, if ($\uparrow$CASE) is distributed across the set elements, then it succeeds for each element. As languages do allow the coordination of elements whose feature values differ, the result of distribution is linguistically preferred to that of generalization.

Another situation which illustrates the difference is when a negative constraint such as ($\uparrow$PASSIVE)$\neq$+ is asserted of a set where some elements have PASSIVE + and others do not. Since some elements satisfy the condition that there be no PASSIVE +, generalization over the negative constraint succeeds and the coordination is judged to be successful. However, under distribution, the requirement that ($\uparrow$PASSIVE)$\neq$+ will be distributed over each element of the set. In this case, the coordination is illformed, since it fails for any element that has PASSIVE +. Once again, the result of distribution is linguistically preferred to that of generalization.

However, while the distribution mechanism captures many of the coordination facts, it cannot account for all of them. In some cases, the conjunct as a whole will be characterized by a certain feature like NUM PL, while each of its elements is actually singular. Following Dalrymple and Kaplan 1997, attributes may therefore be specified as *nondistributive*. A nondistributive attribute can be asserted of a coordination set as a whole, without having it distribute across the individual conjuncts. This is particularly useful for NP coordination, where the number and person attributes of each conjunct usually differ from those of the set as a whole (see 8.3 below). Another example is with the CONJ-FORM provided by the conjunction. There is a potential conflict in CONJ-FORM in cases of same category coordination where different conjunctions are involved, as in (3).

(3) The light flashes *and* the beacon either turns to the right *or* flashes repeatedly.

The conjuncts and the conjunctions in (3) jointly head the whole coordination. Since each conjunction provides a CONJ-FORM, there is a clash between the values provided by *or* and *and*, and the coordination fails. This problem is solved by defining CONJ-FORM as a nondistributive attribute, thus avoiding the clash.

8.2 Same Category Coordination

We first consider the coordination of categories other than nominals. Due to the way in which the number, person, and gender of nominal conjuncts interact with that of the coordination as a whole, coordinated nominals are considered separately (see section 8.3).

8.2.1 General Schema

The general coordination schema was described above in 8.1. However, this schema must be expanded in two ways. First, it must allow for more than two conjuncts, as in (4).

(4) They closed the door, locked it, and walked to the car.

The coordination rule must be formulated differently, according to whether the nonfinal conjuncts are separated from one another only by commas, or whether a conjunction is also required. The rule in (5) allows for commas separating the conjuncts.[3]

(5) SCCOORD(CAT) =

$$
\begin{array}{cccc}
\text{CAT} & ([\text{COMMA} \quad \text{CAT}]+ \quad (\text{COMMA})) & \text{CONJ} & \text{CAT} \\
\downarrow\in\uparrow & \downarrow\in\uparrow & \uparrow=\downarrow & \downarrow\in\uparrow
\end{array}
$$

Second, the rule must allow for two-part conjunctions, such as *either ... or, ni... ni* 'neither ... nor' (French). In these constructions, the first half of the conjunction is of category PRECONJ, which is constrained to occur with a particular CONJ-FORM, provided by its paired conjunction. For conjunctions which require a particular PRECONJ, such as French *ni... ni*, the PRECONJ encodes a PRECONJ-FORM at f-structure which the conjunction is constrained to occur with. This is unnecessary for conjunctions like English *or*, since they can occur alone or with a PRECONJ. The basic coordination rule for two part constructions is in (6).

(6) SCCOORD(CAT) =
$$
\begin{array}{cccc}
\text{PRECONJ} & \text{CAT} & \text{CONJ} & \text{CAT} \\
\uparrow=\downarrow & \downarrow\in\uparrow & \uparrow=\downarrow & \downarrow\in\uparrow
\end{array}
$$

8.2.2 Special Rules for Clauses

Two issues arise with respect to the coordination of clauses, as opposed to other types of same category coordination. The first issue involves the placement of commas (see also Nunberg 1990). Many languages do not allow a comma before the conjunction unless there are more than two conjuncts, as in (7).

(7) a. in the tractor, on the trailer, and next to the barn
     b. *in the tractor, and on the trailer

---

[3]Note that these commas do not provide any information to the f-structure, unlike periods, exclamation marks, or question marks which are also parsed within the ParGram grammars and are used to check for the STMT-TYPE attribute at f-structure (DECLARATIVE vs. INTERROGATIVE).

However, commas are often placed between full clauses even when there are only two conjuncts, as in (8).

(8) The tractor started immediately, and the farmer drove off.

A simple way to deal with this situation is to have clauses call a variant of the usual same category coordination rule, which allows for a comma with only two conjuncts.

The second issue concerning coordination of clauses has to do with cases where only punctuation, usually a semicolon, separates two complete sentences, as in (9).

(9) a. The tractor started immediately; the engine was running smoothly.
     b. Lorsque l'on tourne le   commutateur, les voyants
        when   one turns the switch   the warning lights
        s'allument; ils   s'éteignent lorsque le   moteur démarre.
        light up   they turn off   when   the motor   starts
        'When the switch is turned, the signals light up; they turn off when the motor starts.' (French)

There are a couple of approaches to this problem. One is to have a special coordination rule for the highest category under ROOT, which allows certain types of punctuation in place of a conjunction. Another is to consider each of the two sentences as a separate ROOT clause, one of which ends in nonstandard punctuation.

8.3   NP Coordination

NP coordination often involves number, person, and gender mismatches between the individual conjuncts and the entire coordinated NP. In (10a), each conjunct is singular, but the result is a plural NP, as is evident from the plural verb agreement. In (10b), one conjunct is feminine and the other masculine, but the coordinated NP is masculine, as is clear from the masculine morphology on the adjective.

(10) a. The tractor and the trailer are parked outside.
      b. Jean   et   Marie   sont   gentils.
         Jean.M.Sg and Marie.F.Sg are.Pl nice.M.Pl
         'Jean and Marie are nice.' (French)

Two requirements must be met by an analysis of NP coordination. First, it must be possible to assert constraints about and assign values to attributes in both the individual conjuncts and in the f-structure of the coordination as a whole. Second, there must be an algorithm to construct the number, person, and gender values of the coordinated

NP from the values of the individual conjuncts. These two sides of the analysis are described in 8.3.1 and 8.3.2, respectively.

8.3.1 Basic Structure

The c- and f-structures for NP coordination remain basically identical to those of same category coordination. The simplified rule for NP coordination is shown in (11). As with basic same category coordination, additions must be made for paired conjuncts and for more than two conjuncts (see section 8.2.1).

(11) NPCOORD(CAT) = CAT   CONJnp   CAT
                     $\downarrow\in\uparrow$ $\uparrow=\downarrow$ $\downarrow\in\uparrow$

The schema in (11) differs from that of same category coordination in that it calls a different lexical entry for the conjunction, CONJnp instead of CONJ. The CONJnp and CONJ entries for each conjunction provide a CONJ-FORM attribute at f-structure, as shown in (12).

(12) a. [[the tractor]$_{NP}$ [and]$_{CONJnp}$ [the trailer]$_{NP}$]$_{NP}$

b.

$$
\left[
\begin{array}{l}
\left\{
\begin{array}{l}
\left[
\begin{array}{ll}
\text{PRED} & \text{'TRACTOR'} \\
\text{SPEC} & \begin{bmatrix} \text{SPEC-TYPE} & \text{DEF} \\ \text{SPEC-FORM} & \text{THE} \end{bmatrix} \\
\text{NTYPE} & \text{COUNT} \\
\text{PERS} & 3 \\
\text{NUM} & \text{SG} \\
\text{ANIM} & - \\
\text{CASE} & \text{NOM}
\end{array}
\right] \\
\left[
\begin{array}{ll}
\text{PRED} & \text{'TRAILER'} \\
\text{SPEC} & \begin{bmatrix} \text{SPEC-TYPE} & \text{DEF} \\ \text{SPEC-FORM} & \text{THE} \end{bmatrix} \\
\text{NTYPE} & \text{COUNT} \\
\text{PERS} & 3 \\
\text{NUM} & \text{SG} \\
\text{ANIM} & - \\
\text{CASE} & \text{NOM}
\end{array}
\right]
\end{array}
\right\} \\
\begin{array}{ll}
\text{PERS} & 3 \\
\text{NUM} & \text{PL} \\
\text{CONJ-FORM} & \text{AND}
\end{array}
\end{array}
\right]
$$

The CONJnp entry additionally supplies the number specification for the coordination as a whole. Furthermore, in order to accommodate the number, person, and gender mismatches between the conjuncts and the whole coordination, we have defined the attributes NUM, PERS, and GEND as nondistributive.

This allows statements about the set and about the individual conjuncts without having the one necessarily be dependent on the other. Note that in (12), the elements of the conjunction are both singular, but the coordinated phrase is plural. The NUM PL is supplied by *and*, and does not distribute across the conjuncts.

8.3.2 Agreement

Consider the minimal pair in (13). The only difference between the two sentences is the conjunction, yet (13a) with *and* requires plural verb agreement, while (13b) with *or* requires singular verb agreement. Thus, the type of conjunction involved in the coordinated phrases plays a role in determining agreement.

(13) a. The tractor and the trailer are in the garage.

  b. The tractor or the trailer is in the garage.

Modulo this differing contribution of each conjunction, the general rule in English, French and German for determining the number, gender, and person of a coordinated NP is as follows:

(14)   If any conjunct is plural, the entire NP is plural;

   If any conjunct is masculine, the entire NP is masculine;

   If any conjunct is first person, the entire NP is first person; if there is no first person conjunct and any conjunct is second person, the entire NP is second person; otherwise the NP is third person.

How can this pattern be captured? As seen above, the c-structure of NP coordination is identical to that of basic same category coordination. However, in NP coordination, each of the conjuncts bears annotations as in (15), which illustrates this idea with respect to number agreement:

(15)   CAT
           $\downarrow \in \uparrow$
      $\{ (\downarrow\text{NUM})=_c \text{PL}$
         $(\uparrow\text{NUM})=\text{PL}$
      $| (\downarrow\text{NUM})=_c \text{SG} \}$

The annotation in (15) states that if the conjunct has NUM PL, then NUM PL will be assigned to the f-structure of the coordinated NP as a whole. If the conjunct has NUM SG, then no NUM value is assigned to the f-structure of the NP as a whole. This annotation applies to each conjunct, thus capturing the fact that if any conjunct is plural the entire NP is plural. If all the conjuncts are singular, no number is assigned by these annotations to the coordinated NP. Instead, the conjunction provides the appropriate NUM value, allowing for the difference in (13): *and* always requires NUM PL, while *or* has a default of NUM SG which only applies when NUM PL has not been assigned by (15). Similar rules capture the facts of gender and person agreement in English, French and German.

8.4 Problems

Although this approach works well, there are some remaining problems. Sometimes the conjunction *and* does not produce a plural coordination, as in (16).

(16) This writer and artist has produced many important works.

In (16), writer and artist refer to the same person, so that the conjunct remains singular, as shown by the verb agreement. At present we do not deal with this type of NP coordination.

Since conjuncts map into a set, the linear order in which they appear is lost in the f-structure. Order information can be important for verb agreement and for the temporal sequencing of events. For example, in English, *the lights or the beacon* can be either singular or plural since the second conjunct is singular; however, *the beacon or the lights* can only be plural. The ordering information is preserved in the c-structure, from where it could be recovered. An alternative solution, and the one adopted in later versions of the grammar, is to map conjuncts into an ordered list instead of a set.

9

Special Constructions

There are a number of special constructions in the grammars which warrant discussion but which do not fall under any specific category. These include: tag questions, parentheticals, and headers. They are discussed here to provide the grammar writer with an idea as to how specialized constructions can be handled in the grammar with a minimum of change to the overall structure of the core grammar.

9.1 Parentheticals

Typical parentheticals are illustrated in (1). They are set off from the main part of the clause by parentheses or other types of punctuation.

(1) a. This button (2) is for the oil filter.

    b. Contrôler la   tension (voir page 2).
       check   the tension see page 2
       'Check the tension (see page 2).' (French)

    c. Kühler   auf Blockierungen überprüfen (siehe Seite 42).
       radiator core for blockage   check   see   page 42
       'Check the radiator core for blockage (see page 42).' (German)

    d. A warning light (red) will come on after six seconds.

    e. A warning light—red or green—will come on.

Parentheticals are introduced by a special c-structure rule which includes the required punctuation and allows a limited number of constituents within it, e.g., NPs, imperatives, APs. The PARENP constituent appears in selected c-structure positions depending on the language. Ideally, almost any constituent can be followed by a parenthetical; however, in practice this allows for extensive ambiguity, and so the parentheticals appear only in select positions, as dictated by the corpus at hand.

The PARENP constituent corresponds to an ADJUNCT-PAREN feature in the f-structure, thus rendering it distinct from a plain ADJUNCT (see section 3.3.6 on the division of adjuncts). ADJUNCT-PAREN is defined not to be a set which restricts parentheticals to one per constituent. However, some corpora may allow more than one parenthetical per constituent, which would then require ADJUNCT-PAREN to be defined as a set. Note that constituents which normally do not appear with adjuncts, such as proper names and pronouns, can freely occur with ADJUNCT-PARENs.

The c- and f-structures for the subject NP in (1d) are shown in (2).

(2) a.

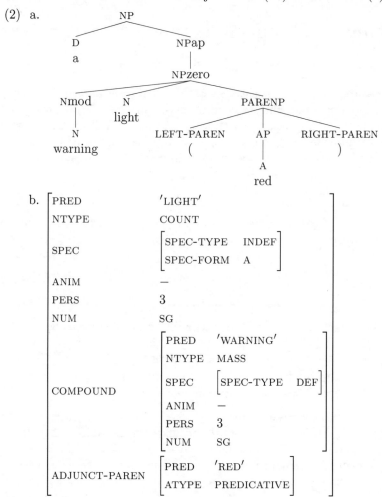

9.2 Headers

Headers are the nominal and clausal elements that appear as section headers in documents, newspapers, chapter titles, etc. Some examples from our tractor manual corpus are given in (3).

(3) a. Hydraulic quadrant control lever

   b. Voyant   de filtre à   air sec
       warning.light of filter for air dry
       'Dry air filter warning light' (French)

   c. Kontrolleuchte Ladekontrolle
       warning.light charge.control
       'Warning light for charge control' (German)

Headers appear as a special c-structure category, HEADER, directly under ROOT. As a root category, they are assigned a STMT-TYPE HEADER. In general, headers are types of NPs, although in certain genres, e.g., newspaper headlines, this would need to be expanded. Unlike regular NPs, headers do not need to have determiners, as seen in (3); as such, the HEADER rule supplies SPEC features to the f-structure in order to satisfy the requirements of NPs which would normally appear with determiners. The c- and f-structures for (3a) are shown in (4).

(4) a.

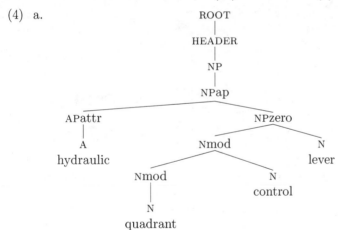

b.
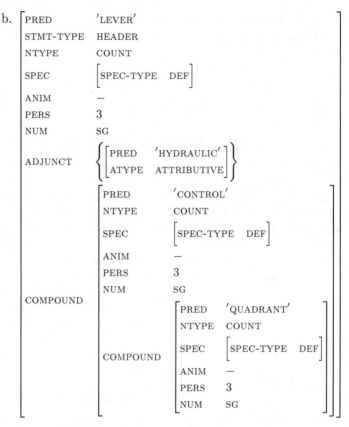

9.3   Tag Questions

The English grammar contains a special set of c-structure rules for tag questions, such as those in (5).

(5)   a. She is flashing the light, isn't she?

     b. They ate all the cake, didn't they?

     c. The lights will not come on, will they?

The basic c-structure of these questions is a declarative clause followed by a comma followed by the appropriate tag. The form of the tag is determined by the features of the subject, the tense and form of the verb, and the polarity (affirmative or negative) of the declarative. The c-structure of (5a) is shown in (6).

The f-structure of tag questions is mostly identical to that of the corresponding yes-no question (see section 2.1.2 on interrogatives). One difference is that the f-structure analysis also includes an attribute TAG whose value in turn is an f-structure which contains information about the form of the tag: its auxiliary, polarity, and pronoun. Constraints on the rules ensure that the correct matching occurs. A slightly abbreviated f-structure analysis (the features of the object have been left out) for the tag-question in (6) is shown in (7).

Note that the tag portion of the question requires a special form of the auxiliary which has both a special c-structure category, e.g., TAGaux, and a special f-structure. This was done largely because the tag itself does not contain the information necessary to satisfy the morphosyntactic requirements of the auxiliary. The necessary information is therefore introduced as part of the rules. On the whole, however, specialized constructions were kept to a minimum in the analysis of tag questions.

(6) a. She is flashing the light, isn't she?

b.

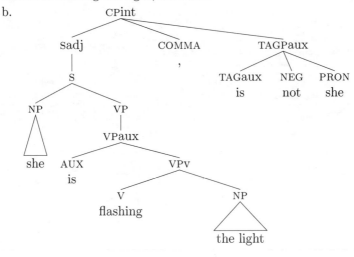

(7) a. She is flashing the light, isn't she?

b.

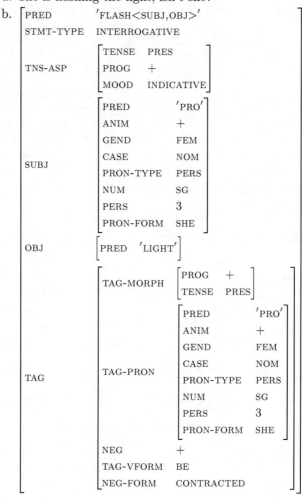

$$
\begin{bmatrix}
\text{PRED} & \text{'FLASH<SUBJ,OBJ>'} \\
\text{STMT-TYPE} & \text{INTERROGATIVE} \\
\text{TNS-ASP} & \begin{bmatrix} \text{TENSE} & \text{PRES} \\ \text{PROG} & + \\ \text{MOOD} & \text{INDICATIVE} \end{bmatrix} \\
\text{SUBJ} & \begin{bmatrix} \text{PRED} & \text{'PRO'} \\ \text{ANIM} & + \\ \text{GEND} & \text{FEM} \\ \text{CASE} & \text{NOM} \\ \text{PRON-TYPE} & \text{PERS} \\ \text{NUM} & \text{SG} \\ \text{PERS} & 3 \\ \text{PRON-FORM} & \text{SHE} \end{bmatrix} \\
\text{OBJ} & \begin{bmatrix} \text{PRED} & \text{'LIGHT'} \end{bmatrix} \\
\text{TAG} & \begin{bmatrix} \text{TAG-MORPH} & \begin{bmatrix} \text{PROG} & + \\ \text{TENSE} & \text{PRES} \end{bmatrix} \\ \text{TAG-PRON} & \begin{bmatrix} \text{PRED} & \text{'PRO'} \\ \text{ANIM} & + \\ \text{GEND} & \text{FEM} \\ \text{CASE} & \text{NOM} \\ \text{PRON-TYPE} & \text{PERS} \\ \text{NUM} & \text{SG} \\ \text{PERS} & 3 \\ \text{PRON-FORM} & \text{SHE} \end{bmatrix} \\ \text{NEG} & + \\ \text{TAG-VFORM} & \text{BE} \\ \text{NEG-FORM} & \text{CONTRACTED} \end{bmatrix}
\end{bmatrix}
$$

Part II

Grammar Engineering

10

Overview

This part of the book discusses issues that arise with respect to the engineering aspects of grammar development. In the first part, we presented analyses of constructions in English, French, and German. In this part, we focus on issues such as the maintainability of grammars, how to achieve robustness in parsing while at the same time avoiding overgeneration, and how a grammar's performance may be measured and improved. These issues are at the heart of much discussion in computational linguistics today and are far from resolved. The material in the following chapters is meant to make a contribution to the discussion by reporting on some of the ideas, solutions, and experiments conducted within our project.

Chapter 11 first recapitulates the architecture of the parser and describes the individual components. Chapter 12 then describes some of the finite state tools we used in more detail. Note that we do not discuss implementation issues with regard to the Xerox Linguistic Environment (XLE). As grammar writers, we saw XLE as a black box whose design and implementation we could not influence directly. We did, however, influence its development indirectly by reporting on various needs such as better debugging tools, a better method for integrating lexical entries with one another, and rule notation that would allow easier maintenance and modularization of the grammar. This interaction has resulted in a platform that caters to many of our needs, and which continues to grow and improve even as this book goes to press. We describe some of the relevant features and functions in the chapter on modularity and maintainability (Chapter 13), and in the chapter on robustness and measuring performance (Chapter 14).

11

Architecture and User Interface

This chapter discusses the architecture and user interface of the Xerox Linguistic Environment (XLE). The architecture of the parser is as shown in (1) (repeated from Chapter 1).

(1)

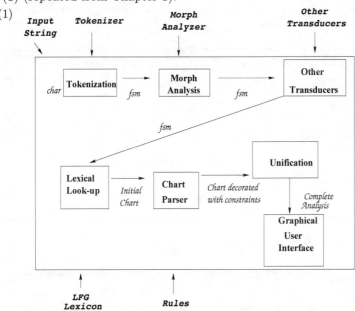

We discuss each of the components in turn, beginning with the tokenizer, and ending with a brief description of a generation component and a fledgling machine translation component. The generation component basically reverses the parsing process shown in (1) and the machine translation component calls up two such grammars: it works on the output from one grammar and sends its result to another grammar for generation.

Before going on to that, however, we briefly describe and illustrate the user interface to XLE in the next section.

11.1 The User Interface

At this point in time, the XLE platform runs within a Unix environment and makes use of such freely accessible software as *emacs* and TCL in order to provide a comfortable and familiar user interface.

Rules and lexical entries are coded as ASCII files. Calls to XLE are instantiated within a Unix shell. In addition, the user can interface with XLE by means of an emacs lfg-mode designed by Mary Dalrymple. This lfg-mode gives the user an easy mechanism of invoking XLE, provides automatic formatting of rules and lexical entries, and allows for a quick retrieval mechanism of rules, templates and lexical entries.

An example of what it would look like to load XLE at the IMS in Stuttgart is shown below. The call to load XLE was accomplished via a command "Start a new XLE process" under the XLE menu bar in the emacs window.

```
emacs@zaunkoenig

Buffers Files Tools Edit Search XLE Complete In/Out Signals Help

xset:  warning, no entries deleted from font path.
xset:  warning, no entries deleted from font path.
xset:  warning, no entries deleted from font path.
xset:  warning, no entries deleted from font path.
XLE loaded from /projekte/pargram/xle/distrib/xle.
XLEPATH = /projekte/pargram/xle/distrib.
XLE release of Jan 15, 1999 10:08.
Type 'help' for more information.
loading IMS patches (under construction)
timeout set to 300 seconds
% create-parser english.lfg
loading english.lfg...
Grammar has 82 rules with 799 states, 2050 arcs, and 3340 disjuncts.

Morph transducer files relative to ./

                    100%^MO%>>>>>>>>>>>>>>>>>>>>>>>>>>>>>>>>>>>>>
                    100%^MO%>>>>>>>>>>>>>>>>>>>>>>>>>>>>>>>>>>>>>
                    100%^MO%>>>>>>>>>>>>>>>>>>>>>>>>>>>>>>>>>>>>>
                    100%^MO%>>>>>>>>>>>>>>>>>>>>>>>>>>>>>>>>>>>>>
3.97 CPU seconds
english.lfg loaded
(Chart)1309d78
%

--**-Emacs: *XLE*        (XLE:run)--L24--All--------------------
```

Once XLE is called, it loads the platform and then waits for the user to do something. In this case, the user has typed "create-parser english.lfg". This command enables the loading of the English grammar defined in the file "english.lfg". XLE reports how many rules, states, arcs and disjuncts the grammar has and then proceeds to load a cascade of finite-state modules (see Chapter 12). In this case there are three such modules, which accomplish the tokenization and the morphological analysis of the input string. Finally, the rules are loaded, XLE reports success and is ready to parse a sentence or constituent.

11.2   The XLE Output

Once a given sentence or constituent has been parsed, XLE returns the result by means of a number of TCL windows. These windows are illustrated and explained in this section.

For example, to parse the NP *the new tractor lights*, the following would be typed in the XLE window shown above.

```
% parse "NP: the new tractor lights"
```

XLE reports that it is now parsing and then returns the parse time and the number of correct analyses produced, as in (2).

(2) 2+4 solutions, 0.52 CPU seconds, 56 subtrees

The "2+4" indicates that there were two optimal solutions plus 4 unoptimal solutions. The unoptimal solutions are filtered out via the o(ptimality)-projection discussed below in section 14.1.3. However, it is useful to let the grammar writer know exactly how many parses were filtered out, as unreasonable analyses or funny rule interactions can often be identified this way.

The "0.52 CPU seconds" indicates how many CPU seconds it took to arrive at the parse. In previous incarnations of XLE this number was computed in terms of "real-time" seconds and would thus vary according to the particular load at that particular time.

The "56 subtrees" indicates the number of subtrees that were explored. This number gives the grammar writer an indication of the complexity of the rule system. In some cases, very simple sentences or constituents may suddenly appear with a very high subtree number. This is usually an indication that something has gone wrong with the rule-writing.

Once XLE has parsed the sentence or constituent, four windows are displayed: the first two contain the c- and f-structures, and the other two show two different packed representations of the valid solutions.

The c-structure and f-structure windows are shown below. In both windows, the "previous" and "next" buttons enable the user to navigate through the different structures for both valid and invalid analyses. The structures can be saved as postscript files or in terms of Prolog code. In the c-structure window, details of the morphology or the parse chart can be viewed by clicking on the "Commands" menu and selecting "morph" or "chart" respectively. The node numbers in the c-structure have corresponding numbers in the f-structure, indicating which part of the f-structure a given c-structure node maps to. The "Options" button allows the user to toggle the display of the numbers since a tree without number annotations is sometimes easier to read.

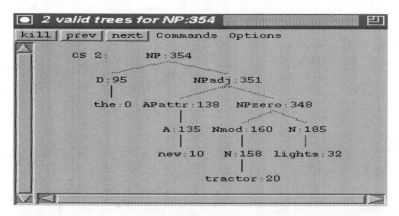

The f-structure window additionally contains the buttons "m::*" and "o::*". Clicking on these opens two more TCL windows. One of them displays the m-structure (see section 3.5.4), and the other registers the number and kind of optimality marks that were encountered during the parse (see section 14.1.3). Again, the display of the node numbers may be toggled under the "Commands" button. The "Options" menu also provides options which only display PREDs or which shows features introduced via constraint equations. These options are very useful debugging tools. Finally, the f-structure can also be used directly as input for the generator (see section 11.6). Choosing the "Generate from this FS" option under the "Commands" menu causes XLE to start another shell which calls the generator and produces an output string.

The c-structure window has a few more features. One is the ability to display sublexical information. As shown below, it is possible to toggle terminal (lexical) nodes to display the sublexical constituents. In our grammars, these sublexical constituents are determined by the output of the finite-state morphological analyzers described in section 11.3.2.

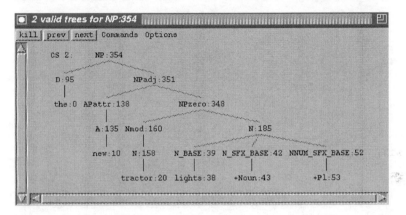

A further feature is that invalid c-structures display boxed nodes, corresponding to where the f-structure notations on the c-structure backbone fail to unify, as shown below. For example, the English grammar allows for the possibility of an NP which has a gerundive head as in *his driving*. So, the parser tries out this possibility with *the new tractor lights*, but this possibility is illformed because the functional information associated with *lights* does not allow a complete and coherent analysis.

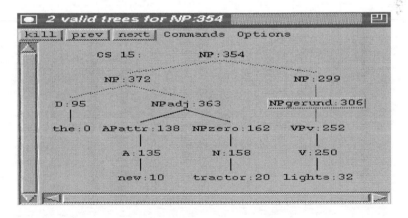

As mentioned at the beginning of this section, XLE displays four windows as the result of a parse. The third and fourth windows show the parsed result in terms of packed representations. One of the windows is illustrated below.

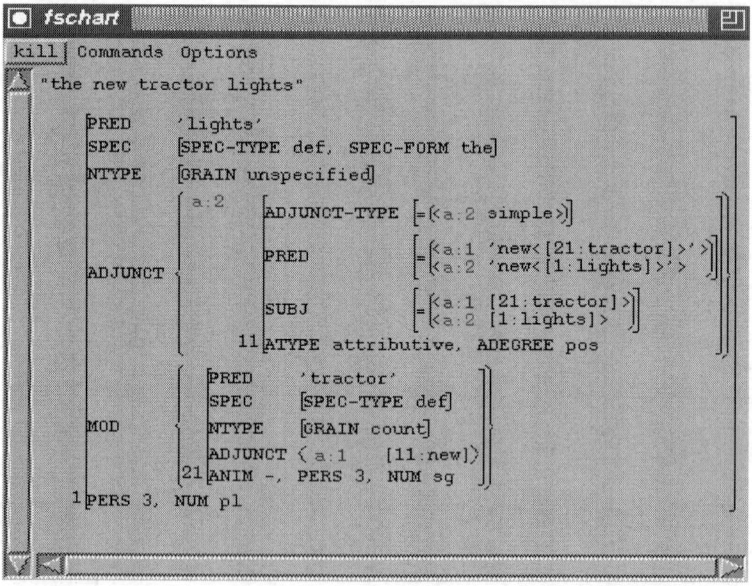

These representations are useful for visualizing parsing ambiguities. A long sentence may have hundreds of valid syntactic analyses; instead of listing them independently, which makes debugging difficult, the XLE chart-parser uses the technique of "disjunctive lazy unification" (see Maxwell and Kaplan 1991 on the notion of disjunctive constraint satisfaction) for sharing pieces of substructure common to several parses. The window above thus displays a packed f-structure, annotated with choices to show where the alternative analyses are. Clicking on a given choice displays the corresponding c- and f-structures in the respective windows.

This concludes the discussion and illustration of the XLE output. In the next section, we move on to describing each individual module of the parser.

11.3 The Architecture

11.3.1 The Tokenizer

One of the first steps in any corpus processing system is applying a tokenizer to the input text. A tokenizer is a device that segments an input stream into an ordered sequence of *tokens*. These tokens can be paragraphs, sentences, words, etc. Since our application involves parsing individual sentences, the relevant tokens correspond to an inflected word form, a number, a punctuation mark, or any other kind of unit to be passed on for subsequent processing. Though most sequences of uninterrupted alphabetic characters constitute a token in most languages, the use of separators inside words varies from language to language. For example, the sequence *l'amour* 'love' might split into two tokens in French while *aujourd'hui* 'today' should be considered as a single unit. On the other hand, a sequence of words (e.g., *ein bißchen* 'a bit', *a priori*, *parce que* 'because', *in order to*) may be considered as a single token for further linguistic treatment (see section 12.2 on multiword expressions).

Our approach to tokenization is to provide a cascade of language dependent finite-state transducing tokenizers (Schiller 1996). These tokenizers segment text by introducing a token boundary (usually a newline) into the output stream. The cascade is composed of a *basic tokenizer* which segments any sequence of input characters into simple tokens (i.e., no multiword units) and one or several *multiword staplers* which identify multiwords and group them together as single units. The development and implementation of a finite-state longest match operator (Karttunen 1996) has made this process both practical and possible. See Chapter 12 on finite-state technology for further discussion.

11.3.2 The Morphological Analyzer

11.3.2.1 The Xerox Finite-State Morphologies

The Xerox finite-state morphological analyzers are used in the German, French, and English grammars (Kaplan and Kay 1994, Koskenniemi 1983, Karttunen et al. 1992, and Kaplan and Newman 1997).[1] In this finite-state technology, transducers directly encode morphological alternations. All inflected forms of the same word are mapped to the same canonical dictionary form (lemma). Morphological categories are represented as part of the lexical form. That is, two-level representations are used: one level containing the surface form of a word and the other con-

---

[1]At the moment there are complete Xerox morphological analyzers using finite-state techniques for several languages: Arabic, Czech, Danish, Dutch, English, Finnish, French, German, Hungarian, Italian, Norwegian, Portuguese, Spanish, and Swedish.

taining the base form (canonical dictionary form) with an attached list of morphological features. The list of morphological features depends on the language. Examples are shown below in (3a, b) for English, (3c, d) for French, and (3e) for German.

(3) a. warning
   1. warn+Verb+Prog
   2. warning+Adj
   3. warning+Noun+Sg
 b. which
   1. which+Pron+Rel+NomObl+3P+SP
   2. which+Pron+Wh+NomObl+3P+SP
   3. which+Det+Wh+SP
 c. clignotant
   1. clignoter+PrPrt+Verb
   2. clignotant+Masc+Sg+Noun
   3. clignotant+Masc+Sg+Adj
 d. que
   1. qui+Acc+InvGen+InvPL+Rel+Int+Pro
   2. que+ConjQue
 e. den
   1. der+Det+Art+Sg+Masc+Akk+St
   2. der+Det+Art+Pl+FMN+Dat+St
   3. der+Pron+Dem+Sg+Masc+Akk
   4. der+Pron+Rel+Sg+Masc+Akk

As seen in the above examples, the Xerox two-level morphologies provide more information (e.g., that the pronoun is a demonstrative one) than what linguists usually expect from a morphological component. However, most of the information provided by the morphological analyzers is extremely useful for the grammar and has been integrated within the ParGram development effort.

11.3.2.2 Interfacing Morphology with Syntax

The finite-state morphological analyzers are interfaced with XLE by means of sublexical rules (see Kaplan and Newman 1997), which parse the output of the morphology. For instance `clignotant+Masc+Sg+Noun` is considered to be a phrase which consists of the stem and each of the morphological tags.

(4) the base form: *clignotant*
   the finite-state symbols: *+Masc*, *+Sg*, *+Noun*

Each item is listed and identified in the lexicon, just like any other lexical item, i.e., it has the item, its category, the XLE tag, and then any relevant equations or template calls. Sample entries for the tags in (4) are shown in (5): +Masc is parsed as a gender tag which is interpreted as contributing the functional information GEND MASC to the f-structure of the stem it appears on, +Sg is a number tag and assigns NUM SG to either the f-structure itself or the subject's f-structure, and +Noun is a word class tag which is interpreted as assigning PERS 3. The reasoning for the latter assignment is that any full noun could not be first or second person, but would necessarily be analyzed as third person. Finally, *clignotant* is parsed as a terminal (lexical) entry of the type noun (N). The template @(NOUN CLIGNOTANT) assigns *clignotant* as the value of a PRED feature (among other things).

(5) +Masc   GEND   TAG   ($\uparrow$GEND)= MASC.
     +Sg   NBR   TAG   ($\uparrow$NUM)=SG;
                 VNBR   XLE   ($\uparrow$SUBJ NUM)=SG.
     +Noun   NTAG   TAG   ($\uparrow$PERS)=3.
     clignotant N   XLE   @(NOUN CLIGNOTANT).

Then, by using sublexical rules which function in the same way as the usual phrase structure rules in LFG, the grammar is able to parse the output of the morphological analyzer. A rule which parses this particular order, which is characteristic of nouns in French, is shown in (6).[2]

(6) N $\longrightarrow$ N_BASE GEND_BASE NBR_BASE NTAG_BASE.

The fragmentary f-structure that results from this parse is shown in (7).

(7) $\begin{bmatrix} \text{PRED} & \text{'CLIGNOTANT'} \\ \text{GEND} & \text{MASC} \\ \text{NUM} & \text{SG} \\ \text{PERS} & 3 \end{bmatrix}$

As should be evident from (7) and the discussion, the integration of the finite-state morphological analyzers with an LFG parser turned out to be quite easy and natural.

Furthermore, if the morphological analysis should produce a tag that is irrelevant (or even wrong due to a mistake in the morphological analyzer), this can be counteracted via an appropriate formulation of the sublexical rule: the offending tag will be parsed by the rule, but will not provide any functional information to be passed to the f-structure.

On the other hand, there are cases where the information encoded by

---

[2]Note that _BASE is added to each sublexical item by XLE so that morphological and syntactic categories can be distinguished. Otherwise, the rule would be N $\longrightarrow$N GEND NBR NTAG, implying a unintended recursion.

the finite-state morphology needs to be enriched. That is, since the finite-state morphological analyzers are meant to be as general as possible, they sometimes lack the information necessary for a specific purpose, e.g., LFG grammar writing in our case. This extra information is provided directly by the grammar writers via annotations and template calls in the lexical entry. This additional information then works together with the information provided by the tags.

The word *slow* in English can be used as an illustration. The English finite-state morphology analyzes *slow* as an adjective and a verb, as seen in (8).

(8) slow
1. slow+Adj
2. slow+Verb+Pres+Non3Sg

However, in the tractor manual we were working on *slow* is also used as a noun in, for example, *To operate the speedshift, press either button to move from fast to slow*. As such, the ParGram lexical entry for *slow* is as in (9). The adjectival and verbal entries include the annotation XLE. This encodes the fact that these stems are relying on a morphological analysis from the finite-state morphological analyzers which have been integrated into XLE. The nominal entry, however, is annotated with an * to encode the fact that here no help from the morphology can be expected and that all of the information must come from this one entry.

(9) slow   A   XLE   @(ADJ SLOW);
           V   XLE   @(TRANS SLOW);
           N   *   @(NOUN SLOW).

As can be gleaned from this discussion, the interaction between lexical items is quite complex within XLE because stems may be coming out of the morphological analyzer, be user-defined, and additionally may span several different word classes, as in the case of *slow*. A more in-depth discussion of the lexicon and the structure of lexical entries follows below in 11.4. However, before we proceed to that discussion, we first introduce another method of introducing stems into the grammar.

11.3.2.3 Extending Capabilities via Unknowns

The morphological analyzers can be further exploited in order to parse words which have not explicitly been entered in the lexicon. Words unknown to the lexicon, i.e., words which lack an explicit lexical entry, are referred to as *unknowns*. From the point of view of XLE, two types of unknowns are distinguished: unknowns which the morphological analyzer knows about but which have not been encoded in the lexicon files; unknowns which the morphology does not recognize and which have not been encoded in the lexicon files either. An example of this latter type are proper names, often foreign ones, which no reasonable morphological analyzer can be expected to recognize.

By way of the morphological analyzer, the grammar can deal with both types of unknowns by means of a series of educated guesses. This allows the grammar to process many more words than are encoded in the lexicons, whether they be hand entered, or automatically generated (section 14.1.1).

Items which are unknown to the grammar (i.e., to the lexicons), but which are encoded in the morphology may be dealt with by matching the information from the morphological analyzer with a type of generic entry in the lexicon. An example of this kind of generic entry is shown in (10) which is an entry for an *-Lunknown* item (unknown to the lexicon).

(10)   -Lunknown
      A XLE   @(ADJ %stem);
      ADV XLE   @(ADVERB %stem)
                        @NOTADJADVMOD;
      N XLE   @(NOUN %stem)
                        ($\uparrow$NTYPE)=COMMON;
      NUMBER XLE ($\uparrow$PRED)='%stem'.

What this entry basically says is the following: try to match the output of the morphological analyzer to one of the following: an adjective, an adverb, a noun, or a number.[3] Closed class items such as auxiliaries or prepositions are not matched via this method. It is assumed that the grammar writer is responsible for taking care of closed class items, but not for encoding every member of an open class.

For example, consider the situation where there is no entry for *red* in the lexicon. The morphology, however, knows that *red* can have the two parses in (11).

(11) red +Adj
     red +Noun +Sg

The grammar can guess at a parse for *red* based on the generic unknown entry, which contains blueprints for both an adjective and a noun. Both of these blueprints make requirements on what kind of functional information an adjective or noun may possess, and both can only be parsed by a particular sublexical rule. Since the output of the morphological analyzer satisfies both the requirements of the adjective and the

---

[3]There is a separate entry for capitalized forms, -LUnknown. In English this has the same possibilities (A, ADV, N, NUMBER) as the lowercase -Lunknown, except that it allows for proper nouns via NAME and titles via TITLE; that is, proper nouns and titles can only be upper cased and so there is no entry for them under -Lunknown.

noun, *red* can be parsed by the grammar after all. Note that the notation "%stem" is a variable which the base form returned by the morphology replaces. In our example, the value of %stem is RED.

Items which are unknown to both the lexicon and the morphological analyzer can be guessed at via another type of generic entry: -*Munknown*. As these unknowns tend to be proper names, foreign words, and acronyms, the grammar writer assumes that any such unknown word is probably a noun and encodes this assumption in terms of an appropriately generic entry for -Munknown. Thus, a large open class of lexical items may be dealt with via a simple, yet useful mechanism.

11.4 Lexical Lookup

11.4.1 Types of Lexicons

As indicated in the above discussion, the grammar uses lexical entries which come from a variety of different sources. All of these lexical entries could in principle be stored in one and the same file. However, separate files tend to be easier to maintain and understand. Within ParGram we have therefore modularized the lexicon by distinguishing the following types of lexicon files:

1. A lexicon file containing core entries that belong to a closed class and lexical exceptions that need to be dealt with via specialized lexical entries.
2. A lexicon file which deals with technical terms or specialized uses of words.
3. Lexicon files of semi-automatically generated verb, adjective, and noun stems.
4. A lexicon dealing with the sublexical tags used by the morphological analyzer.

The core lexicon is (necessarily) hand-coded by the grammar writers. This lexicon includes closed class items such as auxiliaries, determiners, and prepositions. It also includes entries for verbs or nouns which behave exceptionally (e.g., German "coherent" verbs).

Another lexicon file includes the vocabulary specific to a given text. In our case, the tractor manual we used contained a number of technical terms and usages that cannot be considered standard, as seen above with the nominal use of *slow*. These were encoded in a separate lexicon. The advantage of such modularization is that when the grammar is used for a different text or application, the exclusion of this specialized vocabulary simply requires not loading that particular file.

Open class items such as verbs, nouns and adjectives can be coded by hand, but as new nouns (and acronyms) and verbs are constantly entering the language, the grammar writer's job would never be done. As such, it is more satisfying to semi-automatically produce large lexicons for open class items on the basis of corpora extraction methods. This was also done within ParGram (see section 14.1.1).

Finally, the ParGram grammars all define lexical entries which deal with the sublexical tags produced by the morphological analyzers. These entries are all kept in a separate file. Due to this modularization, it is again a simple matter to adapt the lexicon if the morphological analyzer should change for some reason.

11.4.2 Structure of a Lexical Entry

Despite the fact that many different lexicon files are loaded into a given grammar, the structure of any individual lexical entry is the same in all the files. We here briefly discuss what is contained in a typical lexical entry, as exemplified by (12) (see Kaplan and Newman 1997 for details).

(12)   foo   N   XLE   @(NOUN FOO);
       V   XLE   @(VERB FOO);
       P   XLE   @(PREP FOO).

This lexical entry for *foo* specifies the following information.

- The *base form* of the word ('foo' in (12)).
- The *category* or part of speech associated with each particular word. A given item may belong to several different syntactic categories. In our example, *foo* acts as a noun N, a verb V, and a preposition P.
- The *morphcode* is a marker which specifies where the morphological information of the word comes from. The morphcode XLE indicates that the finite-state morphological analyzer is expected to supply the morphological information. The morphcode *, on the other hand, indicates that the item must be parsed as is. No further morphological information can be expected. In this case, all the surface forms of a word together with all the morphological features must be specified in the lexicon. Note that we have not implemented any ParGram specific morphology, but that the generalizable information comes out of independently implemented morphological analyzers.
- Finally, the lexical entry contains a list of possible *attributes* and *values*. In our example, the attributes and values are called via templates. If they were stated directly, they would look as in (13), which is the expansion of the noun template used above in (12).

(13)   ($\uparrow$PRED)='FOO'
       ($\uparrow$PERS)=3.

11.4.3 Interaction between Lexical Entries

The possibility of multiple lexicons brings up the issue of what happens if a given word appears in more than one lexicon (e.g., "water, N" in the noun lexicon, and "water, V" in the verb lexicon). The XLE environment provides detailed notation for manipulating lexical entries. In this section we describe how the lexicons as a whole, and lexical items individually, may interact within XLE.

In the configuration file of the grammar, the lexicons are listed in order; each lexicon overrides information in the previous lexicon(s). Consider what can happen if the first lexicon has the entry in (14) for the word 'foo', and a subsequent lexicon has the entry in (15).

(14)   foo   N   XLE   @(NOUN FOO);
            V   XLE   @(VERB FOO);
            P   XLE   @(PREP FOO).

(15)   foo   A   XLE   @(ADJ FOO).

If nothing else is stated, the entry for the headword 'foo' in (15) will replace that of the earlier entry in (14). Thus, (15) will be the *effective entry* for 'foo'.

However, this may not be the effect we want. In fact, it most often is not: additional information in further lexicons is more often intended to augment, rather than replace, the information that has already been encoded. Upon much feedback of this kind by the grammar writers, the implementation of XLE provides more flexibility with respect to the interaction of lexical entries.

The ETC and ONLY features, for example, control the interaction of entire lexical entries. So, in order to achieve the effect that the adjective entry of 'foo' in (15) should be added to the previous entry in (14), the ETC feature is added to (15). This is shown in (16).

(16)   foo   A   XLE   @(ADJ FOO);
               ETC.

The effective entry for 'foo' will now be as in (17).

(17)   foo   N   XLE   @(NOUN FOO);
            V   XLE   @(VERB FOO);
            P   XLE   @(PREP FOO);
            A   XLE   @(ADJ FOO).

On the other hand, if a particular entry is the only possible entry for a given item, then the ONLY feature is added to the lexical entry.

In addition to the ETC and ONLY notation, which apply to whole entries, there are four operators that allow the grammar writer to manipulate subentries. These are '+', '−', '!', and '='. The operators are placed in front of a subentry, as shown in (18). The '+' adds a new subentry. The '!' replaces an existing subentry. The '=' retains an earlier subentry, while the '−' deletes it.

(18)   a.   foo   !N   XLE   @(NOUN FOO);

                  −P

                  +A   XLE   @(ADJ FOO);

                  ETC.

       b.   foo   =P;

                  +A   XLE   @(ADJ FOO);

                  ONLY.

Note that, as shown in (18), both ETC and ONLY can be combined with each of the four subentry operators to achieve different effects. For example, placing ETC as the final subentry in a later lexicon results in retaining all previous subentries, unless they are explicitly removed with the '−' operator. Placing ONLY as the final subentry in a later lexicon will remove all earlier subentries unless they are explicitly retained with the '=' operator. For example, consider (18a, b) as possible entries for 'foo' in a later lexicon (the earlier lexicon entry continues to be (12)). Note that if one subentry has an operator, all of them must be preceded by an operator.

With (18a) in the later lexicon, the effective entry for 'foo' will be (19a). With (18b) in the later lexicon, it will be (19b). In (19a), the N entry has been replaced by the one in the later lexicon, the P entry has been deleted, and a new entry has been added. In (18b), only the P entry from the earlier lexicon has been retained, while the A entry has been added:

(19)   a.   foo   N   XLE   @(NOUN FOO);

                  V   XLE   @(VERB FOO);

                  A   XLE   @(ADJ FOO).

       b.   foo   P   XLE   @(PREP FOO);

                  A   XLE   @(ADJ FOO).

These tools for manipulating lexical entries are extremely useful when several lexicons are being maintained for different purposes. For example, they allow modification of the effective entries of a core lexicon without having to modify that lexicon directly. Thus, modifications specific to a particular application may be made without having to modify the core entries.

11.5 The Chart Parser

Having discussed the structure and interaction of the lexicons, we now turn to the rules. At the heart of XLE is an efficient unification-based parser based on "contexted unification" (Maxwell and Kaplan 1991). This parser is implemented in C and uses c-structure rules written by grammar writers as a context-free backbone over which the constraints on f-structure (and the other projections implemented within ParGram) are solved on the basis of unification. That is, in order for something to unify, constraints that were stated over certain features must be satisfied, and functional equations must be solved.

This part of the engineering behind the grammar development effort was never modified by the grammar writers: it belongs squarely in the domain of the developers of the XLE platform. As such, we do not discuss this issue here any further, but refer the reader to Maxwell and Kaplan 1991, Maxwell and Kaplan 1993, and the references therein.[4]

The notation and use of the various c-structure rules does not differ notably from the format standardly used in LFG. Some convenient notation for the encoding of generalizations and better grammar maintenance was provided by the implementers. Examples of such notation are discussed in Chapter 13. For a detailed description of the notation used within XLE, see the Grammar Writer's Workbench (Kaplan and Maxwell 1996).

11.6 Generation and Machine Translation

As mentioned in the introduction to this chapter, XLE also provides a generation facility (Kay 1996, Shemtov 1997) which takes Prolog representations of the f-structures as inputs and generates sentence strings. This generation can be done using the same grammar and lexicons that are used for parsing, although some changes usually turn out to be desirable. For example, adverbial clauses can be parsed in a number of positions in the clause, some of which are not suitable for generation: in the English grammar *when* clauses and other clausal adverbs can be parsed when they appear between the subject and the verb, as in *This light, when blinking rapidly, indicates a fault.* The English generator, however, does not allow this placement. Similar problems arise with the tokenizers and morphological analyzers when generation is considered. For instance, tokenizers often take arbitrary white space and turn it into a single space for purposes of canonicalization. Run in the generation direction, this can produce an unbounded amount of ambiguity about how

---

[4]Both of these articles, as well as a number of other papers touching upon this issue, can also be found in Dalrymple, Kaplan, Maxwell and Zaenen 1995.

much white space is in the strings produced by the generator. To deal with this, XLE allows parser and generator specific tokenizers and morphological analyzers. Also, the generation grammar should generally be more constrained than the parsing grammar, since it is often necessary in interest of robustness (see section 14.1) to parse things that one would not want to generate. XLE supports this by having a separate optimality ranking (see section 14.1.3) in the grammar for generation. Thus, one can add "parse-only" optimality marks to the grammar that are used for parsing but ignored during generation.

An interesting use of the generator is as a testing tool for the parsing grammar. When designing testsuites (section 14.2), it is difficult to think of all the possible ungrammatical sentences which the grammar should not parse. As such, the grammar will often allow certain ungrammatical constructions which the grammar writer is unaware of and never intended. These surface when using the generator since XLE has no preconceptions concerning what to test for. For example, extensive testing of the form and order of auxiliaries in English was conducted without the generator and the system appeared to be parsing all and only corrert sequences. However, upon using the generator it was discovered that several ungrammatical combinations were allowed by the grammar. Once identified, these analyses could then be blocked. Thus, the generator can be used as an additional tool for writing constrained grammars.

Since XLE has both a parser and a generator, it is possible to use the system for translation. The translation process fundamentally involves parsing a sentence in one language (the source language), transferring the resulting f-structure to an f-structure in another language (the target language), and then generating from the new f-structure. The process follows the following sequence, in more detail. First the source sentence must be parsed by the relevant grammar. The packed f-structure is then stored as a Prolog file. A set of ordered transfer rules operate on this file, making the required changes to the structure.[5] The transfer rules are hand encoded for a particular language pair so that there is a specific task of writing transfer rules, as there is of writing the grammars. As with grammar writing, the system provides a number of features to aid in this process, such as the use of macros and templates. The result of applying the transfer rules to the f-structure is a new f-structure. This new f-structure is then used as input to the generator of the target language, producing the desired translations.

---

[5]For a shake-and-bake type approach to transfer based on these same packed f-structure representations see Emele and Dorna 1998

12

Finite-State Technology

Finite-state technology has theoretical and practical advantages. The theoretical advantage is that finite-state machines are well understood mathematical entities, with wellknown properties. Finite-state transducers can be composed, intersected or unioned with one another. For example, a transducer which encodes spelling alternations (such as using unaccented characters) can be composed with a transducer which encodes a lexicon. The resulting transducer then allows a different kind of access to a single lexical source. The practical advantage is that the finite-state rules can be efficiently compiled into a passive data-structure, namely a transducer, which possesses the properties of the original rule system. A transducer is a finite-state machine which consumes input while producing output: traversing the data structure transforms the input. These transducers incorporate the context in which the transformations take place, eliminating the need for specifying programming decisions in some type of programming language, and making the natural language processing relatively platform-independent.

12.1 Preprocessing

Certain processing difficulties can be resolved at an early stage, before attempting a parse with a full grammar. Preprocessing can greatly simplify the task of the parser with respect to multiword expressions, or other parts of the grammar which are assembled according to a certain pattern, such as time expressions (e.g., *Monday morning*) or titles (e.g., *Frau Professor Doktor Schmidt*).

In the ParGram project, multiword expressions are dealt with via finite-state preprocessing, as are time expressions (this was limited to the French team). The preprocessing is accomplished in two main stages: tokenization and morphological analysis. Both stages are performed by finite-state lexical transducers. In the next two sections, we first describe our approach with respect to multiword expressions (Breidt, Segond and Valetto 1996, Segond and Tapanainen 1995) and then move on to time expressions.

12.2 Multiword Expressions

Recognizing multiword expressions and passing them on to the parser as single tokens generally reduces parsing ambiguity, allows for more perspicuity in the structure of analyses, and reduces parsing time. One difficulty in judging the effectiveness of preproccessing is the question of what exactly constitutes a multiword. There are some strings of words which may appear to be multiwords, but which the parser needs to access individually in order to provide the right syntactic analysis.

As a general rule, we identified multiwords as those groups of separate morphological words which form a unit at the functional level. Some examples are given in (1), together with the syntactic category they are identified as.[1]

(1) a. fast forward (V), cut off (N), far away (A)

    b. afin que 'so that' (CONJsubj), tr/min 'turns/minute' (N), au fur et à mesure 'gradually as X proceeds' (CONJ) (French)

    c. als auch 'as well as' (CONJ), wie folgt 'as in the following' (ADV) (German)

Although the finite-state morphological analyzer registers the multiword expression in terms of its individual elements, the multiwords are represented as single items at the level of f-structure and c-structure.

An additional advantage of this treatment is that the multiword is usually composed of parts which would not yield the desired surface c-structure category according to the independently motivated rules of the language. Take the English multiword *fast forward* in (1a) as an example. On its own, *fast* can be either an adverb or an adjective, while *forward* is a preposition. These two categories do not productively combine to form verbs in English. That is, there is no rule in the English grammar of the form V ⟶ADJ P or V ⟶ADV P since neither of these is a productive way of forming verbs. Nevertheless, *fast forward* functions as a verb and is thus best treated as a multiword expression.

12.2.1 Technical Terms

Technical terms such as *warning light* or *hydraulic oil filter* are further candidates for multiword treatment. These are not necessarily unproductive expressions, as was the case with the multiwords above. Nev-

---

[1]CONJsubj stands for subordinating conjunction, while CONJ indicates a conjunction which introduces an adjunct.

ertheless, there is good reason for treating them as single tokens since they tend to be used as fixed expressions or names in technical texts.

Precisely because they are used like fixed expressions, technical terms can be easily and successfully extracted from a technical text by partially or fully automated methods (see Brun 1998 with respect to the French experiment). This first stage of extracting terminology from a corpus (in our case the tractor manual) results in a list of items which can then be turned into a lexicon of multiword items.

The extraction within ParGram with respect to the tractor manual was done as follows. Because we had parallel aligned English-French-German texts at our disposal, we used the English translation to decide when a potential candidate was a technical term. The terminology we were dealing with consisted mainly of nouns. To perform the extraction task, we used a tagger to disambiguate the French text (Chanod and Tapanainen 1995), and then extracted the syntactic patterns, N P N, N N, N A, A N, which are good candidates to be technical terms. These candidates were considered as terms when the corresponding English translation formed a unit, or when their translation differed from a word to word translation. Some candidates which passed these tests and were therefore extracted are shown in (2).

(2) vitesses rampantes (gears creeping) 'creepers'
boîte de vitesse (box of gear) 'gearbox'
arbre de transmission (tree of transmission) 'drive shaft'
tableau de bord (table of edge) 'instrument panel'

Once the terminology was extracted, a tokenizer was built which split the input string into tokens using the list of extracted multiwords (Grefenstette and Tapanainen 1994, Ait-Mokhtar 1997). A tokenizer can be set up to provide only the multiword expression analysis of a string (deterministic tokenization), or it can provide both the multiword expression analysis and the canonical one in which each element of the multiword is returned as a separate token (nondeterministic tokenization).

Experience has shown that the first approach is often best in situations in which there is a constrained corpus, such as a technical text, or for words which have no possible canonical (nonmultiword) parse. The second approach is better in the general case where both parses are likely to be encountered. For example, the French conjunction *bien que* can be considered a multiword expression; however, the string *bien que* is also found in situations where *bien* is an independent noun while *que* is a complementizer. In (3a) *bien que* as one two-word unit is clearly wrong; instead *bien* is a noun and *que* is a relative pronoun (the multiword expression use is shown in (3b)).

(3) a. Jean me dit   tout le   bien que Pierre pense de Paul.
       Jean me tells all   the good that Pierre thinks of Paul
       'Jean tells me all the good that Pierre thinks about Paul.'
       (French)

   b. Jean écoute silencieusement bien qu' il ne soit pas
      Jean listens quietly   although he not is   NEG
      d'accord   avec Paul.
      agreement with Paul
      'Jean listens quietly although he completely disagrees with
      Paul.' (French)

Due to the occurrence of such ambiguities in our corpus, we built
a nondeterministic tokenizer within ParGram. The tokenization is performed by applying finite-state transducers on the input string. The Xerox two-level finite-state morphological analyzers were already discussed
in section 11.3.2. In order to provide the reader with a better idea of
how they function, we here go through some examples in detail.

For example, take the sentence in (4). Applying the finite-state transducer to this input results in the following tokenization, where the token
boundary is signaled by the @ sign.

(4) Le tracteur est à l'arrêt.
    the tractor is at the stop
    'The tractor is stationary.' (French)
    Le@tracteur@est@à@l'@arrêt@.@

In this particular case, each word is a token. But several words can
be a unit, as is the case for technical terms. Examples (5) and (6) show
instances of tokenization in which technical terms are treated as units.

(5) La boîte de vitesse est en deux sections.
    the box of speed is in two sections
    'The gearbox is in two sections.' (French)
    La@boîte de vitesse@est@en@deux@sections@.@

(6) Ce levier engage l'arbre de transmission.
    this lever engages the tree of transmission
    'This lever engages the drive shaft.' (French)
    Ce@levier@engage@l'@arbre de transmission@.@

Tokenization takes place in two logical steps. First, the basic transducer splits the sentence into a sequence of single words. Then a second
transducer containing a list of multiword expressions is applied. It rec-
ognizes these expressions and marks them as units. When more than one

expression in the list matches the input, the longest matching expression is marked. We included all the extracted technical terms and their morphological variations in this last transducer, so that the multiwords could be analyzed as single tokens later in the process.

The next step is to associate these multiword units with a morphological analysis in the cases where one is needed. One type of multiword which interacts with morphological analysis is represented by French compounds. These compounds have to be integrated into the morphological analyzer because they may be inflected according to number, as shown in (7). In the tractor corpus, we identified two kinds of morphological variations: either the first part of the compound may be inflected, or both parts of the compounds may be inflected.

(7) • The **first** part varies in **number**:
   gyrophare de toit, gyrophares de toit 'roof flashing beacon(s)'
   régime moteur, régimes moteur 'engine speed(s)'
   • **Both** parts vary in **number**:
   roue motrice, roues motrices 'wheel drive'

This is of course not general for French compounds; there are other patterns of morphological inflection. However, this pattern is reliable for the technical manual we were dealing with. Other inflectional schemes and exceptions can be easily added to the regular grammar as needed (see Quint 1997 and Karttunen, Kaplan and Zaenen 1992 for further discussion).

A cascade of regular rules is applied to the different parts of the compound in order to build the morphological analysis of the whole compound. For example, *roue motrice* is marked with the diacritic +DPL (double plural). A first rule is then applied which copies the morphological tags from the end to the middle if the diacritic is present in the right context:

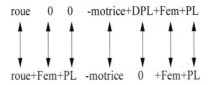

FIGURE 1 Rule 1

A second rule is applied to the output of the preceding one and "realizes" the tags on the surface.

The composition of these two layers gives us the direct mapping be-

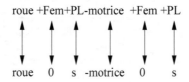

roue +Fem+PL-motrice +Fem +PL

roue   0   s -motrice   0   s

FIGURE 2   Rule 2

tween surface inflected forms and morphological analysis. The same types of rules are used when only the first part of the compound varies, but in this case the second rule deletes the tags of the second word.

The two morphological analyzers for the two variations in agreement marking are unioned into the basic morphological analyzer for French. The result is a transducer that completes the input preprocessing after tokenization has been accomplished. An example of compound analysis is given in (8).

(8) a. > roues motrices
         roue motrice+Fem+PL+Noun

     b. > régimes moteur
         régime moteur+Masc+PL+Noun

This resulting morphological analysis allows multiword terms to be treated as regular nouns by the parser. Parsing constraints on agreement remain valid, for example for relative or adjectival attachment, and nothing special needs to be done within the parser.

12.2.2   Idiomatic expressions

In addition to the simple multiword expressions and to the technical terms which form a word level category, multiword expressions may also include phrasal idioms, as in (9) (see Gross 1975, Nunberg et al. 1994, and Cacciari and Tabossi 1993 on idioms).

(9) a. kick the bucket 'die'
     b. let the cat out of the bag 'tell a secret'
     c. sucrer les fraises 'to be doddery' (French)
     d. ins Gras beißen 'to die' (German)

Phrasal idioms differ from simple multiword expressions in that their syntactic structure is formed according to canonical syntactic principles in the language. The meaning of phrasal idioms, however, is not compositional. For example, the French phrasal idiom *sucrer les fraises* in (9c) is a wellformed VP with a verb *sucrer* followed by an object noun phrase *les fraises*; however, its meaning is "to be doddery," and not the literal translation "to sweeten strawberries." A preprocessor which identifies phrasal idioms as a whole and associates them with their idiosyncratic meanings would therefore be desirable.

However, a difficult problem arises with respect to nonadjacent phrasal idioms. Canonical multiwords have all their subparts adjacent; this allows multiword expressions to be easily recognized. Some phrasal idioms, however, can undergo syntactic operations such as passivization or scrambling (a case in point is the German (9d)). Within ParGram, the problem of phrasal idioms remains to be resolved.

12.3   Time expressions

The application of the finite-state technology with regard to multiwords can be expanded further to expressions which are part of the general syntax, but which at the same time display idiosyncratic syntactic behavior. This is the case of time expressions such as *Monday morning, once every two weeks*, etc. These expressions are peculiar in that they undergo only certain kinds of variation and often behave like adverbs despite their nominal syntax.

Low level methods such as finite-state rules return relatively good results for these (almost fixed) types of expressions. Finite-state local grammars for date-time expressions have been built and experimented with by the French team for use in a preprocessing stage. These analyze *Monday morning* as one unit in the tokenizer, but also simultaneously allow access to the decomposed parts via the morphological analyzer, in a method similar to the one sketched for the French compounds above.

Our conclusion from the various experiments and actual integrations into the grammar is that using different tokenizers and morphological analyzers at a preprocessing stage considerably simplifies the grammars and, as a result, makes them more maintainable.

12.4   Guessers and Normalizers

A normalizer and a guesser have also been integrated into XLE. A normalizer is a component that deals with case conversion, accentuation, and punctuation, among other things helping to identify and correct spelling mistakes or typing errors. For instance, if a French word appears in a title phrase in capital letters and without accents, the normalizer puts the accents back in so that the morphology and hence the LFG lexicon can recognize the word. The header in (10a), for example, cannot be recognized as relating to the base forms in (10b), since there are unexpected capital letters, and missing accents over two of the "e"s which have been removed as part of the capitalization process.

(10) a. EQUIPEMENT SUPPLEMENTAIRE
          equipment   additional
          'additional equipment' (French)
      b. équipement supplémentaire

Without a normalizer to turn form (10a) into form (10b), the grammar cannot recognize the words or parse the header.

A guesser deals with unknown words after the normalizer has done its work. As discussed in section 11.3.2.3, there is a way of incorporating into the grammar words which are not in the LFG lexicon. If the words are known by the morphology, they can be incorporated into the grammar in a constrained manner. However, if they are not known to the morphology, the unknown words will not be provided with morphological tags, making it difficult to incorporate them into the grammar in a productive fashion. A guesser uses morphological tools to guess the part of speech of a word and provides the appropriate tags. For example, an unknown English word ending in *-tion* is likely to be a noun, while one ending in *-ate* is likely to be a verb.

12.5   Part of Speech Preprocessing

Part of speech (POS) ambiguity often leads to analyses that are correct, but which are bizarre in a given context. As such, the parses are still desired, but one will be preferred in a given context. An example is furnished by the following two analyses for the sentence in (11).

(11) a. [The oil filters]$_{NP}$ [light.]$_{VP}$
      b. [The oil]$_{NP}$ [filters light.]$_{VP}$

Now, if the parser is to be applied to a text (technical or otherwise) in which the potential ambiguity never occurs, it would be ideal to never have to consider the ambiguity at all with respect to this text.

One way to do this is to use a POS tagger at a preprocessing stage, which for example would tag the sentence by assigning a POS to each lexical item (Kupiec 1992) and using the disambiguated result as input to the grammar. The drawback of this method is that, while large parsers perform nicely at the word level (97% success) they perform poorly at a sentence level (70% success).

The ambiguity can also be filtered out at the level of the lexicon, (Segond and Copperman 1999), rather than at the level of the parser. The aim is to produce a filtered lexicon out of the larger, standard one. The general idea is as follows. The tagged corpus is sorted into <word, POS> pairs which are run through the morphological analyzer, yielding <base form, POS> pairs. Once duplicates are eliminated, pairs with the same base form are combined to give <base form, POS-list> pairs. Then each entry in the lexicon is compared with the list derived from the corpus and parts of speech which do not occur in the corpus are eliminated.

13

Modularity, Maintainability and Transparency

Our previous discussion of the XLE architecture (Chapter 11) and the interaction of the LFG lexicons with finite-state morphological analyzers and phrase structure rules should have made it clear that modularity is at the heart of our grammar development effort. Given that the projection architecture of LFG as described in the introduction is also founded on the principle of modularity, this is not surprising.

On the other hand, too much modularity can also work against transparency: rules may be more difficult to formulate (and understand) because they access different modules of the grammar, and errors may become more difficult to track down, as they could spring from various different sources. Alternatively, therefore, one could decide to follow an approach similar to that of HPSG, which is to encode the different types of linguistic information within one level of representation and extend this design decision to the grammar implementation so that everything is dealt with within one and the same module.

However, it is clear from general programming experience that a modular approach to software design is generally preferable (see Knuth 1992 on the concept of *structured programming*), as it furthers the maintainability and transparency of the product. Moreover, with respect to grammar design in particular, packing the phrase structure analysis and the unification-based analysis into the same module increases the complexity of the parsing problem. Most implementations of HPSG grammars therefore realize a separate context-free backbone for the phrase structure analysis (as is done in LFG), thus modularizing the grammar (Carpenter 1992, Penn 1993).

Without taking this discussion any further, it seems fair to conclude that some degree of modularity is desirable in the design of a grammar.

The question of exactly how much modularity is beneficial, and in what form, remains to be determined.[1] This chapter is therefore intended as a contribution to the general discussion on modularity, maintainability and transparency. It reports some of the experiences gathered within our grammar development effort. In particular, we discuss two differing perspectives on modularity: one involves the "physical" components of a grammar, such as lexicon and rule files; the other involves the formal means of capturing linguistic generalizations.

13.1 One Grammar, Many Cooks

The three ParGram sites PARC (English), XRCE (French) and IMS (German) all employed differing strategies with respect to how the grammar writers accessed the grammar. At the English site, the grammar writers arranged their schedules in complementary distribution so that the grammar was never worked on by more than one person. At the French site, there was only one main grammar writer: the other people associated with the grammar development process would input ideas or work on lexicon development as a separate module (see section 14.1.1). It was only at the German site that more than one person would be working on the grammar at any given time. This led to multiple copies of the grammar, none of which necessarily remained at the same level of development. This in turn led to major integration problems.

From the early days of painful manual integration and checking, the German team has now progressed to a version control method by using the Unix CVS facility, which is now also used by the French and English groups. Under this approach, only one official version of the grammar exists. Individual grammar writers may check-out copies of the grammar and then check-in changes or additions. The checked-in modules are automatically vetted for compatibility. This method of version control prompted a greater modularization of the rules: the rules for NPs, APs, VPs, etc. are stored in separate files and are coded slightly differently so as to support the greater modularization.

The lexicon, however, is distributed across several files in all of the grammars (as already discussed in Chapter 11). The structure of the distribution follows the same logic at each of the sites:

---

[1] As just one example of the ongoing discussion, note that the topic of modularity was a recurring theme of the 1996 Grammar Engineering Workshop organized by Gregor Erbach, Melanie Siegel, and Hans Uszkoreit in Prague.

1. A small file contains the closed class items and exceptional entries.
2. One file contains the technical terminology or special entries needed for the text at hand. If the text is a specific application like the tractor manual, then this lexicon contains items extracted specifically from that text. If the text to be parsed is of a more general nature, such as a newspaper text, no specialized file is included.
3. One or more large files with semi-automatically generated lexical entries are always included.

This modular division developed naturally within the grammars, as it reflects the different resources and applications that went into the creation of the lexicons. The small file of closed class items contains the core entries that cannot be done without. These entries are hand-coded. The technical terminology, on the other hand, is application-specific and can be extracted semi-automatically from the technical text.

The larger files reflect open class items such as nouns, verbs, and adjectives, which are needed for the parsing of large corpora of a general type (e.g., newspaper texts). These were created through the semi-automatic extraction of subcategorization frames, as is detailed in section 14.1.1.

Another effort at modularization of file systems and storage did not grow naturally out of the development, but came about because of a design decision that was aimed at ensuring transparency across the three parallel grammars. In an effort to encode the fact that some rules and generalizations were in fact valid in all of the ParGram grammars, the grammar writers agreed on a naming convention by which these identical rules and generalizations could be identified in each of the three grammars. That is, generalizations as to how the passive works, or how transitive verbs differ from intransitive verbs, were captured by giving the same name to the relevant lexical rule (section 13.2.3) or template (section 13.2.1) in each of the grammars, and by ensuring that the same material was contained by these rules and templates in each of the grammars.

In effect, however, these rules and templates could easily be experimented with and changed by each individual grammar writer without any consequences for the other grammars. This brought up the problem of continued maintenance and transparency of the three ParGram grammars with respect to one another. It was therefore decided to experiment with locating crosslinguistically valid rules and templates in a single file that would be shared across grammars. That is, the same file containing crosslinguistic generalizations is included as input to every grammar. If a grammar writer now wanted to change an item in this file (for example, if they thought they had come up with a better analysis of the passive), they would first have to check on the consequences for the other grammars, thus ensuring some transparency in the encoding, and not just the output (the analyses presented in Part I) across the three parallel grammars.

13.2 Encoding Generalizations

Another aspect of modularity involves the formal means of capturing linguistic generalizations within a given grammar. That is, if all transitive verbs of a language always share a certain set of properties, then it would be ideal to encode this in a way which allows the grammar writer to generalize over that class of items. This is important with respect to two considerations. For one, it ensures greater transparency as the grammar writer can easily identify the class of items that have something in common. For another, it ensures better maintainability: if the analysis for that class of items changes (for example, a hitherto unnoticed property of transitive verbs is discovered and needs to be added, or the name of a feature changes and needs to be changed in the entries of all transitive verbs) then the grammar writer need only make the change in one place, rather than track down each item of that class and make the change for each item individually.

Examples of this type of modularization are detailed in the next section with respect to the use of templates, complex categories, and lexical rules.

13.2.1 Templates

Templates are defined in a special section of the grammar file and are called mainly from the lexicon. However, rules can also call templates. The benefits of calling templates in the rules are the same as calling them in the lexicon: they allow generalizations to be captured and changes to be made only once, to the template itself.

Formally, templates are macros in that they provide the grammar writer with a short-hand definition of a set of information. However, beyond being just a name for a collection of information, templates are also defined as functions within XLE. This means that they can take arguments and substitute the arguments for variables in the definition of the template.

13.2.1.1 The Lexicon

Templates are meant to express linguistic generalizations. Consider the simple templates in (1). The material before the equal sign, i.e., TENSE(_P) defines the name of the template and the number of arguments (if any). The @ sign precedes the call of a template, as illustrated in (1b) for the template ASSIGN-CASE. This template is defined in (1c) and takes two arguments (see Maxwell and Kaplan 1996 for details on the notation and the formal power of templates).

(1) a.   TENSE(_P)   =   (↑TNS-ASP TENSE) = _P
          (↑FIN) = +.

    b.   FIN(_T)   =   @(TENSE _T)
          @(ASSIGN-CASE SUBJ NOM).

    c.   ASSIGN-CASE(_GF _C)   =   (↑_GF CASE) = _C.

The template in (1a) expresses the generalization that when a clause includes a specification for tense, then it is also finite. This is a true generalization for languages like German, English, and French, but is not necessarily true for other languages (e.g., Japanese). This template takes one argument: a specification of the type of tense involved. So regardless of whether a verb marks present, past, or future tense, this same template can be used.

The template in (1b) expresses another linguistic generalization. Once again, it has to do with tense and finiteness, but looks at things the other way around. In this case, a template FIN is defined, which again takes a tense specification as an argument, but which also specifies that the subject must be marked as nominative. Again, this template captures a generalization that in a finite clause the subject must be nominative. This is true for English, French and German (for German a provision must be added for subjectless clauses), but it does not hold for other languages such as Urdu/Hindi or Icelandic, which may have dative or other kinds of subjects.

Templates are especially useful for describing verb subcategorization and generalizations over verb classes. The lexicons are organized so that each verb subcategorization schema corresponds to a template. These have varying degrees of complexity, depending on issues such as case marking (German), extraction (English), clitic climbing (French), etc. We here illustrate two simple templates for basic intransitive and transitive verbs.

(2) a.   INTRANS(_P)   =   (↑PRED) = '_P<(↑SUBJ)>'
          @NOPASS.

    b.   TRANS(_P)   =   @(PASS (↑PRED) = '_P<(↑SUBJ)(↑OBJ)>').

The templates in (2) specify subcategorization frames. The INTRANS template calls another template that ensures that no passivization will take place, while the subcategorization frame of the TRANS template is fed through a lexical rule that allows for passivization (see section 13.2.3

on lexical rules).

The examples above also demonstrate that templates can call other templates. They can thus be seen as encoding a type of inheritance hierarchy. The concept of an inheritance-hierarchy is used explicitly in HPSG (Pollard and Sag 1987), for example. In our approach, the concept is used more implicitly via a hierarchy of templates. Besides this, there is one other major difference in the approaches: HPSG inheritance-hierarchies tend to be complex and deeply nested; by comparison our template hierarchies are quite flat because information about morphological relatedness is primarily taken care of by the finite-state morphological analyzer and the sublexical rules.

13.2.1.2 Phrase Structure Rules

As with templates called from the lexicon, templates called from rules can also have arguments, allowing for flexibility in the writing of phrase structure rules. For example, there are many places in the English grammar where a null pronoun must be supplied to ensure that the analysis will be wellformed. One such situation is anaphoric control in nonfinite complements (see section 3.3.5 and Bresnan 1982a for some discussion). Here the complement is closed, but does not have an overt subject pronoun. In order to satisfy the subject condition that applies in English, a null subject pronoun must be supplied.

This is done as sketched in (3). A phrase structure rule calls the rule for an infinitive (nonfinite) VP and annotates it with the functional equations bundled together in the macro NULL-PRON. This macro specifies that the predicate of the pronoun be PRO and that the PRON-TYPE be NULL. The macro also takes an argument, namely the grammatical function path that fits the particular situation at hand. Because this path may vary from rule to rule, a more compact coding of the rules is enabled by allowing the path to be a variable.

(3) a. ...
     VPinf: $(\uparrow\text{COMP})=\downarrow$
             @(NULL-PRON $(\downarrow\text{SUBJ})$)
     ...

    b.   NULL-PRON(_PATH) =   (_PATH PRED)='PRO'
                              (_PATH PRON-TYPE)=NULL.

Furthermore, as the features and analysis of null pronominals may change during grammar development, the use of macros guarantees that the relevant changes only need to be made in the macro.

Another example of the use of macros comes from the German grammar. In this case, a number of disjunctions on the right-hand side of a phrase structure rule are bundled together, rather than just the functional annotations, as was the case in (3). As German has relatively free word order, the rules which introduce core arguments and adjuncts of predicates (both verbs and adjectives) are called in numerous places. This wide distribution of essentially the same set of rules over different parts of the grammar poses a maintenance problem: it is easy to realize that an argument must be defined differently or that another condition must be added in one part of the grammar, without realizing that this change must also be made in another part of the grammar. Even if the grammar writer realizes that the same change must be made in other parts of the grammar, it is easy to miss one of the instances, especially as the grammar grows.

Thus, despite all good intentions, the grammar tends to become internally inconsistent quite quickly. The use of macros is one way of ensuring that this problem does not arise. Consider the macro in (4). It disjunctively introduces object arguments, prepositional phrases, and predicative adjectival arguments such as *red* in *The tractor is red.*

(4) ADJ-ARGS = { NP: $(\uparrow\{$ OBJ$|$OBJ2$\})=\downarrow$
     |PP: $\{$ $(\uparrow$OBL$)=\downarrow$
          $|\downarrow\in(\uparrow$ADJUNCT$)$ $\}$
     |AP: $(\uparrow$PREDLINK$)=\downarrow$
          $(\downarrow$ATYPE$)$ $=_c$ PREDICATIVE$\}$.

Whenever this macro is called, it is as if the rules on the right-hand side of the macro were substituted in at the place of the call in the phrase structure rule. The macro thus encodes the linguistic generalization that this particular set of arguments and adjuncts distributes similarly in German.

A slightly different example of this is coordination (Chapter 8) in which the same basic schema is used for coordinating several different c-structure categories. The coordination macro in (5) expresses the general linguistic fact that constituent coordination is composed of constituents of the same category (CAT) separated by a comma or a conjunction.

(5) SCCOORD(CAT) = CAT: $\downarrow\in$ $\uparrow$;
     ([COMMA
     CAT: $\downarrow\in$ $\uparrow$]+
     (COMMA))
     CONJ: $\uparrow=\downarrow$
     CAT: $\downarrow\in$ $\uparrow$.

This macro is called from a rule as in (6) and expands into (7).

(6) sadj ⟶ { s
             |@(SCCOORD sadj)}.

(7) sadj ⟶ { s
             | sadj: ↓∈ ↑;
             ([COMMA
             sadj: ↓∈ ↑]+
             (COMMA))
             CONJ: ↑=↓
             sadj: ↓∈ ↑}.

13.2.2 Complex Categories

Another method of expressing generalizations is the use of *complex categories*. These are phrase structure categories which take arguments, just as templates do. The argument instantiates a variable in the right hand side of the rule.

A simplified example from the German grammar is given in (8). This is a rule which parametrizes across different types of NPs: standard, interrogative and relative NPs. The effect that is being illustrated here is that in German some standard NPs like proper names (*Jonas*) or mass nouns (e.g., *Wasser* 'water') may appear without a determiner. Interrogative and relative NPs, on the other hand, may never appear without a determiner. The rule for the NP in (8) allows the type of the NP to be set via the variable *type*. When the value of the variable is instantiated as *std*, the rule expands to the option in (9a) to allow a standard type of NP with an optional determiner. On the other hand, when the variable is instantiated as *int*, the NP is marked as being of the type interrogative and the determiner is obligatory, as shown in (9b). An instantiation with *rel* works exactly the same way as in (9b) for the purposes of our example. However, with respect to the larger grammar, the identification of an NP as interrogative vs. relative will have consequences in other parts of the grammar.

(8) NP[_type] ⟶ { (D[_type]: _type = std)
                   | D[_type]: { _type = int | _type = rel } }
                   NPap.

(9) a. NP[std] ⟶ (D[std]) NPap.
     b. NP[int] ⟶ D[int] NPap.

The advantage of such parametrization over rules via the use of complex categories is that again large parts of rules can be shared across types of constructions that differ systematically in one respect, but which work in essentially the same way in other respects. In our simplified example, the only shared part is the expansion into an NPap (an NP which contains adjectives). However, if this shared rule should require a large swath of functional annotations, or if the shared part were actually a number of different types of rules, then the gain is already considerable.

In addition, the variables can be specified to hold of a whole family of rules. For example, before the introduction of complex categories into the German grammar, a family of rules existed for interrogative NPs. These rules shared very many characteristics with the family of rules that existed to deal with relative NPs, but as the specifications for each type of NP needed to differ just slightly at crucial points, no systematic sharing of rules across these families was possible. The introduction of complex categories, on the other hand, allowed the collapse of these distinct families of rules into just one set of rules that is parametrized over by the setting of the *type* variable to *int* or *rel*. Thus, the use of complex categories provides another means of expressing generalizations across structures. The modularization of the rules furthermore supports the maintainability of the grammar.

13.2.3 Lexical Rules

Lexical rules have been part of the statement of generalizations within LFG from the beginning (Bresnan 1982a). These rules encode generalizations across grammatical function alternations such as passivization and the dative shift. The lexical rule for passivization as it appears within our grammars is shown in (10).[2] As can be seen from the notation, within XLE lexical rules are treated as a kind of template.

(10)   PASS(SCHEMATA) =   { SCHEMATA
                           @NOPASS
                           |SCHEMATA
                           @PASSIVE
                           $(\uparrow\text{OBJ}) \longrightarrow (\uparrow\text{SUBJ})$
                           $(\uparrow\text{SUBJ}) \longrightarrow \text{NULL}\}.$

The special aspect of this template is that it takes an entire subcategorization frame as an argument (SCHEMATA). With transitive verbs, for example, it takes the predicate, the subject and the object as an argument. The template called by transitive verbs is repeated in (11).

(11)   TRANS(_P)   =   @(PASS $(\uparrow\text{PRED}) = {}'\_P{<}(\uparrow\text{SUBJ})(\uparrow\text{OBJ}){>}'$)

The PASS template allows for a disjunction: either there is a passive,

---

[2]The German grammar employs a more complex rule, due to the more complex set of possibilities with regard to impersonal passives such as *Hier wird getanzt.* 'here is danced', which are considered to be subjectless. However, the basic specifications are the same.

or there is not. If there is a passive, then it turns the object into the subject and suppresses the former subject.

Thus, templates, complex categories, and lexical rules are all used to capture linguistic generalizations, ensuring modularity and transparency in the grammars and thereby also assisting with the problem of grammar maintenance.

14

Performance

Several factors determine performance. One aspect is coverage: does the grammar parse all the sentences in question, assigning them the correct parse? A second aspect is speed: how quickly does the grammar parse what it needs to? Unfortunately there is often a trade off on these issues. If a grammar is constrained to parse a given set of sentences quickly, it is often not broad enough to parse another set of sentences, either because its lexicon is too small or because certain constructions have not been implemented. Conversely, if a grammar can parse a wide variety of sentences, it is often too complex to provide rapid parse times.

In this chapter we discuss how we grappled with these issues in our grammar development effort. We first describe the compilation of large lexicons in order to achieve as much coverage as possible, and go on to the use of optimality marks to achieve robustness in parsing without giving up on linguistic principles and weakening the generator. We then move on to issues of ambiguity and undesirable rule interactions, which tend to slow down the grammar. Finally, we describe our use of treebanks, annotated testfiles and controlled comparisons over different versions of a grammar in order to measure and improve performance.

14.1   Robustness

The notion of robustness in grammar engineering differs slightly from the notion a linguist might entertain. A linguist might consider a grammar robust if it provides an analysis for every grammatical sentence or clause and refuses to provide a parse when the sentence or clause is ungrammatical. From the point of view of grammar engineering, on the other hand, a failure to provide some kind of output is unacceptable as this means that any application depending on output from the grammar will be left floundering. A robust grammar from this perspective is therefore a grammar that never fails to return some output. If the grammar encounters a construction or a lexical item that it has not been equipped to deal with (i.e., the construction has not been implemented, or the lexical item has not been coded in one of the lexicons), then it should be able to provide a "best guess" at what the construction might be. In our grammars we have attempted to compile as large a lexicon as possible via semi-automatic extraction techniques so that the grammar will only very seldom have to stumble over a word. This is described in the next section (section 14.1.1). As described in sections 12.4 and 11.3.2.3, these large lexicons are supported by a guesser in the finite-state morphologies, which takes a best guess at unknown words.

The grammar can be similarly supported to deal with unknown constructions via statistical guessing methods or via a parser that produces coarser-grained output. This type of support has not been integrated within our grammar development effort, but some possibilities that could be envisioned within our project are discussed in section 14.1.2.

In addition to the issue of unknown lexical items or constructions, the grammar is also faced with the issue of what to do about constructions or words that have clearly been marked as ungrammatical (via a NO-GOOD constraint, for example — see section 14.1.3.2). Linguists would be happy with a result that stated: "Sorry, that was ungrammatical." because that would indicate that the grammar does not overgenerate and in fact makes the right predictions. However, if the grammar is to be used in applications, then not providing an output is often the wrong strategy. One area in which the issue can be illustrated quite clealy is machine translation. For example, take the scenario of the machine translation project Verbmobil.[1] This project aims to translate spoken language in business appointment dialogs. Leaving the thorny problem of speech recognition aside, consider some of the properties of spoken speech: there are many stops, starts and corrections, and some of the utterances may be considered ungrammatical. However, it would be extremely uncooperative for the machine translation system to "correct" the users at every turn by informing them that their output had been judged ungrammatical. Instead, the system should attempt to do as well as it can with the input, and only in extreme cases go back to the users and ask them to repeat their utterance. That is, in order to be robust, the system should return some kind of output in every case, even if it marks that output as suboptimal. In our grammars, we have implemented this strategy via the use of optimality marks, as discussed in section 14.1.3.

---

[1]Relevant publications and more information on the project can be found at http://www.dfki.uni-sb.de/verbmobil/

14.1.1 Extraction of Subcategorization Frames

The greater the coverage of a given grammar, the more likely it is to be robust in a good way, i.e., the likelihood increases that the parse is the result of careful linguistic analysis rather than being based on a best guess method. Part of ensuring large coverage (of newspaper texts, for example) is the compilation of a large lexicon. Compiling such a lexicon by hand is unrealistic.

Fortunately, manual compilation is also unnecessary as several tools have been developed that allow the semi-automatic generation of large lexicons. The German and French grammars both have large lexicons which have been incorporated into the LFG grammar. The English grammar is currently compiling a large verb lexicon based on the French and German methods.

The German verb and noun stem lexicons were produced semi-automatically (Eckle and Heid 1996, Eckle 1998) from a combination of data extraction from corpora such as machine readable and tagged newspaper texts and existing resources specifying German verb subcategorization frames such as SADAW (Baur, Oberhauser, and Netter 1994) and CELEX (Baayen, Piepenbrock, and Gulikers 1995). To give an indication of the size of the lexicons, the German verb lexicon to date consists of more than 14,000 entries.

The corresponding French lexicons are based on information extracted from the GSI-ERLI AlethDic French dictionary. AlethDic is written in SGML and contains approximately 72,000 base form entries, 5,730 of which are verbs. It encodes morphosyntactic information, subcategorization frames , and some information about basic semantics. As documented in Brazil 1997, subcategorization information was extracted from this dictionary by applying a cascade of finite-state transducers which reduced ambiguity in the dictionary by filtering out information as to mood, etc. The transducers then further subdivided the subcategorization classes specified in AlethDic into subclasses to meet the needs of the LFG grammar. Finally, in those cases where the distinctions made by AlethDic were irrelevant for the purposes of the LFG grammar, the transducers merged subcategorization specifications.

14.1.2 Statistical Methods and Chunk Parsing

Another way to tackle the robustness issue, as mentioned above, is to ensure that the grammar always produces some useful output, even if the construction being parsed is not covered by the grammar, or is ungrammatical. As Light (1996) puts it, the goal is that "Among other things, a robust system would have broad coverage and its output would degrade gracefully as inputs strayed from the area of coverage." Light's own proposal combines partial parsing strategies with underspecified semantic representations. The partial parsing strategies make use of part-of-speech taggers which operate on the basis of stochastic methods. That is, they go through a text and return their best part-of-speech guess for a given lexical item. The best taggers available to date are around 96-97% accurate.[2]

These part-of-speech taggers can then be combined with so-called shallow or partial parsing techniques, which often rely on finite-state transducers. A good example is again Light's proposal, which is based on the idea of *chunk parsing* (Abney 1991, 1996).[3] Here a cascade of finite-state transducers is given the job of locally identifying "chunks" which could correspond to an NP, PP, or even a clause. As noted in section 12.5, the general problem with such approaches when used in isolation is that the accuracy of the "best guess" for chunks greater than a word degrades to an unacceptable percentage as the accuracy of shallow parsers itself is around the 70% mark, leading to a combined degradation in performance that is unacceptable. However, when used in combination with a deep parser such as XLE and the LFG grammars presented in this book, the shallow or partial parses could be used to back up the deep parser in cases where the deep parse fails either because the construction is ungrammatical, or it is missing from the grammar.

Note that the parsers described were not designed with LFG in mind, though they could be interfaced with an LFG grammar. However, a statistically driven approach to parsing which is based directly on LFG has recently been presented (Bod and Kaplan 1998). This LFG based data-oriented parsing (LFG-DOP) technique calculates probabilities of well-formedness via a competition set, and is able to make guesses about larger, unknown structures based on information about systematic fragments of c- and f-structure analyses. In particular, it is also able to provide analyses for ungrammatical constructions such as *People eats*, where the rule for subject-verb agreement in English is violated. The analysis is based on information extracted from the separate analysis fragments for *eats* and *people*: the model arrives at a best guess of what the sentence might be intended to be, based on its experience with other sentences. Thus, this model for statistical, data-oriented parsing allows the graceful degradation advocated by Light (1996).

---

[2]Two examples of taggers are the LIKELY system employed by Light (1996) for German (Feldweg 1993) and the Xerox tagger for English (Cutting, Kupiec, Pedersen and Sibun 1992).

[3]Another shallow parser which was experimented with for French within ParGram is the finite-state parser discussed in Chanod and Tapanainen (1996, 1997).

14.1.3 Optimality Theory

An integration of the DOP-LFG parsing strategy into our grammars remains a possibility for the future. This section discusses the strategy we have already implemented within our grammars, namely the incorporation of ideas from the theoretical literature on Optimality Theory (OT) (see Prince and Smolensky 1993 on OT in general; Bresnan 1996, 1998b, 1999 on interfacing OT and syntax). This strategy does not involve statistical methods; rather, it makes use of optimality marks which allow the grammar writer to mark certain constructions or lexical items to be either less desirable, undesirable, or completely unacceptable. This is done by positing another projection, the o(ptimality)-projection , on top of the constraint system of the existing LFG grammars. The o-projection determines a preference ranking on the set of analyses for a given input sentence: a relative ranking is specified for the constraints that appear in the o-projection, and this ranking serves to determine the winner among the competing candidates. The optimality constraints are overlaid on the existing grammar and hence do not fundamentally alter the basic tenets of LFG theory.

This OT mechanism can be very effective in filtering syntactic ambiguity. A further advantage of the addition of optimality marks to the LFG architecture is that the robustness of a grammar can be increased by adding low-ranked fallback rules. Such rules can allow for the parsing of common grammatical mistakes (e.g., subject-verb agreement mistakes) and marginal constructions (e.g., misplaced adverbials). Finally, using the same grammar in parsing and generation can be facilitated by applying the OT-style preference mechanism: while a grammar must accept a wide variety of alternative syntactic structures in parsing, generation should be restricted to a subset of 'preferred' construction alternatives.

The discussion and examples that follow are drawn primarily from Frank, King, Kuhn and Maxwell 1998 and the reader is referred to this paper for more details.

14.1.3.1 Notation and Analyses

Optimality marks are explicitly introduced within the grammar as shown in (1), where a VP may take a PP as either an OBL argument or an adjunct.

$$(1) \quad \text{VP} \rightarrow \text{V} \begin{pmatrix} \text{NP} \\ (\uparrow \text{OBJ}) =\downarrow \end{pmatrix} \begin{Bmatrix} \begin{array}{c} \text{PP*} \\ (\uparrow \text{OBL }) =\downarrow \\ \text{MARK1} \in o* \\ \\ \downarrow \in (\uparrow \text{ADJUNCTS}) \\ \text{MARK2} \in o* \end{array} \end{Bmatrix}$$

The optimality marks may be called by whatever mnemonic name the grammar writer wishes. For the purposes of this example, we have simply numbered the optimality marks according to their rank. This rank is determined by an ordering as shown in (2). The optimality ranking divides the constraints into those whose satisfaction will result in a positive mark (those ranked to the left of the NEUTRAL mark) and those whose satisfaction will result in a negative mark (ranked to the right of the NEUTRAL mark). In (2), MARK1 is the most positive and MARK4 the most negative.

(2) OPTIMALITYRANKING   MARK1 MARK2 NEUTRAL MARK3 MARK4.

Applying the ordinary parsing and feature resolution algorithm to an input string produces a set of candidates which enter the competition under the given constraint ranking. The winning structure(s) will be the one(s) containing the fewest instances of the most negative mark. If this does not produce a unique candidate, the second most negative mark is counted, and so on. If all the negative marks fail to single out a candidate, for the remaining structures the positive marks are considered successively, starting from the most positive mark. In this case, the candidates with the *greatest* number of instances win.

As a concrete but simple example, take the rule in (1). For a sentence like *John waited for Mary*, this rule will produce an ambiguity: the PP may be analyzed either as an adjunct or as an OBL argument. However, in the rule, the grammar writer has marked the OBL analysis as being preferable, thus the OBL analysis is the one the grammar returns as being most optimal.

14.1.3.2   Types of Markings

In fact, the XLE implementation allows an even more differentiated treatment of optimality marks than that illustrated in the simple example above. The more differentiated treatment represents an extension of the standard OT method of comparing marks. XLE provides three types of special marks: NEUTRAL, UNGRAMMATICAL, and NOGOOD. They are ranked as shown in (3). The marks defined by the grammar writer, are interspersed between the special marks.

(3) MARK1 NEUTRAL MARK2 UNGRAMMATICAL MARK3 NOGOOD
    MARK4

To facilitate the modification of the ranking without having to edit the grammar and lexicon files, it is also possible to collect marks into an equivalence class by enclosing them in brackets. A declaration as in (4) is interpreted in such a way that MARK1 and MARK1a count as preference marks of identical strength and MARK2 is treated as equivalent to NEUTRAL, i.e., it is effectively ignored.

(4) OPTIMALITYRANKING (MARK1 MARK1a) (MARK2 NEUTRAL)
     MARK3 UNGRAMMATICAL MARK4 NOGOOD MARK5

The four types of marks (preference, dispreference, ungrammatical, and nogood) are discussed below, each one with an brief example of how it might be used in a grammar.

Preference Marks Preference marks are used when one out of two, or more, readings is preferred. For example, preference marks can be used to state a preference for the multiword analysis of technical terms: in general, when the multiword expression reading is possible, it is the preferred one. An example in which both multiword and analytic analyses are possible is shown in (5).

(5) a. The [print quality] of this printer is good.

     b. I want to [print] [quality] documents.

By marking the lexical entries of multiword expressions with a preference optimality mark, the analysis involving the multiword expression is preferred for (5a).

Dispreference Marks Dispreference marks (those below NEUTRAL and above UNGRAMMATICAL) are generally used on rare constructions that are grammatical and as such are parsed by the grammar, but are less likely to occur. The dispreference mark ensures that the construction surfaces only when no other, more optimal, analysis is possible. Consider the case of German headless NPs, as in (6).

(6) Meistens kauft die größere Firma   die kleinere.
    Mostly   buys the larger company the smaller
    'Usually, the larger company buys the smaller (one).' (German)

Sentences like this are dealt within the German grammar via a version of the NP rule which allows an NP to consist of an adjective with an optional determiner. However, this rule also permits the grammar to build such NPs in many places where they are implausible. An example of such a situation is seen in (7).

(7) Nachts fallen helle Farben auf.
at night stand bright colors out (German)

    a. [$_{NP(NOM)}$ helle Farben]
reading = 'At night, bright colors stand out.'

    b. [$_{NP(NOM)}$ helle] [$_{NP(DAT)}$ Farben]
reading = 'At night, the colors notice bright ones/bright ones strike colors.'

The reading in (7a) in which *helle Farben* forms an NP is the desired one. However, the reading in (7b) in which *helle* forms an NP headed by an adjective and *Farben* a canonical NP is also possible (the verb *auffallen* 'be noticeable' can either be intransitive or take a dative object). To constrain this extra, infelicitous reading, a dispreference mark can be introduced in the part of the NP rule which derives the NPs headed by an adjective, as shown in the rule fragment (8).

(8) a. OPTIMALITY RANKING ... NEUTRAL AHEADNP UNGRAMMATI-
CAL NOGOOD.

    b. NP $\longrightarrow$ { ...

$$\begin{array}{cc} (\text{DET}) & \text{A} \\ (\uparrow\text{SPEC})=\downarrow & \uparrow=\downarrow \\ & \text{AHEADNP} \in o* \end{array}$$

... }

Ungrammatical Marks It is also possible mark items as ungrammatical. This strategy is used to mark rules which parse ungrammatical constructions, thus building robustness into the parser.

A simple example of where this might be useful is subject-verb agreement: ungrammatical marks as part of the grammar effectively allow a relaxation of the subject-verb agreement constraint. Consider the entry for the English third singular verbal ending *-s* in (9). In cases where subject-verb agreement is observed, the first disjunct delivers an analysis where no optimality mark is used. However, when subject-verb agreement is violated, only the second disjunct can be chosen, which introduces an ungrammatical mark NOSVAGR (the notation $oM*$ refers to the o-projection of the mother node; see section 3.5.4 for more detailed discussion of this notation). This structure will only surface if there is no grammatical analysis. Similar constraints could be added for other person and number combinations. If the only solutions are ungrammatical, then XLE marks this by adding an asterisk before the number of solutions whenever the number of solutions is reported.

(9) a. OPTIMALITYRANKING NEUTRAL UNGRAMMATICAL NoSVAgr
       NOGOOD.

    b. -s { ($\uparrow$SUBJ NUM)=SG
           ($\uparrow$SUBJ PERS)=3
        | NoSVAgr $\in oM*$ }

The difference between dispreference marks and ungrammatical marks is that analyses that are marked as ungrammatical are ignored unless there are no grammatical analyses, either preferred or dispreferred.

Another use of ungrammatical marks which is applicable to more technical contexts is to mark rules which are used only in parsing and not in generation. UNGRAMMATICAL marks are a clear instance of this since even though it may be desirable to have the grammar parse ungrammatical sentences to improve robustness, it is unlikely that one would wish to have such ungrammatical structures produced. Another use is for punctuation control: in general, it is good to be able to parse punctuation in a large number of positions, but to generate it in a much more restricted domain. For example, although commas appear with reckless abandon in many texts, they can be generated in a more controlled fashion. Finally, certain constructions may be technically grammatical but not be ones that one wishes to generate. For example, it is possible to place a *when* clause after the subject and before the verb in English, as in (10a). However, the grammar could be restricted to only generate *when* clauses in sentence-initial and sentence-final positions, as in (10b).

(10) a. The rear burner, when left on for too long, will tend to overheat.

    b. S $\longrightarrow$ NP   CONJPsub   VP
          ($\uparrow$SUBJ)=$\downarrow$ ($\uparrow$ADJUNCT)=$\downarrow$ $\uparrow$=$\downarrow$
                    ParseOnly $\in o*$

NOGOOD Marks The NOGOOD marks indicate that the analysis is always bad, even if there is no other analysis. The purpose of this is to allow fine-grained filtering of the grammar. For instance, a grammar might be annotated with certain marks that indicate constructions only used in special domains, such as a particular technical text. If these marks are listed after NOGOOD, then these constructions are treated as being inconsistent and are not processed any further by the grammar.

For example, a special rule to parse section headers might be written for a corpus which contains many such headers, but this rule might be undesirable for other uses of the grammar. Rather than painstakingly removing (or commenting out) the relevant header rules from within the grammar, the use of optimality marks provides a simple yet effective way of rendering parts of the grammar ineffective by moving a mark into the

NOGOOD category.

Thus, the introduction of OT marks into the grammars opened up several possibilities for grammar modularization, flexible filtering of syntactic ambiguity, and increased robustness in parsing. Furthermore, an additional application of constraint ranking is the parametrization of a single grammar for use in parsing vs. generation by specifying two different rankings for these two processes.

14.2 Testing

Testing the grammar is an indispensable part of ensuring robustness and increasing the performance of a grammar. Although individual constructions can be tested with a few sample sentences as they are developed, more systematic testing is required to maintain the quality of the grammar over time and to catch unexpected results of the addition of new rules and lexical items. Much of the methodology of grammar testing is dictated by common sense. However, issues do arise with respect to what kinds of testsuites to use, what other kinds of methods apart from testsuites one might use to test the grammar for continued consistency, and how to get a stable measure of the grammar's performance as it grows and changes. In the following sections we address these issues as they arose within our grammar development effort.

14.2.1 Types of Testsuites

14.2.1.1 Testsuites Internal to ParGram

One of the hazards of developing large grammars is that although a construction may be tested relatively thoroughly while it is first being implemented, subsequent changes may alter the grammar in such a way as to affect the behavior of the construction. That is, the addition of rules may inadvertantly block already implemented constructions or allow them to occur in contexts where they should not. The best way to ensure that this does not go unnoticed is by developing and utilizing testsuites, in addition to extensive commenting and documentation of the grammar.

A testsuite is a series of sentences (or NPs, PPs, etc.) which can be fed to the grammar. For example, in the XLE environment, the command `parse-testfile` <name-of-file> results in the grammar parsing all of the sentences in the specified file and recording the number of parses, the time it took to parse the sentence, and the number of subtrees for the sentence (a measure of complexity). That is, this system allows the grammar tester to see some information from the results of the analysis, but not the analysis itself. An example from a testfile of the English auxiliary system is shown in (11). The numbers in parentheses provide information on performance: the first number indicates the number of parses, the second the number of seconds the parse took, and the third the number of subtrees that the parser considered.

(11) ROOT: It has appeared. (1 1.3 283)
 ROOT: It has been actuated. (1 2.15 294)
 ROOT: It has been appearing. (1 1.23 294)
 ROOT: It has been being actuated. (1 2.45 308)

Within XLE these results are automatically stored in a separate file, thus providing a benchmark for future users of the grammar.

In order to thoroughly test a grammar, a variety of testsuites is necessary. It is best to have testsuites for each of the major types of constructions which the grammar handles. For example, there might be testsuites for the auxiliary system, for coordination, for questions, for relative clauses, for different types of verb subcategorization frames, etc. Each testsuite should contain simple examples of all possible versions of the construction in question. In addition, ungrammatical variants of the construction should be included in order to ensure that the grammar is not overgenerating. For example, a testsuite for the English auxiliary system should contain ungrammatical sentences like those in (12) in addition to grammatical sentences like those in (11).

(12) ROOT: It has appearing. (0 1.38 283)
 ROOT: It have is actuated. (0 2.3 294)
 ROOT: It is having actuates. (0 2.36 312)
 ROOT: It has been appears. (0 1.15 294)

The sentences constructed for the basic testing of a construction type should be very simple, to ensure that the fundamentals of the construction are correct. However, in order to test the grammar properly, naturally occuring complex examples as in (13) should also be tested at regular intervals.

(13) NP: the two-speed blower which provides increased air circulation for the heating system (8 2.525 605)
 NP: a deflector that may be opened to permit greater directional control of the airflow (1 4.611 581)

This allows for the testing of constructions the grammar writers may not have thought of themselves, and also tests interactions between parts of the grammar, such as relative clauses in combination with embedded clauses. This issue of complex rule interactions is further addressed in section 14.3.1.

14.2.1.2 Testsuites External to ParGram

Besides testsuites established by the grammar writers within a grammar development effort, a good method of measuring the grammar's performance and coverage is to test it by means of an unseen corpus. In order to subject our grammars to such tests, we availed ourselves of testsuites available the public domain. We additionally created testsuites by extracting sample sentences from standard grammar descriptions.

Some of the public domain testsuites we used to test our grammars are a result of the efforts of the TSNLP (Testsuites for Natural Language Processing) consortium, which provides a database of testsuites for English, French and German.[4] The existence of such testsuites is due to a broader effort at finding standardized evaluation measures for natural language applications. Some projects concerned with these issues are EAGLES (Expert Advisory Group on Language Engineering Standards) and DiET (Diagnostic and Evaluation Tools for Natural Language Applications).[5] As in previous chapters, the discussion in this section and the following section on measuring performance should be seen as a contribution towards the ongoing effort and discussion about finding good tools and a good methodology for evaluating grammars.

One of the testing methods used in ParGram was to compile statistics on the unseen corpora. An example, compiled by Norbert Bröker in December 1998 for the German grammar, is shown below in (14) and (15). The corpus consisted of sentences extracted from Buscha and Helbig 1989.

(14)

	number	percentage
items	1561	100
items parsed	1130	72.39
items parsed grammatical	1130	72.39
items parsed ungrammatical	0	0
items unparsed	431	27.61
items unparsed grammatical	431	27.61
items unparsed ungrammatical	0	0
massive ambiguity (>25 optimals)	1	0.06
long parse time (>30 seconds)	0	0
timeout exceeded during parsing	0	0

[4]Further information about the TSNLP project can be found at
http://cl-www.dfki.uni-sb.de/tsnlp/index.html.
[5]More information on these projects can be found at
http://www.ilc.pi.cnr.it/EAGLES/home.html and http://www.dfki.uni-sb.de/.

(15)

	average	median
optimal solutions	1.742	1
suboptimal solutions	3.778	1
runtime	0.718	0.540
words per test item	0	0
ratio runtime/subtree	0.004	0.004

These two tables break up the data in a number of ways. The first table shows that of a total number of 1,561 sentences, about 72% were parsed. All of the sentences that were parsed were indeed grammatical sentences of the language (i.e., the features of the grammar that are designed to ensure robustness did not kick in to parse ungrammatical sentences). The grammar could not deal with about 28% of the corpus. Furthermore, there was only one sentence that displayed massive ambiguity, there was no sentence which required a parse time of over 30 seconds, and no sentence timed out during parsing. The second table calculates averages for the results shown in table (14). The average number of optimal solutions was 1.7 with an average runtime of 0.7 seconds.

14.2.2 Further Tools and Databases

While the type of statistics illustrated in the previous section go a long way towards measuring the performance of a grammar (see also section 14.3) and providing the grammar writer with information as to where the grammar needs to be cleaned up or developed further, there are a number of things such statistics cannot be used for. For example, while we know that the German grammar was able to parse 72% of the sentences, we do not actually know whether it parsed the sentences correctly, or whether the grammar simply came up with an analysis that would be considered wrong by most linguists. In cases of massive ambiguity, as with the one sentence that had more than 25 optimal solutions in table (14), it is furthermore very difficult for the grammar writer to determine whether the desired analysis is even among the many analyses the grammar has produced.

14.2.2.1 Treebanks

One way of storing information about the desired analysis or analyses for a given construction is the use of a treebanking system. In our project, the use of treebanks was inspired by the Penn Treebank. However, given that in LFG much of the useful information about the analysis is represented in the form of AVMs, our treebank contained both trees (the c-structure) and the AVMs (the f-structure).

In order to establish a treebank, testsuites were run through the grammar and the resulting analyses were manually checked for the correct analysis or analyses. If the desired analyses were among the parses produced by the grammar, they were stored in Prolog form. If not, the grammar was either fixed or extended to include the desired analysis and the treebanking went through another cycle, resulting in a number of stored analyses that the grammar writers could use as a means to ensure that future instantiations of the grammar not only continued to cover constructions that had already been tested, but also continued to cover them correctly.

14.2.2.2 Selectional Tools

The use of treebanks provides the grammar writer with complete analyses that have been stored and can be compared to current parses. Another tool, dubbed TASTE (Kuhn 1998), was developed in order to provide grammar writers with the possibility of specifying partial information about the desired parse. Take the sentence *It was said that he smokes*. Now, consider a scenario in which the grammar returns many optimal solutions for this sentence, none of which seemed to contain an analysis in which the matrix clause *it was said* is correctly analyzed as having been passivized and the embedded clause as active.

In order to find the correct analysis, or to find out what might have gone wrong, the grammar writers could now painstakingly flip through the many possibilities presented by the grammar. Or, they could simply annotate the sentence to be parsed with the desired information, as in (16) (taken from Kuhn 1998).

(16) T: It was said that he smokes = Pass(Plus) Comp(Pass(Minus))

This annotation builds on the fact that XLE stores the output of the parse in Prolog. Thus, the desired information is encoded in list form, as in (16), and also allows levels of embedding to be specified, as in the case of the embedded clause: the COMP is specified to be PASSIVE −.

From the point of view of XLE, the annotations in (16) simply function as constraining equations, which restrict the space of possible analyses to only contain those that satisfy the annotations, i.e., a matrix clause that is passive and an embedded clause that is not. The grammar thus concentrates on satisfying these constraints, and the grammar writer can focus on a subset of all possible analyses in order to debug the grammar, or develop a treebank.

The TASTE tool allows the grammar writer to manipulate f-structure information. However, often it is also useful to be able to preselect c-structure information. XLE provides for this possibility as well by means of a bracketing tool in which the grammar writer can specify which constituent groupings are expected as part of the desired analysis.

14.3 Measuring Performance

As discussed in section 14.2, the establishment of testsuites and an evaluation of the parsing results provide one indication for the measurement of grammar coverage and performance. Further methods include analyses of the interactions between different rule systems in the grammar. For example, is the grammar written in a way that allows for undesirable interactions of rules? Can one part of the grammar be identified as the cause of a blow-up in parsing times? Can commonalities in rule interactions be identified across grammars? And how can grammars be compared to one another in terms of performance?

This section reports on some of the experiences gathered within ParGram and the experiments that were conducted in order to establish a window on the complex system of interactions that constitutes a grammar of natural language.

14.3.1 Rule Interactions

The greatest effort in writing a grammar often lies not in describing the constructions but rather in restricting the interactions between them. The computational system is relentlessly thorough: it identifies unforeseen interactions and requires that they be handled in full detail, whether they are of theoretical interest or not.

14.3.1.1 Undesirable Interactions

In this section, we describe some examples of undesirable interactions which were ultimately eliminated from the grammars. A first and rather simple example comes from an interaction of verbal templates with the phrase structure rules of English. Initially, the verbal templates in the English grammar only contained basic information as to the subcategorization frame, as in (17).

(17) $\text{TRANS}(P) = (\uparrow \text{PRED})='P<\text{SUBJ},\text{OBJ}>'$

As additional verb types were introduced, sentential subjects (*That the tractor would not start upset the driver.*) and particles (*He threw out the manual./He threw the manual out.*) were added. However, the information provided by the sentential subjects and by the particles in no way conflicted with the information of the template for simple transitive verbs. As such, a simple transitive verb like *see* could appear in the desired structure, as in (18a), but also in undesired structures, as in (18b) and (18c).

(18) a. I saw it.
      b. *That it is red saw it. (sentential subject)
      c. *I saw it on. (particle)

That is, the phrase structure rules allowed for all the structures in (18) since these structures are needed for other verbs. In addition, a template of the type in (17), which was sufficient when the phrase structure rules were simpler, has no constraints against the type of information provided by the sentential subjects or particles. This problem can be easily fixed by providing the TRANS template with constraints against sentential subjects (e.g., against subjects with tense and/or complementizers) and against particles (e.g., against having a PRT-FORM value). However, it was only through testing that such interactions were found. Next consider examples of how lexical entries can interact with the phrase structure rules to give undesirable analyses. Originally, the only complementizer in the English grammar was *that*, which was followed by a finite clause, as in (19).

(19) She knows that it is flashing too quickly.

As the grammar was expanded to include embedded questions and *for-to* complements, two new complementizers were added (*whether* and *for*) as well as new c-structure rules to allow for infinitival complements, as in (20).

(20) a. I want to know whether to leave now.
      b. They arranged for Mary to drive the tractor.

Although obvious in hindsight, the distribution of *that* can no longer be simply constrained by its complementizer c-structure category since this could incorrectly result in its appearing with infinitival complements. Instead, the different complementizers (and verbs) need to be constrained to appear only with certain types of complements.

Another example of lexical entries interacting with rules comes from the use of unknowns to increase the available number of lexical items (sections 11.3.2.3, 14.1.1). The English grammar uses unknowns for nouns and for numbers, both of which can be called by the NP rule. Unfortunately, at the time of publication the English morphology is such that every number has two sets of tags, one which resembles that of ordinary nouns like *cat* and one which is unique for numbers. As such, every time a number is parsed in an NP position, it has two possible analyses, roughly as in (21).

(21) a. [[three]$_N$]$_{NP}$
      b. [[three]$_{NUMBER}$]$_{NP}$

Ideally, numbers should always have a tag indicating that they are numbers, even if they also have a noun tag. As such, it would be possible to block the surfacing of numbers as nouns and instead have them always be numbers and picked up by the NP rule that way, i.e., only analysis (21b) would surface. (The NUMBER option is needed independently for places in which only numbers, and not common nouns, are allowed, e.g., in dates.) Unlike the other interactions discussed in this section, there is no way to block this undesirable overgeneration without either giving up the power of using the unknowns or requesting a significant modification to the morphology provided. Instead, optimality marks (see section 14.1.3) were used to constrain this ambiguity.

Finally consider an example of two rules interacting in an undesirable manner. This occurred in both the English and French grammars with the introduction of headers (section 9.2) into the grammars in conjunction with the rule allowing noun-noun compounds. Headers are designed to allow certain NPs to be root level categories, as in (22a), while noun-noun compounds occur in NPs like (22b).

(22) a. ROOT: Gearshifts
      b. NP: the oil filter

When both of these exist, roots such as (23) have two analyses, one which forms a sentence S (the dominant reading in both the French and English case) and one which forms a header (the less common reading).[6]

(23) a. ROOT: the beacon flashes
          S = [the beacon]$_{NP}$ [flashes]$_{VP}$
          HEADER = [the [beacon]$_N$ flashes]$_{NP}$
      b. ROOT   Le   tracteur   part
                  the   tractor   leaves/portion
          S = [le tracteur]$_{NP}$ [part]$_{VP}$ ('the tractor left')
          HEADER = [le tracteur [part]$_N$]$_{NP}$ (#'the portion tractor')

However, there is a difference between sentences and headers which can be exploited to block this double parse. Namely, sentences end with punctuation marks, at least in written text such as the tractor manual, while headers do not. As such, if punctuation is made obligatory at the end of sentences, then (23) will only have one parse: S if there is a

---

[6]Some sentences have the header reading dominant, as with the French example in (i) which is structurally equivalent to (23b).

(i) Le   code   barre
     the   code   obstruct/bar
     S = [le code]$_{NP}$ [barre]$_{VP}$ ('The code obstructs (it).')
     HEADER = [le code [barre]$_N$]$_{NP}$ ('the bar code')

punctuation mark and HEADER if there is not.

In sum, as the grammar is expanded to include a wider variety of constructions, these can interact in unpredictable ways, resulting in ungrammatical parses of grammatical constructions and parses of ungrammatical constructions. As these can be detected by rigorous testing, they should be eliminated whenever possible before the grammar increases further in complexity.

14.3.1.2 Legitimate Interactions

Consider next the case of interactions which are unforeseen and result in a proliferation of analyses, but which are legitimate. Although it is usually not desirable to block such interactions, it is important to know that they exist, since they can result in unexpectedly large numbers of analyses.

An example of a legitimate, but unanticipated, interaction between rules arises from the introduction of present participles as adverbial modifiers in conjunction with the NP rule which allows present participles to act as adjectival modifiers of nouns. Both rules are needed independently for constructions like those in (24).

(24)   a.   S = [Turning the wheel to the left]$_{\text{ADVP}}$ the driver should gently press the brake.

   b.   NP= the [turning]$_{\text{AP}}$ wheels

In certain circumstances, sentences can have two parses, one in which an initial present participle is interpreted as heading a sentence adverbial and one in which it is interpreted as the adjectival modifier of the subject NP. Such an example is seen in (25).

(25) Flashing lights can be seen for miles around.
   [Flashing]$_{\text{S.ADV}}$ [[lights]$_{\text{NP}}$ can be seen for miles around.]$_{\text{S}}$
   [[Flashing]$_{\text{A}}$ lights]$_{\text{NP}}$ can be seen for miles around.

Since both types of constructions legitimately occur, there is no means, or reason, to block one parse or the other. In fact, (25) could have either parse, depending on the context in which it appears. However, knowing that such interactions occur can help to explain sudden increases in parses when running testsuites.

A similar type of example comes from the German grammar in which the inclusion of adverbs, which morphologically resemble their adjectival counterparts, allows for additional interpretations of certain sentences. So, (26) has two readings, one in which *früh* 'early' is an adjective modifying *Montag* 'Monday' (in both sentences this is a noun phrase acting as an adverb) and one in which it is an adverb modifying the VP.

(26) Wir fangen Montag früh an.
  we start Monday early PART
  Wir fangen [Montag [früh]$_{AP}$]$_{ADVP}$ an.
  (='Early Monday we start.')
  Wir fangen [Montag]$_{ADVP}$ [früh]$_{ADVP}$ an.
  (='Monday we start early.')

Once again, since both constructions occur legitimately, one parse cannot be blocked in favor of the other.

Thus, as a grammar becomes more complicated, covering a wider variety of constructions with a greater number of lexical items, predicting how the rules and lexical entries interact becomes increasingly difficult. Some of these interactions are desirable because sentences often combine more than one construction, e.g., a question with a particle verb. Others are undesirable and need to be removed from the grammar by adding in appropriate constraints, modifying the rules, etc. Regardless, it is necessary to determine what interactions occur and how they affect the performance of the grammar. One way of gauging the problem is to test a wide variety of sentences and perform statistical analyses of the results, as was already seen in section 14.2.1.2. Another way is to perform controlled experiments with different versions of a grammar, or the judicious use of optimality marks (section 14.1.3). Such controlled experiments have been carried out primarily with respect to the German grammar and are briefly described in the next sections.

14.3.2 Grammar Internal Performance

The use of headless NPs in German is a known source of rule interactions that result in marked degradation of performance. It was clear early on, even without controlled experimental methods, that the inclusion of headless NPs (as already discussed in section 14.1.3.2) resulted in a marked loss in efficiency. The experiment reported in Kuhn and Rohrer 1997 used optimality marks not only as a diagnostic method, but also as a method of exploring the use of optimality marks to constrain possible analyses and thereby arrive at a more efficient grammar.

In particular, Kuhn and Rohrer 1997 used NOGOOD marks to create different grammar versions in which differing subsets of rule systems were switched off. They then compared the behavior of the manipulated grammar versions. The results are shown in table 14.3.2.[7]

---

[7]The English equivalents of the German sentences in the table are as follows: (i) He is looking for the middlesized (ones); (ii) She likes those (ones); (iii) Cozy pubs are missing in the city; (iv) The nice, small, comfortable, cozy pubs are missing in the city; (v) He sees the child; (vi) He sees the child with the cap; (vii) He sees the child

Grammar Version	A no ranking		B ranking		C *empty N		D *dem. pronoun *empty N	
(i) Er sucht die mittelgroßen.	1	0.442	1	0.548	0	0.299	0	0.275
(ii) Die gefallen ihr.	1	0.305	1	0.305	1	0.463	0	0.194
(iii) In der Stadt fehlen gemütliche Kneipen.	2	0.483	1	0.473	1	0.450	1	0.384
(iv) In der Stadt fehlen die schönen kleinen angenehmen gemütlichen Kneipen.	6	5.404	1	5.471	1	1.248	1	0.938
(v) Er sieht das Kind.	1	0.312	1	0.301	1	0.334	1	0.278
(vi) Er sieht das Kind mit der Mütze.	2	0.673	2	0.673	2	0.696	2	0.395
(vii) Er sieht das Kind mit der Mütze in der Hand.	5	1.505	5	1.516	5	1.603	5	0.594
(viii) Die Erfahrungen sollen später in die künftigen Planungen für die gesamte Stadt einfließen.	2	12.625	2	14.944	2	4.542	2	1.186
(ix) Hinter dem Betrug werden die gleichen Täter vermutet, die während der vergangenen Tage in Griechenland gefälschte Banknoten in Umlauf brachten.	92	217.418	20	222.776	20	35.580	20	4.632

TABLE 1 Results of a controlled comparison based on marked constraints

The grammar was annotated with optimality marks. In Version A of the grammar, these optimality marks were simply treated as NEUTRAL. That is, they had no effect. With this base-line grammar version, all the items in the testsuite could be parsed, and most of them within a reasonable time frame. Sentence (ix), however, exploded both in terms of parse time and in the number of analyses the grammar produced.

In Version B of the grammar, the optimality marks were allowed to play a role in that analyses with an empty nominal head were dispreferred. This version of the grammar was still able to cover the sample testsuite in table 14.3.2 while at the same time producing only 20 analyses for sentence (ix). However, there was no marked increase in efficiency.

Version C of the grammar looked at what would happen if one gave up trying to parse empty nominal heads. This was accomplished by moving the optimality mark for emtpy nominal heads from the dispreferred ranking to a NOGOOD ranking. In this case, sentence (i), whose only good parse contained an empty head, is not covered by the grammar anymore. On the other hand, parse times decrease markedly for sentence (ix), without any loss in coverage. Furthermore, in grammar Version D, in which not only empty nouns were excluded, but *der, die, das* 'the/that' were restricted to the determiner reading only (suppressing the demonstrative reading), performance increased even further, without a loss of coverage as compared to grammar Version C.

Thus, the source of the performance increase can be pinpointed fairly exactly via the use of optimality marks. An efficient method of dealing with the problem can then be undertaken as a second step.

Another experiment was conducted in order to gauge the impact of the introduction of complex categories (see section 13.2.2) on a grammar. Would the introduction of this type of modularization indeed speed up a given grammar? In the following experiment, reported in Kuhn 1999 and summarized in tabular form in table 14.3.2, three versions of the grammar were compared. Version A assumed a very general type of clause structure based on the notion of a CP, which subsumes interrogative, indicative and relative types of clauses. Version B parametrized the clause types by means of complex categories. In Version C, the parametrization was taken even further to include a parametrization over different declension classes of determiners and adjectives.

---

with the cap in its hand; (viii) The experiences are supposed to enter into the future plans of the entire city; (ix) The same suspects that brought counterfeit money into circulation in Greece in the last few days are thought to be behind the fraud.

Grammar Version	A general CP analysis	B clause types parameter- ized	C additional NP-internal parametri- zation
Results based on entire testsuite (25 sentences)			
parsing time average [sec] standard deviation [sec]	> 300 > 370	> 75 > 220	1.19 1.13
median [sec] quartile distance [sec]	> 130 > 730	> 3 > 14	0.94 1.01
maximal time [sec] # sentences beyond timeout	> 900 6	> 900 1	5.6 —
Results based on the 19 "easiest" sentences			
parsing time average [sec] standard deviation [sec]	121.19 163.38	4.83 6.82	0.92 0.65
median [sec] quartile distance [sec]	69.89 161.62	2.15 4.70	0.88 0.69
maximal time [sec] # sentences beyond timeout	720.76 —	29.2 —	5.6 —

The three versions of the grammar were run on a testsuite that included phenomena known to pose difficulties for computational grammars, such as relative clauses, coordination, and headless constructions.[8] The result of the experiment clearly indicates that the introduction of complex categories in order to achieve greater modularity in the grammar via a parametrization over linguistically relevant categories is very desirable.

14.3.3 Cross-grammar Performance

Comparing grammars to one another is a more difficult problem than determining grammar internal performance over time because the internal structure of the different grammars may not be accessible to the tester to create different versions for comparison. On the other hand, the methodology developed by Kuhn should be extendable to cross-grammar performance, as the comparison of different versions of one grammar is not so far removed from a comparison of grammars based

---

[8]The entire testsuite is provided in an Appendix in Kuhn 1999.

on similar premises written for different languages. This latter scenario is precisely that of the ParGram grammar development effort, in which the French, German and English grammar writers together worked out parallel analyses and set common guidelines and standards to be met by the grammars.

While we have not as yet conducted the types of experiments described in the previous section on the three ParGram grammars, some cross-grammar evaluation has been done in cases where a performance or coverage problem appeared to be shared by all grammars. One such example is coordination. As discussed in Chapter 8, coordination is treated in the ParGram grammars. However, with regard to performance issues, the treatment of coordination currently implemented remains less than satisfactory. A recent evalution of the English, German, and French grammars shows that coordination is indeed a problem for each of the three grammars: the grammars perform faster and have to deal with much less complexity (measured in terms of how many subtrees were dealt with) when a testsuite containing no examples of coordination is processed.

(27)

	Average #		
	words	subtrees	runtime
with coordination			
German	9.29	254	5.89
English	9.10	304	3.62
French	10.36	526	8.17
without coordination			
German	6.33	172	2.12
English	6.69	163	0.88
French	7.31	264	1.31

In this comparison, the French grammar has the most difficulties with coordination. This could perhaps be due to coordination being more difficult to treat in French than in English or German. Or the difference in parsing times might stem from an unforeseen rule interaction that takes place in French, but not in German or English. Whatever the cause ultimately turns out to be, cross-grammar comparison clearly yields results that can point the grammar writer towards both weaknesses and strengths in the grammar.

Cross-grammar comparison with grammars that are not based on similar linguistic theories, frameworks, or even basic premises provides a greater challenge than the type of cross-grammar comparison conducted within ParGram. As already mentioned previously in section 14.2.1.2, the need to establish standardized methods and tools for cross-grammar evaluation is recognized within the computational community and is currently being addressed by projects such as TSNLP or EAGLES. We hope that the methodology currently being experimented with within Par-Gram, including the use of optimality marks to create different versions of a grammar, and especially the focus on the parallelism across languages and grammars, will complement and extend the methodologies and tools developed in the ongoing discussion of grammar engineering and grammar development.

A

Appendix: Feature Standardization

This appendix provides the basic guidelines we used for positing features and their values in the ParGram project, as well as sample features.

A.1 General Guidelines

TYPE We allow all categories to be classified for TYPE; this is useful for constraining the applicability of rules. Sample TYPEs seen in Part I include: ATYPE, PTYPE, VTYPE, NTYPE, SPEC-TYPE, STMT-TYPE, ADV-TYPE, and ADEG-TYPE.[1]

FORM We allow all categories to be classified for FORM. FORM features are generally used to preserve surface information which may be needed for transfer. For example, all *wh*-phrases have PRED PRO and it is the PRON-FORM which indicates the value of the *wh*-phrase (*who, what, how, why*, etc.). Sample FORMs seen in Part I include: VFORM, COMP-FORM, CONJ-FORM, PRT-FORM, PRON-FORM, and SPEC-FORM.

A.2 Sample Features

This section lists some of the features and their possible values as used in the ParGram project. Note that this list is meant to be representative, not exhaustive, in order to provide the grammar writer with an idea of what types of features might be needed in designing and implementing a large scale grammar of a language.

Verbal Features

Semantic

ASPECT: PROG, STATIVE, PERF

MOOD: IMPERATIVE, INDICATIVE, SUBJUNCTIVE

---

[1]THE HYPHENATION CONVENTION: for greater readability, hyphens are inserted in names with a prefix of two or more letters. For example, PRON-FORM but VFORM.

PASSIVE: ±

STMT-TYPE: DECLARATIVE, HEADER, IMPERATIVE, INTERROGATIVE

TNS-ASP: ASPECT, MOOD, TENSE

TENSE: FUT, PAST, PRES

VSEM: UNACC, UNERG

Morphological

FIN: ±

INF: ±

VFORM: BASE, INF, PERFP, PRESP

VTYPE: AUX, MAIN, MODAL

Nominal Features

ANIM: ±

CASE: ACC, DAT, GEN, NOM

GEND: FEM, MASC, NEUT

NTYPE: COUNT, MASS, PROPER

NUM: PL, SG

PERS: 1, 2, 3

REFL: ±

Adjectival Features

ADEGREE: COMPARATIVE, EQUATIVE, SUPERLATIVE

ADEG-TYPE: EQUATIVE, NEGATIVE, POSITIVE

ATYPE: ATTRIBUTIVE, PREDICATIVE

Prepositional Features

PCASE: IN, ON, UNDER, etc.

PSEM: DIRECTIONAL, LOCATIVE, TEMPORAL, UNSPECIFIED

PTYPE: NOSEM, SEM

Others

ADV-TYPE: ADJADVMOD, SADV, VPADV

NEG: ±

POSTNEG: ±

TOPIC-INT: the fronted portion of an interrogative clause

TOPIC-REL: the fronted portion of a relative clause

A.3 Grammatical Functions

There are a few attributes whose status between features and grammatical functions was unclear, e.g. COMPOUND, ADJUNCT, and SPEC. Below are listed only the grammatical functions which can be subcategorized for, i.e., governable grammatical relations.

COMP: Subordinate clauses which provide their own subjects; usually finite.

OBJ: Direct objects and objects of certain prepositions.

OBJ2: Indirect objects that are not PPs.

OBL: There is only one kind of OBL in the ParGram grammars. What kind of OBL it is can be retrieved from the PCASE; this avoids redundant representation of information and makes rule-writing more compact.

PREDLINK: The nonsubject argument of linking verbs.

SUBJ: Subjects.

XCOMP: Subordinate clauses whose subject is provided from elsewhere in the sentence; usually nonfinite.

References

Abney, Steven. 1987. *The English Noun Phrase in its Sentential Aspects.* Doctoral dissertation, MIT.

Abney, Steven. 1991. Parsing By Chunks. In *Principle-Based Parsing*, ed. Robert Berwick, Steven Abney, and Carol Tenny. Dordrecht: Kluwer Academic Publishers.

Abney, Steven. 1996. Partial Parsing via Finite-State Cascades. In *Proceedings of the ESSLLI '96 Robust Parsing Workshop.* http://www.sfs.nphil.uni-tuebingen.de/~abney/.

Abush, Dorit. 1994. Sequence of tense. In *Ellipsis, Tense and Questions*, ed. Hans Kamp. IMS, Stuttgart. DYANA deliverable R 2.2.3.

Ait-Mokthar, Salah. 1997. Du Texte ASCII au Texte Lemmatisé : la Présyntaxe en une Seule étape. In *Proceedings TALN97.* Grenoble, France.

Alshawi, Hiyan (ed.). 1992. *The Core Language Engine.* Cambridge, Massachussetts: The MIT Press.

Alsina, Alex. 1996. *The Role of Argument Structure in Grammar: Evidence from Romance.* Stanford, California: CSLI Publications.

Andrews, Avery. 1983. Constituent Coordination in LFG. Unpublished manuscript, Australian National University.

Andrews, Avery. 1990. Unification and morphological blocking. *Natural Language and Linguistic Theory* 8(4):508–558.

Baayen, R.H., R. Piepenbrock, and L. Gulikers. 1995. The CELEX Lexical Database (CD-ROM). Linguistic Data Consortium, University of Pennsylvania.

Baker, Mark. 1983. Objects, Themes, and Lexical Rules in Italian. In *Papers in Lexical-Functional Grammar*, ed. Lorraine Levin, Malka Rappaport, and Annie Zaenen. Bloomington, Indiana: Indiana University Linguistics Club.

Baker, Mark. 1988. *Incorporation: A Theory of Grammatical Function Changing.* Chicago, Illinois: The University of Chicago Press.

Baur, Judith, Fred Oberhauser, and Klaus Netter. 1994. SADAW Abschlußbericht. Technical report. Universität des Saarlandes and SIEMENS AG.

Bech, G. 1983. *Studien über das deutsche Verbum infinitum.* Tübingen: Max Niemeyer Verlag. First published in 1955.

Berman, Judith. 1996. Topicalization vs. Left Dislocation of Sentential Arguments in German. In *Proceedings of the LFG96 Conference,* ed. Miriam Butt and Tracy Holloway King. Grenoble, France, August. http://www-csli.stanford.edu/publications/LFG/lfg1.html.

Berman, Judith, and Anette Frank. 1995. *Deutsche und französische Syntax im Formalismus der LFG.* Tübingen: Max Niemeyer Verlag.

Bod, Rens, and Ronald Kaplan. 1998. A Probabilistic Corpus-Driven Model for Lexical-Functional Analysis. In *Proceedings of 17th International Conference on Computational Linguistics ACL/COLING-98.* Montreal, Canada.

Brazil, Keith. 1997. Building Subcategorisation Lexica for an LFG Grammar of French. Technical report. Grenoble: Xerox Research Centre Europe. Summer Internship Report.

Breidt, Lisa, Frédérique Segond, and Giuseppe Valetto. 1996. Formal description of Multi-word Lexemes with the Finite State formalism: IDAREX. In *Proceedings of the 16th International Conference on Computational Linguistics (COLING-96),* 1036–1040. Copenhagen, Denmark.

Bresnan, Joan. 1982a. Control and Complementation. In *The Mental Representation of Grammatical Relations,* ed. Joan Bresnan. 173–281. Cambridge, Massachussetts: The MIT Press.

Bresnan, Joan (ed.). 1982b. *The Mental Representation of Grammatical Relations.* Cambridge, Massachussetts: The MIT Press.

Bresnan, Joan. 1996. LFG in an OT Setting: Modelling Competition and Economy. In *Proceedings of the LFG96 Conference,* ed. Miriam Butt and Tracy Holloway King. Grenoble, France, August. http://www-csli.stanford.edu/publications/LFG/lfg1.html.

Bresnan, Joan. 1998a. *Lexical-Functional Syntax.* Oxford: Blackwell. Forthcoming.

Bresnan, Joan. 1998b. Morphology Competes with Syntax: Explaining Typological Variation in Weak Crossover Effects. In *Is the Best Good Enough? Proceedings for the Workshop on Optimality in Syntax,* ed. Pilar Barbosa, Danny Fox, Paul Hagstrom, Martha McGinnis, and David Pesetsky. 59–92. Cambridge, Massachusetts: The MIT Press.

Bresnan, Joan. 1999. Explaining Morphosyntactic Competition. In *Handbook of Contemporary Syntactic Theory*, ed. Mark Baltin and Chris Collins. Oxford: Blackwell. To appear.

Bresnan, Joan, and Jonni Kanerva. 1989. Locative Inversion in Chicheŵa: A Case Study of Factorization in Grammar. *Linguistic Inquiry* 20(1):1–50.

Bresnan, Joan, Ronald Kaplan, and Peter Peterson. 1985. Coordination and the Flow of Information through Phrase Structure. Unpublished manuscript, Xerox PARC.

Bresnan, Joan, and Lioba Moshi. 1990. Object asymmetries in comparative Bantu syntax. *Linguistic Inquiry* 21:147–186.

Bresnan, Joan, and Annie Zaenen. 1990. Deep Unaccusativity in LFG. In *Grammatical Relations: A Cross-Theoretical Perspective*, ed. Katarzyna Dziwirek, Patrick Farrell, and Errapel Mejías-Bikandi. 45–57. Stanford, California: CSLI Publications.

Brun, Caroline. 1998. Terminology Finite-State Preprocessing for Computational LFG. Unpublished manuscript, Xerox Research Centre Europe, Grenoble.

Buscha, Joachim, and Gerhard Helbig. 1989. *Linguistische und didaktische Grammatik*. Leipzig: Verlag Enzyklopädie.

Butt, Miriam, Mary Dalrymple, and Anette Frank. 1997. An Architecture for Linking Theory in LFG. In *Proceedings of the LFG97 Conference*. San Diego, California, July.
http://www-csli.stanford.edu/publications/LFG2/lfg97.html.

Butt, Miriam, María-Eugenia Niño, and Frédérique Segond. 1996. Multilingual processing of auxiliaries in LFG. In *Natural Language Processing and Speech Technology: Results of the 3rd KONVENS Conference*, ed. Dafydd Gibbon, 111–122. Bielefeld.

Cacciari, C., and P. Tabossi (ed.). 1993. *Idioms: processing structure and interpretation*. New Jersey: Lawrence Erlbaum Associates.

Carpenter, Bob. 1992. ALE user's guide. Technical Report CM-LCL-92-1. Laboratory for Computational Linguistics: Carnegie Mellon University.

Chanod, Jean-Pierre, and Pasi Tapanainen. 1995. Tagging French–Comparing a Statistical and a Constraint-Based Method. In *Proceedings of the 7th Conference of the EACL*, 149–156. Dublin, Ireland.

Chanod, Jean-Pierre, and Pasi Tapanainen. 1996. A Non-Deterministic tokeniser for Finite-State Parsing. In *Proceedings of ECAI 96, Workshop on Extended Finite State Models of Language*. Budapest, Hungary.

Chanod, Jean-Pierre, and Pasi Tapanainen. 1997. Finite-State Based Reductionist Parsing for French. In *Extended Finite State Models of Language*, ed. András Kornai. Cambridge: Cambridge University Press.

Chomsky, Noam. 1970. Remarks on nominalization. In *Readings in English Transformational Grammar*, ed. R.A. Jacobs and P.S. Rosenbaum. The Hague: Mouton de Gruyter.

Cutting, Doug, Julian Kupiec, Jan Pedersen, and Penelope Sibun. 1992. A Practical Part-of-Speech Tagger. In *3rd Conference on Applied Natural Language Processing*, 133–140. Trento, Italy.

Dalrymple, Mary. 1993. *The Syntax of Anaphoric Binding*. Stanford, California: CSLI Publications. CSLI Lecture Notes, number 36.

Dalrymple, Mary (ed.). 1998. *Semantics and Syntax in Lexical Functional Grammar*. Cambridge, Massachussetts: The MIT Press.

Dalrymple, Mary, and Ron Kaplan. 1997. A Set-based Approach to Feature Resolution. In *Proceedings of the LFG97 Conference*. San Diego, California, July.
http://www-csli.stanford.edu/publications/LFG2/lfg97.html.

Dalrymple, Mary, Ronald Kaplan, John T. Maxwell III, and Annie Zaenen (ed.). 1995. *Formal Issues in Lexical-Functional Grammar*. Stanford, California: CSLI Publications.

Dalrymple, Mary, John Lamping, and Vijay Saraswat. 1993. LFG Semantics Via Constraints. In *Proceedings of the 6th Meeting of the EACL*, 97–105.

Eckle, Judith, and Ulrich Heid. 1996. Extracting Raw Material for a German subcategorization lexicon from newspaper text. In *Proceedings of the 4th International Conference on Computational Lexicography (COMPLEX '96)*. Budapest, Hungary.

Eckle-Kohler, Judith. 1998. Methods for quality assurance in semi-automatic lexicon acquisition from corpora. In *Proceedings of EURALEX '98*. Liège, Belgium.

Emele, Martin, and Michael Dorna. 1998. Ambiguity Preserving Machine Translation using Packed Representations. In *Proceedings of 17th International Conference on Computational Linguistics ACL/COLING-98*. Montreal, Canada.

Feldweg, Helmut. 1993. Stochastische Wortartendisambiguierung für das Deutsche: Untersuchungen mit dem robusten System LIKELY. Technical report. Tübingen: Seminar für Sprachwissenschaft.

Frank, Anette. 1996. A Note on Complex Predicate Formation: Evidence from Auxiliary Selection, Reflexivization, and Past Participle Agreement in French and Italian. In *Proceedings of the LFG96 Conference*.

Grenoble, France, August.
http://www-csli.stanford.edu/publications/LFG/lfg1.html.

Frank, Anette, Tracy Holloway King, Jonas Kuhn, and John T. Maxwell III. 1998. Optimality Theory style constraint ranking in large-scale LFG grammars. In *Proceedings of the LFG98 Conference*, ed. Miriam Butt and Tracy Holloway King. Brisbane, Australia, June/July. http://www-csli.stanford.edu/publications/LFG3/lfg98.html.

Grefenstette, Gregory, and Pasi Tapanainen. 1994. What is a Word, What is a Sentence? Problems of Tokenisation. In *Proceedings of the 3rd International Conference on Computational Lexicography (COMPLEX '94)*, 79–87. Budapest, Hungary. Research Institute for Linguistics, Hungarian Academy of Sciences.

Grimshaw, Jane. 1982. On the Lexical Representation of Romance Reflexive Clitics. In *The Mental Representation of Grammatical Relations*, ed. Joan Bresnan. 87–148. Cambridge, Massachussetts: The MIT Press.

Grimshaw, Jane. 1990. *Argument Structure*. Cambridge, Massachussetts: The MIT Press.

Gross, Maurice. 1975. *Méthode en syntaxe*. Paris: Hermann.

GSI-ERLI. 1994. Le dictionnaire AlethDic, version 1.5.3. Technical report. GSI-ERLI.

Halvorsen, Per-Kristian. 1983. Semantics for Lexical-Functional Grammar. *Lingusitics Inquiry* 14:567–615.

Halvorsen, Per-Kristian. 1987. Situation semantics and semantic interpretation in constraint-based grammars. Technical Report 101. Stanford, California: CSLI.

Helbig, Gerhard. 1984. Probleme der Beschreibung von Funktionsverbgefügen im Deutschen. In *Studien zur deutschen Syntax*, ed. Gerhard Helbig. Leipzig: Verlag Enzyklopädie. Volume II.

Johnson, Mark. 1986. The LFG Treatment of Discontinuity and the Double Infinitive Construction in Dutch. In *Proceedings of the Fifth West Coast Conference on Formal Linguistics*, ed. Mary Dalrymple, Jeffrey Goldber, Kristin Hanson, Chirs Piñón Michael Inma and, and Stephen Wechsler, 102–118. Stanford, California. Stanford Linguistics Association.

Kamp, Hans, and Uwe Reyle. 1993. *From Discourse to Logic*. Dordrecht: Kluwer Academic Publishers.

Kaplan, Ron, and Joan Bresnan. 1982. Lexical-Functional Grammar: A Formal System for Grammatical Representation. In *The Mental Representation of Grammatical Relations*, ed. Joan Bresnan. 173–281. Cambridge, Massachussetts: The MIT Press.

Kaplan, Ronald, and John T. Maxwell III. 1988a. An Algorithm for Functional Uncertainty. In *Proceedings of the 12th International Conference on Computational Linguistics (COLING-88)*, 297–302. Budapest, Hungary. Reprinted in Dalrymple et al. 1995, pp. 177–198.

Kaplan, Ronald, and John T. Maxwell III. 1988b. Constituent Coordination in Lexical-Functional Grammar. In *Proceedings of the 12th International Conference on Computational Linguistics (COLING-88)*, 303–305. Reprinted in Dalrymple et al. 1995, pp. 199–210.

Kaplan, Ronald, and John T. Maxwell III. 1996. LFG grammar writer's workbench. Technical report. Xerox PARC.
http://www.parc.xerox.com/istl/groups/nltt/medley/.

Kaplan, Ronald, Klaus Netter, Jürgen Wedekind, and Annie Zaenen. 1989. Translation by Structural Correspondences. In *EACL 4*, 272–281. University of Manchester.

Kaplan, Ronald, and Paula Newman. 1997. Lexical resource reconciliation in the Xerox Linguistic Environment. In *Proceedings of the ACL Workshop on Computational Environments for Grammar Development and Engineering*.

Kaplan, Ronald, and Annie Zaenen. 1989. Long-distance Dependencies, Constituent Structure, and Functional Uncertainty. In *Alternative Conceptions of Phrase Structure*, ed. Mark Baltin and Anthony Kroch. 17–42. Chicago, Illinois: University of Chicago Press. Reprinted in Dalrymple et al. 1995, pp. 137–165.

Kaplan, Ronald M, and Martin Kay. 1994. Regular Models of Phonological Rule Systems. *Computational Linguistics* 20(3):331–378.

Karttunen, Lauri. 1996. Directed replacement. In *Proceedings of the ACL*, 108–115. Santa Cruz, California.

Karttunen, Lauri, Ronald Kaplan, and Annie Zaenen. 1992. Two-level Morphology with Composition. In *Proceedings of the 14th International Conference on Computational Linguistics (COLING-92)*, 141–148. August.

Kathol, Andreas. 1995. *Linearization-Based German Syntax*. Doctoral dissertation, Ohio State University.

Kathol, Andreas. 1996. Concrete Minimalism of German. Unpublished manuscript, UC Berkeley.

Kay, Martin. 1996. Chart Generation. In *Proceedings of the 34th Annual Meeting of the ACL*. Santa Cruz, California.

Kay, Paul, and Charles Fillmore. 1994. Grammatical constructions and linguistic generalizations: The What's X Doing Y? Unpublished manuscript, UC Berkeley.

Kayne, Richard. 1984. *Connectedness and Binary Branching*. Dordrecht: Foris.

Kehler, Andrew, Mary Dalrymple, John Lamping, and Vijay Saraswat. 1995. The Semantics of Resource-Sharing in Lexical-Functional Grammar. In *EACL95*. University College Dublin.

King, Tracy Holloway. 1995. *Configuring Topic and Focus in Russian*. Stanford, California: CSLI Publications.

Kiss, Katalin É. 1995. *Discourse Configurational Languages*. Oxford: Oxford University Press.

Knuth, Donald E. 1992. *Literate Programming*. Stanford, California: CSLI Publications.

König, Ekkehard. 1991a. Gradpartikeln. In *Semantik: Ein internationales Handbuch der zeitgenössischen Forschung*, ed. Arnim von Stechow and Dieter Wunderlich. 786–804. Berlin: de Gruyter.

König, Ekkehard. 1991b. *The Meaning of Focus Particles: A comparative Perspective*. London: Routledge.

Koskenniemi, K. 1983. *Two-level morphology: A general computational model for word-form recognition and production*. Department of General Linguistics, University of Helsinki.

Kuhn, Jonas. 1998. Towards data-intensive testing of a broad-coverage LFG grammar. In *Computers, Linguistics, and Phonetics between Language and Speech, Proceedings of the 4th Conference on Natural Language Processing – KONVENS-98*, ed. Bernhard Schröder, Winfried Lenders, Wolfgang Hess, and Thomas Portele, 43–56. Bonn. Peter Lang.

Kuhn, Jonas. 1999. Meta-descriptions of rules for generalization in constraint-based grammar design. Unpublished manuscript, IMS, Universität Stuttgart.

Kuhn, Jonas, and Christian Rohrer. 1997. Approaching ambiguity in real-life sentences – the application of an Optimality Theory-inspired constraint ranking in a large-scale LFG grammar. In *Proceedings of the DGfS-CL*. Heidelberg, Germany.

Kupiec, Julian. 1992. Robust part-of-speech tagging using a hidden Markov model. *Computer Speech and Language* 6:225–242.

Light, Marc. 1996. CHUMP: Partial Parsing and Underspecified Representations. In *12th European Conference on Artificial Intelligence*, ed. Wolfgang Wahlster, 28–30.

Maxwell III, John T., and Ronald Kaplan. 1991. *A Method for Disjunctive Constraint Satisfaction*. 173–190. Dordrecht: Kluwer Academic Publishers. Reprinted in Dalrymple et al. 1995, pp. 381–402.

Maxwell III, John T., and Ronald Kaplan. 1993. The Interface between Phrasal and Functional Constraints. *Computational Linguistics* 19(4):571–590. Reprinted in Dalrymple et al. 1995, pp. 403–429.

Maxwell III, John T., and Ronald Kaplan. 1996. An Efficient Parser for LFG. In *Proceedings of the LFG96 Conference*. Grenoble, France, August.
http://www-csli.stanford.edu/publications/LFG/lfg1.html/.

Maxwell III, John T., and Christopher D. Manning. 1996. A Theory of Non-constituent Coordination based on Finite-State Rules. In *Proceedings of the LFG96 Conference*. Grenoble, August.
http://www-csli.stanford.edu/publications/LFG/lfg1.html/.

Milsark, G. 1988. Singl-ing. *Linguistic Inquiry* 19:611–634.

Mohanan, Tara. 1994. *Argument Structure in Hindi*. Stanford, California: CSLI Publications.

Nolke, Henning, and Hanne Korzen. 1996. L'ordre des mots. *Langue Française* 111. Larousse.

Nunberg, Geoff, Thomas Wasow, and Ivan Sag. 1994. Idioms. *Language* 70(3):491–538.

Nunberg, Geoffrey. 1990. *The Linguistics of Punctuation*. Stanford, California: CSLI Publications.

Penn, Gerald. 1993. A comprehensive HPSG grammar in ALE. Technical report. Laboratory for Computational Linguistics: Carnegie Mellon University.

Perlmutter, David. 1978. Impersonal Passives and the Unaccusative Hypothesis. In *Proceedings of the 4th Annual Meeting of the Berkeley Linguistics Society*. University of California, Berkeley.

Pollard, Carl, and Ivan Sag. 1987. *Information-Based Syntax and Semantics, Volume 1: Fundamentals*. Stanford, California: CSLI Publications.

Pollard, Carl, and Ivan Sag. 1994. *Head-Driven Phrase Structure Grammar*. Chicago, Illinois: The University of Chicago Press.

Prince, Alan, and Paul Smolensky. 1993. Optimality Theory: constraint interaction in generative grammar. Technical Report 2. Piscateway, New Jersey: Rutgers University Center for Cognitive Science.

Pullum, Geoffrey. 1982. Syncategorematicity and English infinitival *to*. *Glossa* 16:181–215. Preliminary version published as 'The category status of infinitival *to*'. University of Washington Working Papers in Linguistics 6.55-72, 1981.

Quint, Julien. 1997. Morphologie à deux niveaux des noms du français. MA Thesis. Grenoble: Xerox Research Centre Europe.

Quirk, Randolph, Sidney Greenbaum, Geoffrey Leech, and Jan Svartvik. 1985. *A Comprehensive Grammar of the English Language*. New York: Longman.

Rambow, Owen. 1996. Word Order, Clause Union, and the Formal Machinery of Syntax. In *Proceedings of the LFG96 Conference*, ed. Miriam Butt and Tracy Holloway King. Grenoble, France, August. http://www-csli.stanford.edu/publications/LFG/lfg1.html.

Sag, Ivan, Gerald Gazdar, Thomas Wasow, and Steven Weisler. 1985. Coordination and how to distinguish categories. *Natural Language and Linguistic Theory* 3:117–171.

Schiller, Anne. 1996. Multilingual Finite-State Noun Phrase Extraction. ECAI'96 Workshop on Extended Finite State Models of Language, August 11-12, Budapest.

Segond, Frédérique, and Max Copperman. 1999. Lexicon Filtering. In *Recent Advances in Natural Language Processing: Selected Papers from RANLP '97*, ed. R. Mitkov and N. Nicolov. John Benjamins. Special issue.

Segond, Frédérique, and Pasi Tapanainen. 1995. Using a finite-state based formalism to identify and generate multiword expressions. MLTT-19. Grenoble: Xerox Research Centre Europe.

Sells, Peter. 1985. *Lectures on Contemporary Syntactic Theories*. Stanford, California: CSLI Publications.

Shemtov, Hadar. 1997. *Ambiguity Management in Natural Language Generation*. Doctoral dissertation, Stanford University.

Siegel, Muffy E. A. 1976. *Capturing the Adjective*. Doctoral dissertation, University of Massachusetts at Amherst.

Vallduví, Enric. 1992. *The Informational Component*. New York: Garland Press.

van Genabith, Josef, and Dick Crouch. 1996. Direct and Underspecified Interpretations of LFG f-structures. In *Proceedings of the 16th International Conference on Computational Linguistics (COLING-96)*, 262–267. Copenhagen, Denmark.

von Stechow, Arnim, and Wolfgang Sternefeld. 1988. *Bausteine syntaktischen Wissens*. Opladen: Westdeutscher Verlag.

Zaenen, Annie. 1989. Nominal arguments in Dutch and WYSIWYG LFG. Unpublished manuscript, Xerox PARC.

Zaenen, Annie, and Ronald Kaplan. 1995. Formal Devices for Linguistic Generalizations: West Germanic Word Order in LFG. In *Linguistics and Computation*, ed. Jennifer Cole, Georgia Green, and Jerry Morgan. 3–27. Stanford, California: CSLI Publications. Reprinted in Dalrymple et al. 1995, pp. 215–239.

Subject Index

Name Index